Invisible Presence

Invisible Presence

The Representation of Women in French-Language Comics

Catriona MacLeod

Bristol, UK / Chicago, USA

First published in the UK in 2021 by
Intellect, The Mill, Parnall Road, Fishponds, Bristol, BS16 3JG, UK

First published in the USA in 2021 by
Intellect, The University of Chicago Press, 1427 E. 60th Street,
Chicago, IL 60637, USA

Copyright © 2021 Intellect Ltd

All rights reserved. No part of this publication may be reproduced, stored in a retrieval system, or transmitted, in any form or by any means, electronic, mechanical, photocopying, recording, or otherwise, without written permission.

A catalogue record for this book is available from
the British Library.

Copy editor: MPS Limited
Cover designer: Aleksandra Szumlas
Production manager: Helen Gannon
Typesetter: MPS Limited

Hardback ISBN 978-1-78938-390-4
ePDF ISBN 978-1-78938-391-1
ePUB ISBN 978-1-78938-392-8

Printed and bound by TJ Books, UK

To find out about all our publications, please visit our website. There you can subscribe to our e-newsletter, browse or download our current catalogue and buy any titles that are in print.

www.intellectbooks.com

This is a peer-reviewed publication.

For Allan J. MacLeod. QED.

Contents

List of Figures	ix
Acknowledgements	xi
Introduction: Women Problems	1

SECTION 1:   PRIMARY WOMEN CHARACTERS — 13

1. Bécassine to Barbarella … But What Came in Between? An Introductory History of Female Primary Characters in the Francophone *Bande Dessinée* — 14
2. Bécassine: The First Lady of *Bande Dessinée*? — 34
3. Barbarella: Study of a Sex-Symbol — 49
4. Solving the Mystery of Adèle Blanc-Sec — 61

SECTION 2:   SECONDARY WOMEN CHARACTERS — 77

5. Beyond Bonemine: An Introductory History of Female Secondary Characters in the Francophone *Bande Dessinée* — 81
6. A Study of Stereotypes: The Secondary Female Characters of *Astérix* — 96
7. Secondary Women in Urban Realism: *La Vie de ma mère* — 108
8. Black Secondary Women in the Works of Warnauts and Raives: The Eroticization of Difference — 119
9. Secondary Women in the BD New Wave: The Female Figures of *Le Combat ordinaire* — 130

SECTION 3: WOMEN CHARACTERS BY WOMEN CREATORS   139

10. The Women that Women Draw: An Introductory History of Female Characters Drawn by Women Artists in the Francophone *Bande Dessinée*   140
11. The Rise and Fall of *Ah! Nana*: France's First and Only All-Female *illustré*   152
12. Murdering the Male Gaze: Chantal Montellier's *Odile et les crocodiles*   166
13. Everyday Extremes: Aurélia Aurita's *Fraise et chocolat*   180

Conclusion: Problem Solved?   189
Figures   194
Notes   207
References   230
Index   239

Figures

Figure 1:	Forest, *Barbarella* (Edition Intégrale: Premier tome) (1994), p. 3 © 2019 Humanoids, Inc. Los Angeles.	194
Figure 2:	Forest, *Barbarella* (Edition Intégrale: Premier tome) (1994), p. 14 © 2019 Humanoids, Inc. Los Angeles.	194
Figure 3:	Forest, *Barbarella* (Edition Intégrale: Premier tome) (1994), p. 6 © 2019 Humanoids, Inc. Los Angeles.	195
Figure 4:	Forest, *Barbarella* (Edition Intégrale: Premier tome) (1994), p. 53 © 2019 Humanoids, Inc. Los Angeles.	195
Figure 5:	Extrait de l'ouvrage *Adèle et la bête*, Tardi (2007), p. 27 © Casterman. Avec l'aimable autorisation des auteurs et des Editions Casterman.	196
Figure 6:	Extrait de l'ouvrage *Adèle et la bête*, Tardi (2007), p. 21 © Casterman. Avec l'aimable autorisation des auteurs et des Editions Casterman.	197
Figure 7:	Extrait de l'ouvrage *Adèle et la bête*, Tardi (2007), p. 22 © Casterman. Avec l'aimable autorisation des auteurs et des Editions Casterman.	197
Figure 8:	Extrait de l'ouvrage *La Vie de ma mère: Face B*, Chauzy et Jonquet (2003), p.11 © Casterman. Avec l'aimable autorisation des auteurs et des Editions Casterman.	198
Figure 9:	Larcenet, *Le Combat ordinaire* (2004), p.13 © DARGAUD 2003 – www.dargaud.com. All rights reserved.	199

Figure 10:	Claveloux, 'La Conasse et le Prince Charmant' in *Ah! Nana* (no.2) (1977), p. 29 © Nicole Claveloux (many thanks to the artist for allowing the reproduction of this image).	200
Figure 11:	Capuana, Untitled Strip in *Ah! Nana* (no. 6) (1977), back cover. © Cecilia Capuana (many thanks to the artist for allowing the reproduction of this image).	201
Figure 12:	Capuana, 'Visite inattendue' in *Ah! Nana* (no.3) (1977), p.24. © Cecilia Capuana (many thanks to the artist for allowing the reproduction of this image).	202
Figure 13:	Capuana, 'Visite inattendue' in *Ah! Nana* (no.3) (1977), p.25. © Cecilia Capuana (many thanks to the artist for allowing the reproduction of this image).	203
Figure 14:	Montellier, *Odile et les crocodiles* (2008), p. 19 © Actes Sud 2008.	204
Figure 15:	Aurita, Fraise et chocolat (2006), p. 72 © Les Impressions Nouvelles – 2006.	205
Figure 16:	Aurita, Fraise et chocolat (2006), p. 75 © Les Impressions Nouvelles - 2006.	206

Acknowledgements

This book began as a Ph.D. dissertation. I'd like to extend heartfelt thanks to my supervisors, Laurence Grove and Keith Reader, for all of their help and support and to my examiners Ann Miller and Rachel Douglas for their very useful feedback, in addition to the University of Glasgow and, finally, the AHRC for funding the project. Thanks also go to the University of London Institute in Paris for awarding me a period of research leave in order to make the book a book, and my colleagues at ULIP for being indefatigable sources of advice and encouragement. Several research colleagues helped me greatly with their advice on specific chapters: thanks go to Ann Miller (again), Armelle Blin-Rolland and Lise Tannahill.

A version of Chapter 8 previously appeared as an article in *Contemporary French Civilization*. Many thanks are due to Liverpool University Press for granting permission for its reproduction in this book. Several artists and publishing houses were also kind enough to waive their fee for reproducing images in this book. Thanks are due to Cecilia Capuana, Nicole Claveloux, Les Humanoïdes Associés, Les Impressions Nouvelles, Dargaud and Casterman.

I'd like to personally thank my friends and family, especially my parents, Jennifer and Allan MacLeod, for all their support on everything (all the time) and Granny, Mary King, for being so generous in support of all our educations. Final thanks go to my very visible little women, Nora and Inès, for being constant reminders of why this work is important.

Introduction: Women Problems

The problem of woman is the most marvellous and disturbing problem in all the world[1]

—André Breton (1962: 213n)

In 2009, during an event in Glasgow, the artist Lewis Trondheim was asked why there were few women characters to be found in his many French-language comic strip, or *bande dessinée* (BD),[2] créations. He shrugged and answered: '[w]omen are harder to draw'.[3] The audience tittered at Trondheim's rueful confession, but were perhaps unaware that he was articulating a difficulty already expressed by several of the most recognized names in the history of Franco-Belgian comics. Like Trondheim, Moebius, an undisputed master of sequential art, admitted to having trouble drawing female characters, stating in 1993 that he had 'never successfully drawn a real woman' (quoted in Peeters 1994: 52n80).[4] Before Moebius, *Astérix* co-creator René Goscinny expressed a difficulty with the idea of 'caricaturing' women to include in his strips, claiming that his respect for women prevented this (Pilloy 1994: 11; see also Groensteen 2013) – a point of view that mirrored almost exactly the words of the most famous of artists in *bande dessinée* history, Hergé, who added that 'women characters rarely lend themselves to comedy' anyway (quoted in Peeters 1994: 52n80).[5] Drawing woman, it seems, has long posed a variety of problems in the *bande dessinée* medium.

These 'women problems' are complex, but, when examined, may be broadly broken down into two principal and interconnected issues: the problem of creating images of, and thus a gaze directed towards, 'real' – to borrow Moebius's expression – women, and the problem of doing so within the specificities of the *bande dessinée* medium.

The first of these – the notion that creating images of women to be looked at is problematic in a male-centred world – is not specific to drawn art; exploring the theoretical basis for this has been a particular focus of feminist art criticism. In an early example of such criticism, John Berger explained in his now-famous BBC series, *Ways of Seeing* (1972), that 'a woman, in the culture of privileged Europeans, is first and foremost a sight to be looked at' (*Ways of Seeing* (Episode 2) 1972), whether in oil paintings and photographs, or on the street. Certainly, images of women abound in the visual arts. Renoir, for example, is said to have once stated that without the female body, he would never have become a painter (Nochlin 2006: 4). However, in a traditionally male-dominated society, such as that of privileged Europeans, *really* looking at a woman is not easy to do. In such a society, the looker – an active, and, thus, powerful, consumer of images – is imagined to be (and, thus, regardless of gender, is positioned as) male and heterosexual; images are therefore created and coded by artists specifically in order to please this male viewer. In *Ways of Seeing*, Berger gave the example of the female nude in European pre-modernist painting, one category of fine art in which women were the principal focus. He claimed that amongst tens of thousands of examples of female nudes, only twenty or thirty exceptions showed the woman 'revealed as herself': the majority showed women wearing the disguise of hairless, idealized, passive nudity, all designed to appeal to the sexuality of the male 'spectator-owner' ([Episode 2] 1972). The *idea* of women was present in this art, then, but 'real' women were very often not. Summarizing the wider findings of feminist art criticism much later, in 2003, Griselda Pollock agreed, noting that in modern society, still dominated by the notion of male, heterosexual primacy, 'the visual sign "woman" does not describe female people with changing bodies, intellects, desires, capacities' (2003: 178). Rather, 'Woman' as image is a creation of masculine fantasy and fear and is, thus, 'neither natural nor viable. It is clearly historical/political' (2003: 178).

Laura Mulvey, the most well-known proponent of feminist visual criticism, used psychoanalytic theory in order to examine the presence – or, rather, the absence – of women in modern imagery more deeply. Lacanian psychoanalysis posits that, in a phallocentric system – that is, one that is based on the primacy of the phallus, a notion representing the ideological conception of the masculine (power, authority, presence) – the feminine exists as a negative value. Rather than seeing two sexes – man and woman – phallocentrism identifies one and its negative – man and not-man. 'Not-man' is seen as lacking (a phallus) and, thus, as incomplete and, as Pollock again states, '[is] damaged, reduced, unfit for full participation, weaker, a mere vessel; the object not the subject of desire, the seen and not the see-er, the spoken and not the speaking' (2003: 179). Phallocentrism is also oculocentric: based on sight. This means that the act of looking at women (and, indeed, at images of women) is key to defining their negative position in the phallocentric system: looking confirms their non-man-ness. However, looking at women also creates a problem – in a system that creates meaning in reference to, and allies positive presence, power and authority with, the phallus, its absence becomes distressing and signifies 'lack' or 'loss'. This is linked to the fact that, according to psychoanalytic theory, the psychosexual development we undertake as infants is replayed in various, unconscious forms throughout adulthood. Woman's visual lack of a phallus (either anatomically or symbolically) reminds the now-mature viewer (again, traditionally positioned as male) of the anxiety caused in childhood when it was believed that the woman's discovered difference indicated castration – the loss of something it was imagined she originally had – and, thus, replays this traumatic experience. This anxiety and the techniques used to counteract and contain it determine the understanding of womanhood and the representation of women in the Symbolic order, the stage of development humans enter into once they understand language, societal rules and laws.[6] This last point is crucial when considering images of women in a phallocentric system: these images do not simply reflect the anxiety provoked by women's lack and the notion, to borrow Pollock's words, that they are damaged, weaker, the object and not the subject of desire. They also contribute to, and renew, these fears and assumptions.

Mulvey explained in two key essays the construction of images of women and the techniques used to overcome the anxiety of their 'lack' in certain examples of twentieth-century art adhering to a traditionally phallocentric mode of representation. In 'Fears, Fantasies and the Male Unconscious or "You Don't Know What is Happening, Do You, Mr Jones"', an article analysing Allen Jones's sculptures of female figures, Mulvey explained that the anxiety provoked by women can be (as in the case of Allen's work) replaced by dressing women in, or depicting women alongside (or being punished by) fetish objects that reassuringly 'stand-in' for the missing phallus (2009: 6–13). In a further article, 'Visual Pleasure and Narrative Cinema', Mulvey extends this theory to go beyond static imagery, noting the visual and narrative strategies used to neutralize the veiled threat of 'woman' in examples of classic Hollywood films, explaining how female characters are, in these stories, investigated, punished, killed or, themselves, visually fetishized – that is, unrealistically beautified and 'overvalued' to such an extent that their own body becomes a reassuring fetish, thus neutralizing the distress caused by their lack (see Mulvey 2009: 22). This latter example of fetishism, although identified by Mulvey in a study of classic cinema, is equally visible in the pre-modern nudes of which Berger speaks, which are often idealized to the point of appearing unreal or angelic. Mulvey neatly summarizes in the earlier of the two noted articles the reality of the visual representations of women she studies: '[w]omen are constantly confronted with their own image in one form or another […] Yet, in a real sense, women are not there at all. The parade has nothing to do with woman, everything to do with man [...] Women are simply the scenery onto which men project their narcissistic fantasies' (2009: 13). Again, then, feminist art criticism shows that creating an image of a 'real' woman, from within a male-dominated, heterosexual paradigm, is not easy. The *bande dessinée*, as another form of visual expression, is certainly not exempt from the creative concerns linked to the societal context that determines its production and, thus, the apparent fact that artists drawing women in this medium may also encounter the anxiety of this 'woman problem' is unsurprising. However, unlike several forms of visual art that have now been analysed by feminist visual critics, how artists may overcome (or not) the traditional challenges of depicting women in the *bande dessinée* remains to be fully examined.

The second part of the problems with depicting women faced by *bande dessinée* artists is more particular to the medium itself, and concerns the construction of images of women to be looked at within the formal and historical specificities of the art form. Indeed, some of the reflections of the artists quoted above reveal a layer of perceived difficulty in portraying women that is more specific to drawn images. The statements of both Goscinny and Hergé largely imitate the reflection of caricaturist and photographer Nadar in the nineteenth century, when he asked of drawing 'beautiful' women: '[h]ow can the clumsy, oafish pencil ever translate into the lowliest of languages their subtle delicateness, their exquisite finesse?' (quoted in Peeters 1994: 51n80).[7] The caricaturist's pondering, later echoed by the two most well-known *bande dessinée* creators of the twentieth century, reveals his concern about portraying women, often (unnaturally) idealized, as we have seen, in 'high' arts such as painting, in the 'low' medium of caricature, created with the simple pencil. Both the practical tools with which drawn art can be created and its status, whether in the single panel form of caricature or its multi-panel French-language descendent, the *bande dessinée*, have evolved since the era of Nadar's reflection and, in turn, Hergé and Goscinny's respective reconfigurations of it. However, their concerns indicate one historical explanation for the difficulties expressed in depicting women and remind us that the *bande dessinée*'s specific history, reception and creative processes impact on its representations.

The *bande dessinée*, born in the nineteenth century but largely popularized in the twentieth, indeed lived its early life as a 'low' cultural product,[8] partly due, and unlike caricature in this respect, to its consistent pre–Second World War direction towards a young readership. *Illustrés* for children – mixed-media weekly publications containing illustrated stories, games and *bandes dessinées* – were the first means of disseminating the burgeoning medium and were generally specific in their direction towards either girls or boys. Nevertheless, across both 'types' of *illustrés*, male characters featured more prominently in their strip content than women figures, and boys' illustrés, which would become more numerous than those for girls, eventually developed to contain a larger proportion of BDs per issue than their female-directed counterparts (Reyns-Chikuma suggests this to be more visible after 1945 [2016: 156]), both of these factors progressively defining the medium as principally 'for boys'.[9] This gendered direction of the art form provides a second, related, historical explanation for the 'women problems' alluded to by the artists above: with a principally male audience in mind, artists (also mostly male) were more inclined to draw male characters with whom their readers were more likely to identify.[10] An additional complication to drawing women 'for boys', but equally important here, is the notion discussed above that in a traditionally phallocentric society, images of women always express sexual difference and symbolize male desire – elements perhaps deemed 'unsuitable' for publication to children (indeed, as will be discussed more fully in Chapters 1 and 2, following a legal change in 1949 meant to protect young readers, female characters were sometimes entirely removed from strips because of their perceived indivisibility from their sexual presence).

A final reason linked to the early and mid twentieth-century development of the *bande dessinée* that, to an extent, explains the difficulty of artists (particularly Hergé and Goscinny, who were active during this era and, indeed, cite the following as a particular worry) in drawing women concerns the direction of the medium principally towards comedy (hence the Anglo-American terms 'comics' and 'funny pages') and action. Both are genres that tend towards a focus on male figures. Women, traditionally viewed as 'passive' creatures, have rarely been associated with action narratives, except as, unsurprisingly, victims needing to be saved. The idealized woman of the Western imagination has also traditionally been viewed as incompatible with the 'aggression' of comedy, explained by Regina Barecca thus: '[y]ou can't be fragile and traffic in humour, and conventional femininity insists on fragility and delicacy as trademarks' (2013: xv) (one also thinks of the persistent idea, still repeated in the twenty-first century, that women themselves are 'not funny').[11]

Thus, the establishment of some of the key characteristics of the early medium – cultural status, audience and reception, and dominant genres – contribute, alongside the anxiety associated with representing women noted earlier, to the difficulty in depicting them in the *bande dessinée*. The simplest and most visible response to this compound problem found in examples of the early medium is the apparent decision on the part of many artists to include few (or, indeed, no) female figures in their strips (see Chapters 1, 5 and 10 for evidence of this). When the *bande dessinée* began to direct itself towards an adult audience in the 1950s and 1960s, an evolution that was accompanied by diversifications in style, genre and, eventually, cultural status, a strong trend for very sexualized depictions of women was established – one which endured (and, arguably, still does) for decades, leaving *bande dessinée* theorist and creator Benoît Peeters to lament in 1994 of the medium in general that '[i]n most albums, female faces and bodies remain devoid of individual existence due to their constant depiction using the same patterns and clichés of expressionless seduction'[12] (Peeters 1994: 52n80). Women were more frequently present following this evolution of the medium, but realistically flawed human women – 'real' women – once again, were not.

A more detailed historical account of women's depiction in the medium throughout the twentieth century, including exceptions and nuances to the above, is set out in this book and, as such, this introduction includes only a simplified sketch of the most important and relevant details. Presenting these general points briefly here, however, is useful in explaining the persistence of the perceived difficulties in drawing women that has been noted amongst artists of the later twentieth (and twenty-first) centuries like Moebius and Trondheim. It is reasonable to imagine, in addition to the anxiety caused by looking at women (and, thus, in creating images of women to be looked at, as the artist is always the first to see their creation) posited by previous feminist art criticism, that the depiction of women (or, often, the absence of women entirely) throughout the earlier medium impacted greatly upon the creative processes of later artists (male or female) – indeed Jacques Tardi has indicated that the lack of female characters previously in the *bande dessinée* significantly complicated the task of creating Adèle Blanc-Sec (Finet and Tardi 2010: 8), his most famous character creation and an exceptional female figure in the medium (see Chapter 4 of this book). Thus, these 'women problems' have, to a notable extent, endured and been reproduced in a cyclical fashion.

The previous pages have set out, in broad strokes, two sources of the difficulties expressed by some key artists of the twentieth-century *bande dessinée* medium in drawing women – that of creating images of 'real' women and that of creating these images within the specificities of the *bande dessinée* form. One simple but important point remains to be made in reference to each of these sources, however, and that is that they are both products of artistic creation within, and traditionally adhering to, a male-dominated and, more importantly, a masculine-valorizing system.[13] This means that, despite their appearance of inevitability within this system, they are contingent and, thus, able to be challenged. Griselda Pollock (2003: 181) reminds us in her work that the anxiety provoked by women's 'lack' – and, of course, the notion of this 'lack' itself – is merely symbolic in origin and that 'it is only within social and cultural framing that the feminine becomes a masculine fetish'. In 'Visual Pleasure and Narrative Cinema', Mulvey (2009: 16) claimed that new forms of political and alternative filmmaking could contend the assumptions encoded into mainstream Hollywood narratives fixated on the contradictory fear and desire directed towards the sight of women. This is also true of the narrative-visual form *bande dessinée* but is necessarily achieved using techniques specific to the medium. Similarly, the influence of, and eventual adherence to, traditional historical modes of representing women in the medium is able to be challenged as well as followed (this does not negate the importance of influence but, rather, raises the possibility of consciously identifying and reacting against these modes of depiction).

The primary goal of this book is to study, for the first time, the two facets of the 'women problems' outlined above in reference to the *bande dessinée*. It undertakes this task by examining key examples of the medium from 1905, the year of the first appearance of Bécassine – the first popular, recurring female character – to 2008, the year in which work on this project began. It both analyses the visual and narrative strategies used in these examples to contain and defuse the problematic presence of woman and reflects in detail on the historical evolution of female depiction within the medium. In line with the last point made regarding the contingency of the norms of female representation, however, it also examines certain modern examples of the *bande dessinée* that challenge the persistent trends and techniques of female depiction and propose new means of 'seeing woman' in this art form.

***

The research presented in this book began, as noted, in 2008 and eventually became a Ph.D. dissertation. At this time, there were very few publications to cite as evidence of existing study into depictions of women in the *bande dessinée*. Today, in 2017, this research landscape is still sparsely populated in comparison to other areas of women's visual studies, but has certainly been improved. A 2016 special issue of the journal *Alternative Francophone* entitled 'La bande dessinée au féminin', for example, offered a variety of perspectives on certain female authors and their characters, in addition to a brief overview of women figures in the medium more generally – the latter adding to a similarly useful summary written by Thierry Groensteen for *neuvième art 2.0* in 2013. A gradually increasing variety of articles (and some postgraduate research dissertations) exist that examine the work of francophone female artists and the figures they depict (see, for example, Miller 2001; Carrier 2004; Boy 2009; Brogniez 2010) – the notable success of, and wider scholarly interest in, Marjane Satrapi's *Persepolis* should be noted as a factor in this increase – and a smaller number of publications are available that study women characters in specific male-created strips (Davreux 2006; Laity 2002; Lipani-Vaissade 2009). Regarding the latter field of study, Annie Pilloy's *Les Compagnes des héros de B.D: Des femmes et des bulles* (1994) remains a rare example of a full-length monograph that takes a broader stance in examining the representation of women characters in the *bande dessinée*, but limits itself to the study of children's strips published by Belgian companies Lombard and Dupuis in the second half of the twentieth century.

A wider range of research concerning women in, and as creators of, Anglo-American comics exists than that which focuses particularly on examples of the *bande dessinée*, despite attempts by francophone industry figures such as Chantal Montellier to raise the profile of women artists.[14] Trina Robbins, a self-proclaimed 'herstorian' of American comics, has long championed the study of women in sequential art (cf. Robbins and Yronwode 1985; Robbins 1993, 1999) and a recent vogue for 'Women in Comics' studies has seen the launching of reading groups, the holding of several symposia and the publication of some useful texts over the last ten or so years, particularly focusing on female-created autobiographical comics (Tensuan 2006; Cvetkovich 2008; Lightman 2014; Oksman 2016). Hillary Chute's *Graphic Women: Life Narrative and Contemporary Comics* (2010) is perhaps the most well-known of these, and is undoubtedly an invaluable contribution to the study of self-representation and trauma in women's graphic life writing.

What is clear from this brief summary of the current scholarly landscape, however, is that studies of women characters in comic art generally are primarily contained within studies focusing on female artists; still very little research exists, particularly in the context of the francophone-specific *bande dessinée*, on depictions of women throughout the medium, drawn by the majority-male pool of artists. It is interesting to note that the direction taken by *bande dessinée* studies in this respect is opposite to that taken in feminist literary criticism, which began with 'Images of Women' analysis in the 1970s, examining the depiction of female characters through male-dominated literary history, before progressing on to studies of women's writing. The rise of academic attention to the *bande dessinée* notable from the 1990s onwards with the publication of texts such as those by Peeters (1991), Groensteen (1999), Grove (2005) and Miller (2007), however, occurred alongside the rise in numbers and visibility of women artists in the medium at the turn of the millennium. Thus, the focus in the contemporaneously burgeoning field of feminist *bande dessinée* criticism on works created by women (noted in references above) is appropriate and understandable. Nevertheless, developing the under-examined 'Drawn Images of Women' field of studies is an important undertaking for two key reasons. As already indicated, images of women not only reflect the assumptions and fears held about women, but also contribute to the continual re-forming of these attitudes. Depictions of female figures in the *bande dessinée* are not immune from these processes and, therefore, investigating the images displayed of women in the medium is valuable as a contribution to the wider field of feminist art criticism. Second, examining the representation of women in the *bande dessinée*, including the visual and narrative processes used to counteract the noted 'woman problems' and, in turn, those used to challenge the notions behind these problems, gives critical insight into the history of the *bande dessinée*, into the formal construction of the sequential art medium and how this construction may be artistically manipulated. This book undertakes these tasks, analysing female figures drawn by male and female artists, thus taking a first step towards examining the representation of women across the modern *bande dessinée* as a whole.

***

This book is divided into three sections. Two study the representations of women as characters in works by male artists and the third examines depictions of women figures by female artists. Feminist literary critic Elaine Showalter addressed the need to study women authors separately from their male counterparts in 1971:

> Women writers should not be studied as a distinct group on the assumption that they write alike, or even display stylistic resemblances distinctively feminine. But women do have a special history susceptible to analysis, which includes such complex considerations as the economics of their relation to the literary marketplace; the effects of social and political changes in women's status upon individuals, and the implications of stereotypes of the woman writer and restrictions of her artistic autonomy.
>
> (quoted in Moi 1995: 50)

This reasoning equally applies to female creators of the *bande dessinée* who, as will be discussed in detail in Chapter 10, have been a marked minority within the medium throughout the twentieth century and, thus, have experienced a different relation to the process of *bande dessinée* creation and publication than their male counterparts.

The two sections studying female figures drawn by male artists are divided between those figures occupying 'primary' and 'secondary' character roles. For the reasons explained above (amongst others), women characters are much more likely to inhabit secondary or minor roles (relative to one or more male leading characters) in strips across the history of the *bande dessinée* – Pilloy (1994, p. 16) states, for example, that in her study of strips published by Lombard and Dupuis (and, as she notes, there is nothing to indicate that other publishers do things differently) male characters occupied the principal roles in some 90% of the series studied. This being the case, where female characters do occupy the starring role of a strip or series, particular attention needs to be paid to this rather exceptional occurrence, resulting in the separate study of principal and secondary figures. Furthermore, the way in which one gazes upon a leading character (usually towards whom the look of the reader is most often directed) and a minor figure (generally depicted less frequently, placed below the main character in the representational hierarchy) is necessarily different – the stylistic and narrative strategies used to depict (and neutralize the presence of) women in each correspondingly varies. The final section, studying women characters created by women, takes as its focus female principal characters, with female secondary characters at times analysed alongside, where appropriate.

Each section begins with a history of female representation and then is divided into chapters that analyse women characters from carefully chosen *bandes dessinées*. Section 1 examines the three most well-known leading ladies of the *bande dessinée* medium thus far – Bécassine, Barbarella and Adèle Blanc-Sec. It analyses the visual and narrative processes used in their depiction both throughout the series of *bandes dessinées* in which they appear and, in order to provide a more concentrated study, in one specific narrative per character. All of these analyses show that, despite their positions as exceptional female principal characters in a medium dominated by male figures, their presence as women is continually, in differing ways, denied. Bécassine, the first popular recurring female character of the *bande dessinée*, was originally conceived in 1905 by a male-female creative team, Jacqueline Rivière and Joseph-Porphyre Pinchon. The principal creative pair behind the long-running series and the most well-known depictions of the character was to be artist Pinchon alongside Maurice 'Caumery' Languereau, however, and, thus, Bécassine is discussed in this section focussing on male-drawn strips. This chapter analyses the evolution of, and, exceptionally for a female BD figure, the existing studies dedicated to, Bécassine. It combines these analyses with a close study of the 1915 album *Bécassine pendant la Grande Guerre* to show that, despite being retrospectively dubbed as a pioneering, emancipated female figure of the burgeoning medium, Bécassine is stylistically and narratively defeminized and, indeed, dehumanized. These manipulations effectively work to remove the presence (and thus the problem) of 'woman' from this most well-known of female *bande dessinée* characters.

This is followed, in Chapter 2, by a study of Jean-Claude Forest's Barbarella and a close-study of the 1964 album *Barbarella* – a watershed album for the Franco-Belgian industry, credited as proof of the financial viability of adult-directed *bande dessinée* in a previously almost entirely juvenile market. This analysis considers the narrative evolution of the character across all her adventures and her gradual 'grounding', in addition to closely examining the visual techniques used by Forest in *Barbarella* to eroticize and fetishize the eponymous figure again resulting, but in a markedly different manner to Bécassine, in the neutralizing of the female presence.

This first section closes with a study of Jacques Tardi's Adèle Blanc-Sec and a detailed analysis of her depiction in *Adèle et la bête* (1976), finding that Tardi employs several narrative and visual techniques to, paradoxically, both idealize and demonize the character of Adèle, once again resulting in the diffusion and destabilization of her femaleness.

Section 2 studies the representation of secondary women characters in a diverse range of strips, aiming to provide an overview of this most common form of female depiction across the medium. Whereas the works studied in Section 1 all show varying examples of how 'woman' has been neutralized in the characterizations of these most well-known female figures, the *bandes dessinées* of this second collection of studies principally show how the noted 'women problems' may be counteracted by the 'containment' implicit in many forms of traditional female typing. It begins with the most famous French series in the history of the medium, *Astérix le Gaulois*, created by René Goscinny and Albert Uderzo in 1959, and analyses its collective secondary women figures before presenting a close study of the 1991 album *La Rose et le glaive*, which uncharacteristically builds its narrative around the actions of these female characters. This chapter studies how the female presence of this long-running series is constrained within mostly negative domestic stereotypes, whilst also acknowledging the importance of female presence (originally entirely omitted from the strip) to the overarching *Astérix* narrative and the imaginary world created by Goscinny and Uderzo.

This section then studies a quite different example of the form, a two-part *bande dessinée* adaptation entitled *La Vie de ma mère* (2003) by Jean-Christophe Chauzy and Thierry Jonquet, developed from Jonquet's 1994 novel of the same name. This narrative contains female characters of different class backgrounds and the analysis shows how these women are typed and, thus, contained accordingly. A comparative study of certain elements of Jonquet's novel adapted into this *bande dessinée* allows for theoretical reflection on what is specific about typing in the sequential art format and how elements of the form are used to contribute to this depiction of women.

Chapter 8 then takes as its focus short story 'Congo blanc' (1992) and full-length one-shot *Lettres d'Outremer* (1996) by Warnauts and Raives, two *bande dessinée* narratives that feature secondary women characters of African origin. These close-studies analyse how predominantly stylistic aspects specific to sequential art are manipulated by Warnauts and Raives in order to present the women depicted as representations of the 'Black Venus' – a type specific to black women, emphasizing eroticism and Otherness as a means to neutralize the compounded fear generated by their femaleness and 'exotic' difference.

This study of secondary female characters concludes with a close analysis of Manu Larcenet's four-part series *Le Combat ordinaire* (2003–08). This narrative allows for a reflection on depictions of women of different generations and social backgrounds. The analysis identifies both the typing used in the representation of these secondary women and also the evolution and eventual dissipation of certain of these types as the narrative progresses, presenting an example of the use of the medium and its expressive capabilities as a means of challenging female depictions traditional in earlier examples of the *bande dessinée* and of recognizing the changing place of both women and men in post-industrial France.

The final section of this book concentrates on representations of women drawn by women artists. It is not the contention of this book that there exists a specifically female *bande dessinée* aesthetic, nor that women artists are, by the simple fact of their sex, immune from the anxieties of drawing women or from drawing women in adherence to traditional modes of representation. However, due to women's positioning as 'not-men' and, thus, as 'outsiders' in the masculine-centred societal system, which has, and continues to, govern artistic production, women's creations may contain a particular political challenge to these dominant modes of representation that is worthy of study. While recognizing the existence, then, of female artists' work that does not question the traditional status quo (and, as in the case of Larcenet's *Le Combat ordinaire*, certainly recognizing the existence of male artists' work that does), the case studies of the closing section of this book examine women characters created by women who manipulate the formal properties of the medium and consciously interrogate standard narrative tropes used to define and neutralize the female presence.

Chapter 11 studies the *bandes dessinées* of *Ah! Nana*, the first (and only) feminist *bande dessinée* magazine, published from 1976 to 1978. A comparative analysis of selected strips from this magazine shows a wide variation of female representation, whilst also exhibiting a particular focus on examining the notion of women as victims, showing them both as helpless before, and complicit in, their own symbolic and physical oppression.

Chapter 12 then studies the work of Chantal Montellier – one of the most prolific *bande dessinée* creators of the French-language tradition – with a close study of her 1984 album *Odile et les crocodiles*. This analysis examines how Montellier uses the highly unconventional female figure of Odile and a complex web of artistic and literary references to critique the representation of women in textual and modern art, most specifically the *bande dessinée*.

Finally, Chapter 13 examines Aurélia Aurita's 2006 work *Fraise et chocolat*, an often-explicit autobiographical account of the artist's relationship with another *bande dessinée* creator. This analysis shows how Aurita interweaves everyday and comedic narrative aspects, in addition to a frequently bare and simplistic visual style, to normalize and, thus, desexualize the sight of female nudity, thereby challenging one of the most dominant trends of women's representation in the *bande dessinée* medium (and, indeed, the wider world of visual art).

As a first step in the domain of *bande dessinée* 'Images of Women' criticism, this book of course cannot examine every aspect of female depiction throughout the medium. It is intended, however, as a study that provides a useful framework for thinking about the intricacies and specificities of female depiction within the art form, in response to the difficulties in representing women laid out above, and one that might serve as a jumping-off point for further study of female figures in, and women's visual relationship to, the *bande dessinée*.

SECTION 1

PRIMARY WOMEN CHARACTERS

1

Bécassine to Barbarella ... But What Came in Between? An Introductory History of Female Primary Characters in the Francophone *Bande Dessinée*

Although there now exist several encyclopaedic volumes cataloguing the *bande dessinée* (BD) throughout the twentieth century alongside various monographs amassing among them a comprehensive picture of the medium's evolution, gathering information on the representation and development of female characters in the BD from this existing research is far from straightforward. As previously noted, still relatively few scholars make specific mention of female pictorial presence (or absence) in the *bande dessinée* in their theoretical works, whilst in encyclopaedic historical tomes, a proportion of strips that have been produced in the last hundred years featuring women as principal characters are not included. This may be a consequence of authors basing their choice of included material on sales, or the perceived influence of strips on the medium as a whole. Whatever the reason, the omission of these female-led *bandes dessinées* from apparently comprehensive histories further contributes to an obscuring of the female character's place in the medium, underlining and perpetuating the circular relation of cultural memory to academic attention. In what follows, a detailed chronology of recurring principal female characters by male creators will be outlined in order to establish the progression of these previously ignored figures within the *bande dessinée*, charting how evolving styles, trends and, indeed, changing legal restrictions influenced their depictions. This historical grounding will also provide the necessary context for close analysis of specific women characters in the following section.

The starting point in charting the presence of women in the *bande dessinée* begins, as one might expect, with that of the mass-produced, modern medium itself: in the pages of the turn-of-the century children's press. Towards the end of the 1800s, weekly *illustrés* for children, featuring what would now be referred to as *bandes dessinées* (the term itself not widely used until the 1950s) began to flourish (see Miller 2007: 15–17). Following publications for young, gender-unspecified audiences, which nonetheless seemed distinctly directed towards boys – in the first five issues of *La Jeunesse Illustré* in 1903, for example, only one strip out of its sixteen-page mixture of *bandes dessinées* and text-based stories centred around a female character – certain *illustrés* were created that directly targeted a young female readership. These publications were of mixed format combining stories, illustrations, rainy-day ideas, instructions for the fabrication of doll clothes etc., with content designed specifically for a particular social class targeted by each journal. These publications for girls were to provide platforms for some of the first regularly recurring children's *bandes dessinées* and, unsurprisingly, due to the gender of the target readership, the first female principal characters of the developing medium.

The first journal of the twentieth century created to focus solely on a young female audience was *La Semaine de Suzette*, which made its inaugural appearance in February 1905 with a set goal to provide a 'quality publication for girls from good families' (Gaumer 2010: 765).[1] From this class-driven motivation, the editor-in-chief of *La Semaine de Suzette*, Jacqueline Rivière, in collaboration with artist Joseph Pinchon, created the character and strip *Bécassine*: the first, and to this day most well-known, regularly recurring female principal *bande dessinée* character, who made her debut alongside the journal on the back page of its first publication.[2] *Bécassine* would eventually become very popular with the journal's readers, and the resultant albums, figurines and films would ensure the strip's status as a veritable phenomenon beyond the confines of its parent publication. However, in the early days of *La Semaine de Suzette*, the *bande dessinée*'s appearance was far from regular, with months occasionally passing between episodes of the strip. In the meantime, the journal continued to publish a limited number of *bandes dessinées* per instalment, but none which featured characters who were to re-appear regularly in the long term.

On the whole, *La Semaine de Suzette* was to remain a more text-based journal than its future competitors. Examples of the *bande dessinée* were, particularly initially, limited within its pages, perhaps thought too proletarian for the publication's class-inspired motivation (Gaumer 2010: 765). However, the growing popularity of the medium generally, and that of the *Bécassine* series in particular, meant that over time more of the journal was devoted to the adventures of the Breton maid and other stories in strip form.[3]

Following the pioneering introduction of *Bécassine* in 1905, another notable strip featuring a regularly recurring female principal character made its entrance before the end of the decade. *L'Espiègle Lili* appeared for the first time in 1909 in the first issue of the illustrated journal *Fillette*. Created with a strong Christian backing, *Fillette* was destined for an audience with a more modest income and education than *La Semaine de Suzette* (Lipani-Vaissade 2009: 155), with its content differing accordingly. From the outset appearing as a publication with more of an image-based focus than its bourgeois competitor, the first issue of *Fillette* featured *bandes dessinées* of varying lengths on ten out of its sixteen pages. Presumably anticipating a lower literacy rate amongst its readers than that of *La Semaine de Suzette*, this new *illustré* for girls continued its elevated proportion of image to text throughout its long publication span (1909–64). It contained, like its earlier counterpart, many single-episode strips featuring female characters that would never re-appear. *L'Espiègle Lili*, however, became a popular drawn strip feature. Originally drawn by André Vallet and Jo Valle, this series featured the cheeky exploits of the young eponymous figure. Although it garnered neither the fame nor the sales of *Bécassine*, this strip was to outperform its more successful counterpart in terms of longevity and album-production, ending in 1988 after 73 published hard-backed books. It was principally drawn by three artists, with René Giffey taking over from Vallet in 1921 and, in turn, Al.G taking the artist reins in 1947. Two entirely new tales significantly modernizing the series were published in 1996 and 1998 drawn by Anne Chatel, entitled *Lili chez les top models* and *Lili à Chérie FM*. Since the appearance of these albums, however, no further episodes featuring Lili have been published.

The character of Lili was reinvented several times over her considerable lifespan, with each of her artists interpreting her focus and temperament differently. Initially, under the partnership of Vallet and Valle, Lili proved to be worth her 'mischievous' title, spending her time playing practical jokes. Following her artistic adoption in 1921 by René Giffey, however, Lili began to grow up, and even married in episodes published in 1923. Her progression into adulthood was short-lived, however, as from 1925 Giffey chose to return Lili to her original infantine incarnation (Moliterni et al. 2004: 1106). Under Al. G's direction following the Second World War, Lili again evolved to shake off her *enfant terrible* roots and the strip became more adventurous, featuring episodes of its main character travelling and trying a multitude of different jobs as she tries to earn her own living. The '*espiègle*' epithet was eventually abandoned from the title of the *bande dessinée* and its structure and style was considerably modernized, with Al. G introducing the use of speech bubbles to replace the original format of above-panel captions (Moliterni et al. 2004: 1106).

It is interesting to note that despite being one of the longest-running francophone *bande dessinée* characters, with a span of 89 years between her first and last appearance, Lili is often omitted from non-encyclopaedic histories of the twentieth-century *bande dessinée*. As has become the case for many of the female-led strips from the pre-1960 period, the retrospectively bolstered iconic status of *Bécassine* seems to have overshadowed, if not all but erased, the memory of other early women principal characters from the medium's collective consciousness. The original mischievous incarnation of Lili, however, seems to have provided a blueprint for the future depiction of female primary characters during the first half of the century in France and Belgium, as, as shall be seen, almost all were to be drawn as little girls in light-hearted adventures, drawn in traditionally structured strips that separated text and image, a recipe not mirrored in either style or substance by pre-war US imports featuring female leads and one which certainly did not survive the turning point that was to be 1949.

Following the introduction of *L'Espiègle Lili* in 1909, no popular recurrent female *bande dessinée* figures are identifiable until a decade later. In November 1919, a new journal for girls was published, its first issue appearing as a free supplement to *Le Petit Vingtième*.[4] The journal, named *Lili* after the character of the same name, made a brief claim to unisex appeal in a sub-heading on its first cover page that encouraged adults to '[g]ive this magazine to a little girl or boy and make them smile' (Anon. 1919: 1).[5] However, this request was never repeated in subsequent issues and even within this first publication the uniquely female direction of the *illustré* was clear. Despite the name of the journal, the series *Lili* was never to appear in it, continuing its pre-publication in *Fillette*. The name of this new journal was connected to Jo Valle's mischievous creation, however, as explained in a letter from the character Lili to the readers of the *illustré* in its first issue in which she described her pleasure at becoming 'the inspiration for a new magazine' (Anon. 1919: 3).[6] *Lili*, which was to have a much shorter lifespan than the publications discussed above (it was discontinued in 1926), produced one strip notable for its regularity, which it introduced in its first issue: *Ninette et Clo-Clo*. This new series followed the humorous and harmless exploits of the 8-year-old Ninette and her younger sister Clo-Clo. Jo Valle, the original writer of *L'Espiègle Lili*, provided the texts alongside André Galland's drawings. A rigidly formatted structure saw each story composed of three strips, divided into two rectangular panels on either side of a circular panel with text in prose, equally divided and placed below its corresponding illustration. The *bande dessinée* featuring female figures and directed towards a female readership remained, at this time, stylistically traditional.

Following *Ninette et Clo-Clo*, the next notable female-led *bande dessinée* to be regularly included in a French-language publication did not appear until 1929, with the *Fillette* strip *Nigaude et Malicette*.[7] There are no strips featuring women principal characters from earlier in the 1920s in France or Belgium identified in any reference book or source consulted in the compilation of this history, suggesting a dearth of production apparently not experienced throughout the wider international medium as the appearance in the United States of popular strips *Winnie Winkle* (1920) or *Little Orphan Annie* (1924) attests (both of these American strips *are* featured in such *bande dessinée* dictionaries as those of Gaumer and Moliterni).[8] This lack of comparably remembered female figures implies a particular reluctance on the part of the Franco-Belgian medium in the early twentieth century to include female characters in its strips. This reluctance would continue, to varying extents, throughout the century. *Nigaude et Malicette* made its debut in the twenty-first year of *Fillette*'s production, in the issue of 29th January 1929, signed by Ribémont. Occupying a double page in each issue, it followed the format of the francophone strips created before it, with frame-less images separated by sizeable gutter spaces rather than occupying distinctly outlined panels, and all text placed below the illustrations. From the pages of *Fillette*, and later through the course of four albums published by the Société Parisienne d'Edition (SPE), it told the story of two cheeky young girls who, after creating continual mischief in their rural village, are each sent to work as maids for rich families. The pair is sometimes accompanied in their adventures by Zoé, a chef to one of the families. Zoé is a rotund, middle-aged black woman, drawn with excessively large lips, commanding a poor level of French and described as 'lazy and greedy'[9] (Ribémont 1929: 3), reminiscent to the modern-day reader of the Congolese inhabitants of Hergé's later *Tintin au Congo* and to the 1920s reader of African characters in the work of Alain de Saint-Ogan.[10] Her appearance and occupation strongly suggest her to be a *bande dessinée* incarnation of the 'black mammy' stereotype, and it is interesting to note that she is not the first to grace the pages of *Fillette*: in its publications from the mid-1920s the journal included characters of African origin in non-recurring or short-term strips in several of its issues, with the 'black mammy' figure featuring among them. The mother of Mokoko, Peggy's black friend from the strip *Les Aventures du bébé Peggy* (1926), for example, is very similar to Zoé in appearance and behaviour. The presence of this stereotype in these *bandes dessinées* would seem to clash with Jan Nederveen Pieterse's assertion in *White on Black: Images of Africa and Blacks in Western Popular Culture* that the black mammy stereotype was largely confined to the United States, with European popular culture overwhelmingly sexualizing its images of the black female (Pieterse 1995: 178).[11]

Whilst *Nigaude et Malicette* is absent from both Moliterni and Gaumer's encyclopaedic volumes on the *bande dessinée* (1994, 1997), as with *Winnie Winkle* and *Little Orphan Annie* the imported American strips featuring female principal characters which appeared, translated, in French-language publications from the 1930s and would dominate female-centred *bande dessinée* until the Second World War receive complete entries. The first to appear was *Little Annie Rooney*, translated into French as *La Petite Annie* or *Les Malheurs d'Annie* (Gaumer and Moliterni 1997: 483), which made its debut in *Fillette* in 1933. It then moved to *Le Journal de Mickey* the following year, making it the first regularly published female-led strip to appear in a French-language publication not specifically directed towards girls, and the only strip prominently featuring a female character to be included in the early issues of the era-defining *Journal de Mickey*. *Little Annie Rooney* told the story of a young orphan girl and her survival throughout a series of dramatic adventures with her dog Zéro. It first appeared in 1927 in the United States, written and drawn by Verd, and was largely influenced by Harold Gray's *Little Orphan Annie*. The style of the *bande dessinée* differs significantly from those strips featuring female principal characters discussed above, with its clearly outlined panels encasing both images and text, and frequent encircling of dialogue in speech bubbles, more reminiscent of the modern medium than the strip's noted predecessors.

The year 1937 saw the introduction of *Polly and her Pals* (translated into French as *Poupette et son fiancé* then *Poupette et sa famille*) in the relatively short-lived *Journal de Toto* (1937–40). A comic strip in the literal sense, *Polly and her Pals* based its humour around the flirtatious antics of the beautiful young Polly and, of course, her friends. It embodied in its principal character a modern, emancipated young woman quite removed from the troublesome little girls featured in earlier French strips, particularly those of *La Semaine de Suzette* such as *Ninette et Clo-Clo*. It should be noted, however, that as this comic developed, it increasingly shifted its focus away from its eponymous female character towards the figure of Polly's diminutive father (Gaumer 2010: 687). Following the classic American strip format of defined panels containing text and image as seen with *Little Annie Rooney*, *Polly and Her Pals* distinguished itself from its contemporaries by its graphic style, described as 'an interesting geometric style, close to futurism' (Gaumer 2010: 687).[12] Such innovative stylistic features, in addition to its initial representation of women, underlined the difference between this imported strip and its more traditional francophone counterparts. This aesthetic and thematic gulf between US and Franco-Belgian strips was then further underlined by the publication of Frank Godwin's *Connie* in *Le Journal de Mickey* from 1938, a strip that distinguished itself via its innovative, asymmetrical format and saw its primary character evolve from sentimental and love-struck towards an adventurous, more mature role as the strip developed (Moliterni et al. 2004: 1156).

Despite the American domination of the *bande dessinée* throughout the 1930s, original French-language strips featuring female principal characters still appeared in the weekly journals, mostly in short-term serializations or one-off strips that were generally less popular and are certainly less remembered than their US-created counterparts. One strip that did run regularly in *Fillette* from 1937, and was subsequently published in four albums by the SPE, was *Les Aventures de la petite Shirley*. This was another artistic product from the pen of René Giffey, a man who was responsible for many of the francophone female-centred strips of the era, but who was also, interestingly, a noted creator of risqué cartoons featuring nude women for various popular adult publications (see Filippini 2006: 150–51).

Les Aventures de la petite Shirley contributes to the notable divide visible between US and Franco-Belgian female-led strips in the pre-war period in both its traditional style and format (featuring a notable divide between image and text and no clear outline of panels) and its focus on a 6-year-old girl.

The 1940s were far from rich in their creation of new strips featuring female central characters. The industry was severely disrupted by the Second World War until its conclusion, with many *illustrés* forced to fold (Grove 2005: 19). However, the limited *bande dessinée* production from this decade nonetheless attested to the beginning of an important rupture in trends regarding the representation of women within the Franco-Belgian market. One leading female figure who appeared in the early 1940s – and whose creation and demise was a definite product of this exceptional period in history – was Zoubinette, from the strip of the same name drawn by Auguste Liquois (using the pen name Robert Ducte). Described by Albert Algoud as 'an anti-Resistance and anti-Semitic heroine' (Algoud 2010: n.pag.),[13] Zoubinette's adventures appeared in the French pro-Nazi publication *Mérinos*. The sometimes sexualized nature of her exploits as 'a patriotic French girl who fell prey to the dishonest abuses of Resistance terrorists and other such bandits' (Grove 2005: 139) indicates that Zoubinette was an early, but now mostly forgotten, example of a French-created eroticized female BD character, prefiguring what was to become the dominant characteristic of female depiction in the second half of the twentieth century.

Following the conclusion of the war, *bande dessinée* production remained relatively limited throughout the remainder of the decade with two new notable female-led strips identifiable from this five-year span. The first, *Durga-Rani, reine des jungles*, made its first appearance in *Fillette* on 19th December 1946. Written by fantasy literature author Jean Sylvère and drawn by *Pieds Nickelés* artist Pellos, *Durga-Rani* presented the story of a female Tarzan-esque character who abandons civilization as a child to become the 'queen of the jungle'. The series follows her adventures in which her 'duty to save the innocent' sees her emerge from the jungle to save young princes and stop the misdeeds of evil sultans. Drawn by Pellos in a more realistic artistic style than that used in *Les Pieds Nickelés*, the pages of *Durga-Rani* appearing in *Fillette* did not follow a standard format. Some, like the first strip to appear in *Fillette* in 1946, contained neither panels nor strips, resembling more with their unspecified structure an illustrated story than a *bande dessinée*. Others, particularly as the story developed (although there was no consistent progression of the strip's format towards the unwavering adoption of a classically recognizable *bande dessinée* format) were organized into three strips of images with text below, with some further examples displaying distinct, outlined panels. Although not a strip that would later yield a lengthy succession of albums like the *Bécassine* series, *Durga-Rani* was published and re-published outside of *Fillette* several times and over the course of more than fifty years. Three collections of pages were published by the SPE in 1949, and further re-edited into two versions in 1976 by Serg. The 1990s saw the appearance of three *Durga-Rani* booklets following on from the Serg publications, edited by *Les Amis de Pellos*, while two further collections, collating strips from *Fillette* between 1949 and 1953, were published in 2003 by Regards (Gaumer 2010: 285). One reason for the continued publication of *Durga-Rani* no doubt stems from the quality of Pellos's illustrations. Another, however, perhaps concerns the exceptional place the strip's central figure occupies in the French *bande dessinée* tradition. Durga-Rani is not strictly a super-heroine, as like Tarzan she has no supernatural powers, but as a supposed consequence of living her life in the jungle, she is shown to possess an array of heightened 'natural' powers – such as speed, strength, agility and the ability to communicate with animals – which places her nonetheless within the definitive domain of the 'superhero character'. As such, she represents a unique figure in *bande dessinée* creation as the only French-devised female superhero. None are discernible either before or after *Durga-Rani*, the superhero/ine genre remaining almost exclusively the domain of American creators.

The exceptional characterization of Durga-Rani finally suggests an influence of imported US strips on French-created female figures, after many years of starkly contrasting characterization. The influx of such strips continued in the 1940s, as four months after the introduction of *Durga-Rani* in December 1946, *Fillette* again launched within its pages a strip featuring an American female principal character, this time the translated version of the Chicago Tribune's *Aggie Mack* (a story about the Cinderella-esque teenage Aggie), re-titled *Pauvre Aggie!…* in the French publication.

Durga-Rani and *Pauvre Aggie!…* remained in *Fillette* until the end of the 1940s and beyond. They were not the only *bandes dessinées* to feature within the *illustré* during the immediate post-war period. The adventures of *Oscar le petit canard* closed each issue with a single-page story on the back page, while serialized strips featuring male central characters also appeared in this period – Kline's science-fiction tale *Stany Beule dans la Lune* and the American *Aventures de Miki* ran for many months. The post-war *Semaine de Suzette*, however, which recommenced on 30 May 1946, featured almost no *bande dessinée* content. Bécassine re-appeared in the issue of 1st January 1948 for the serialization of her adventure *Les Petits Ennuis de Bécassine*, but this would appear to be the only prominent strip in the journal until the end of the decade.

Thierry Groensteen (2013) notes the presence in this immediate post-war era of a trend particularly found in the Christian press of pairing a boy and girl (normally a pair of relatives) as lead figures of a strip and suggests that this trend, in fact, contributes the largest place to the depiction of women in the *bande dessinée* of the time. One key example of this, *Fripounet et Marisette* (principally serialized in the Action catholique des enfants–sponsored *illustré* of the same name) exhibited a practice that would become more visible in the 1950s (see Chapter 5 of this book) as it began in 1943 featuring only the male character Fripounet before adding Marisette later, in 1945. Certainly in this strip, as in Maurice Cuvillier's *Sylvain et Sylvette* (which from 1941 appeared in *Coeurs Vaillants*, an *illustré* created by l'Union des œuvres catholiques de France) and another, later example of the trend, *Moky et Poupy* (first serialized in *Cœurs Vaillants* from 1958), the female half of the eponymous partnership is a prominently featured character. However, the male figure is often more active and acts in the 'hero' role – as seen, for example, in *Moky, Poupy et le volcan* (published in album format in 1960), in which Moky (a Native American boy) must save Poupy and his friends from the actions of the unscrupulous 'pale-faces'. Thus, the female figure takes, to an extent, the secondary role of the strip.

The last year of the 1940s saw the introduction in France of official restrictions on artistic content directed towards a young audience with the promulgation of the *Loi du 16 juillet 1949 sur les publications destinées à la jeunesse*. An interesting side effect of this new law was the reduction of the already understated appearance of women compared to men in the *bande dessinée*, with long-lasting effects. Ostensibly, this law was promulgated to protect children from harmful influences in the media, but, in reality, it presented two major restrictions to the representation of women in the Franco-Belgian drawn strip. The first was a huge reduction in the importation of American strips, due to the new condition that all foreign material for children be vetted before distribution with a view to prohibiting 'negative influences' such as 'banditry, lying, theft, laziness, cowardice, hatred, debauchery' (Grove 2010: 134),[14] which were easily interpreted as appearing in many American strips.[15] The introduction of the law therefore signalled the end of the dominance of American strips in the representation of women central characters in the interconnected French and Belgian markets, and allowed francophone artists again to come to the fore.

The second and more important consequence of the 1949 law for female representation in the *bande dessinée* concerns the interpretation of its ruling against the last of the negative influences noted above: 'debauchery'. Publishers began by warning their artists against the portrayal of 'seductive' female characters; however, fearful of censorship, this caution at times took an extreme turn, encouraging certain artists to avoid representing female characters altogether. According to René Goscinny in a 1976 interview, '[w]ell-meaning editors insisted that we mustn't include women with cleavage or characters who hit on girls. So, we got used to not putting women in our stories, or at least not very many, but it was to comply with the censorship' (quoted in Pilloy 1994: 11).[16] This over-cautious artistic reaction affected the representation of female secondary characters more visibly, as they were progressively removed from the background of strips following the promulgation of the law (see p. 85 of this book). In terms of primary female character representation, the effect was still clear, however, from the fact that very few notable new women principal characters are identifiable from the decade following the introduction of the legislation.

As the 1950s dawned, a further change specific to the history of female *bande dessinée* representation presented itself – perhaps as another side-effect of the 1949 law – concerning the primacy of *Fillette* and (to a lesser extent) *La Semaine de Suzette* in the (pre-)publication of new strips featuring female central characters. Of the four notable *bandes dessinées* introducing new women principal figures discernible from this decade – *Arabelle*, *Sylvie*, *Line* and *Prudence Petit-Pas* – each debuted in a different publication, with none appearing in either of these two previously prevalent *illustrés*. Connected to this is the fact that in the 1950s, *bandes dessinées* in daily newspapers began to appear regularly. Groensteen notes in *Astérix, Barbarella et Cie* that most newspapers during this era printed 'rather unoriginal syndicated BDs, but publications like *L'Humanité* and especially *France-Soir* […] [were] committed to creating something new' (2000: 156).[17] It is in the pages of *France-Soir* that Jean Ache's *Arabelle* first appeared in 1950, with Martial's *Sylvie* following in 1952 in the woman's weekly *Bonnes Soirées*. Although earlier in the history of female principal characters, strips were largely divided in their structure and format according to the national market from which they emanated – as discussed above, those *bandes dessinées* produced by francophone creators adhered much less to a standard strip/panel structure than their American counterparts and separated more distinctly their textual and visual elements – the stylistic construction of these strips, with text integrated into panels and the use of speech-bubbles, was indicative of a very definite shift in structure throughout female-focused strips away from the traditional French format and towards an 'American structuring style'.[18] Both also featured young, attractive women rather than little girls as their principal figures, building on *Zoubinette*'s example and taking female-focused *bande dessinée* creation a step closer to the sexualization of the 1960s. The figures of Arabelle and Sylvie most likely escaped the (often artist-imposed) censorship of female figures following the 1949 law because of their publication in the adult-oriented *France Soir* and *Bonne Soirée*, the new law only applying to children's publications.

Following the introduction of *Sylvie*'s distinctly middle-class adventures (a family strip, it followed the happy daily life of Sylvie, her husband and her son), no further notable female principal characters are identifiable until the appearance of *Line* in 1956. Published in the journal of the same name (which began several months before the introduction of its namesake strip), *Line* was created by

Nicolas Goujon and Françoise Bertier – artistic teams Charles Nugue and André Gaudelette and Paul Cuvelier and Greg later took over in 1957 and 1962 respectively (Gaumer 2010: 524) – and featured a vibrantly coloured, quasi-realist style that demarcated the strip more clearly for a younger audience than either *Arabelle* or *Sylvie*. *Line* followed the adventures of its eponymous character, a feisty blonde teen that solves police mysteries. Although the journal *Line* was fairly short-lived, folding in 1963, the influence of its star strip seems to have outlived it: following the *bande dessinée Line*'s mystery-solving theme, several more examples of female principal characters occupying detective-type roles were to emerge over the following decade, suggesting the evolution of female characterization towards somewhat more intelligent roles. *Prudence Petitpas,* the 'Miss Marple of the *bande dessinée*' (Gaumer 2010: 696), followed *Line*, appearing in *Tintin* in 1957. Petitpas, conceived and created by Maurice Maréchal, although aided from time to time by Greg and René Goscinny, amongst other artists, was a truly original addition to the progression of female principal characters in the *bande dessinée* due to her age. Whereas previously all leading women were young adults or, more often, children, Prudence Petitpas appeared as a kindly, grey-haired old lady, whose age nonetheless did not stop her from being a prolific mystery solver. Following Petitpas's arrival in the medium, the next notable elderly principal female character seems not to have appeared until 1982, in the guise of Jean-Marc Lelong's curmudgeonly *Carmen Cru*.

Into the 1960s, the trend for detective-style female characters continued with secretary-turned-investigator *Mam'Zelle Minouche*, by Roger Lécureux and Raymond Poivet, which launched in the pages of daily paper *L'Humanité* in 1961, boasting an elegantly realist black-and-white style. The evolution of female leading figures in the *bande dessinée* was soon to be revolutionized in terms of both characterization and quantity, however, as several months later, in January of 1962, Jean-Claude Forest's *Barbarella* would be printed in the tri-monthly *V-Magazine*. Forest is often credited with creating via *Barbarella* the first truly 'adult' francophone *bande dessinée* and heralding, alongside journal *Pilote*, the new mature direction of the medium from the 1960s onwards.[19] However, to attribute to the serialized 1962 *Barbarella* the status of inaugural adult strip is, as Grove has suggested, to ignore the appearance of *Zoubinette* during the war (2005: 138–39) and, as Groensteen attests, the presence of strips in newspapers across the 1950s that displayed notably mature directions (2000: 156). Forest's real feat with *Barbarella* in terms of the evolution of the BD market lay in proving the sales potential of a *bande dessinée* album for a mature readership, made clear by the popularity of the first hard-backed edition of the space-faring heroine in 1964, published by Eric Losfeld. The influence of the character Barbarella for the progression of female primary characters in the *bande dessinée* is less debatable, however. The popularity of

Barbarella's overtly exposed and eroticized portrayal, which ignored previously upheld standards of modesty in the representation of female characters – even more stringently respected since the introduction of the 1949 law – opened the door for openly sexualized female figures to be introduced into the mainstream French-language *bande dessinée*. Following Barbarella's example, several similar female principal characters appeared later in the 1960s, all printed by *Barbarella* publisher Eric Losfeld.[20] Two, *Jodelle* and *Pravda*, introduced in 1966 and 1968 respectively, were drawn by Guy Peellaert. *Jodelle*, scripted by Pierre Bartier, followed the exploits of the eponymous character, a beautiful red-headed spy who conducts much of her business in her underwear. This character was short-lived, appearing only in the album bearing her name (pre-published in satirical monthly magazine *Hara Kiri*). Over the course of her eponymous adventure, however, Peellaert's signature pop-art-inspired style was displayed, a distinctive artistic approach that would re-appear in 1968's *Pravda* (co-written with Pascal Thomas and also featuring a scantily dressed red-head), characterized by curved lines and bright, contrasting blocks of primary colours. The technique of pairing a bold artistic style with eroticized depictions of a female primary character is visible for the first time in these 1960s strips, but it would re-appear continually over the decades of the twentieth century (particularly in the 1980s, see below). Perhaps employed to artistically legitimize strips featuring particularly eroticized – and thus controversial – representations (this would become particularly true of strips by Italian erotic *bande dessinée* 'masters' Guido Crepax and Milo Manara whose work is consistently praised for its impressive draughtsmanship), this pairing was not evident across all sexualized representations of women in the late 1960s, however. *Epoxy,* drawn in 1968 by Cuvelier and the first *bande dessinée* written by Jean Van Hamme, told the story of a young woman, Epoxy, who finds herself in a parallel universe as an erotic plaything for the ruling Olympic gods. Contrasting with its thematic mix of fantasy and mythology – a combination that would come to dominate the *bande dessinée* production, particularly that featuring sexualized women, of the 1980s – this work displayed a realist style in muted colours, strikingly different from that of *Pravda* published in the same year.

Despite this sudden explosion of sexualized characters across the 1960s, the newly introduced female principal figures of the decade were not solely limited to eroticized figures. While the medium worked towards establishing a more mature audience over this decade and into the 1970s, strips for younger readers continued to be produced. New *bandes dessinées* featuring female leading roles such as *Sophie* (1964) and *Isabelle* (1968) were particularly found amongst the pages of Belgian *illustré Spirou*, a journal that, after the turn of the decade, went on to introduce two of the most well-known female leading characters destined for a young audience since Bécassine. The first was Natacha, from the strip of the same name, who made her *bande dessinée* debut in February of 1970, created by Gos and François Walthery. A pretty air-hostess drawn in a rounded, cartoony manner similar to the *École de Marcinelle* style,[21] Natacha travels the globe over the course of her adventures and is adept at finding herself in tricky situations. The popularity of the strip assured the publication of its first hard-backed album just a year after its serialized introduction, in 1971, with the series since producing a further twenty albums. This best-selling *bande dessinée* prefigured a sub-trend that would become more visible from the 1980s onwards of female characters appearing in publications destined for young readers but bearing somewhat sexualized depictions. Although *Natacha* was launched in *Spirou*, a journal for a juvenile readership, the character is sartorially eroticized – her standard air-hostess uniform includes a mini-skirt, showing off her long, tanned legs, and she appears in a tiny red bikini on the cover of her second album: *Natacha: Envol vers l'aventure*. This tendency recalls the trend in American pre-war 'action hero' strips, such as *Tarzan* and *Flash Gordon*, which – although aimed at young readers – featured scantily dressed female love-interests such as Jane Porter and Dale Arden and confirms the near-constant focus on the attractive appearance of female characters in the *bande dessinée* following the Second World War.[22]

Natacha's entry into *Spirou*'s ever-growing ranks was supplemented by that of new strip *Yoko Tsuno* in September of 1970. Created by Roger Leloup who, after the publication of 28 albums, continues to draw the strip, this *bande dessinée* illustrates via stark lines and detailed backgrounds Leloup's fidelity to the Hergéen *ligne claire* style. However, whilst Leloup's strip forms part of an established stylistic tradition, nothing is traditional about his choice of principal character, Yoko Tsuno. In addition to being an intelligent, technically capable engineer with a black belt in martial arts – thus proving her characterization already far removed from that of the pouting, mishap-prone air hostess Natacha – as a Japanese-born figure, Yoko is a rare example of an Asian character in the Franco-Belgian *bande dessinée*. Interestingly for two such different *bande dessinée* figures, Hélène Davreux briefly suggests in *Bécassine ou l'image d'une femme* that a common influence behind the creation of both Yoko Tsuno and Natacha was the strengthened voice of the Women's Liberation Movement in France following the political turmoil of May '68 (2006: 12), as both contributed to the increased visibility of women in visual art. The future influence (as noted above) of the somewhat sexualized Natacha does not indicate her creation to be a useful step in any progression towards balanced, less physically objectified female figures, however.

The vogue for sexualized female characters destined for more mature readers continued into the 1970s, a decade that, in terms of the wider medium, was characterized by expansion, experimentation and the pursuit of artistic freedom (Miller 2007: 25). *Paulette* (1970), drawn by Georges Pichard and written by Georges Wolinski and *Hypocrite* (1971), Jean-Claude Forest's female-focused follow-up to *Barbarella*, were both characters whose adventures often involved undressing on a whim.

Several short-lived strips appeared in the mid-1970s featuring female principal characters that are now largely forgotten, such as *Aymone* (1975) (although the character of Aymone is notable for being a young black woman in a medium populated almost exclusively by white female figures). Other figures such as Isabelle Fantouri and Julie Wood, both central characters of strips bearing their names, appeared in 1976, but achieved neither the longevity nor the impact of another eponymous character making her entrance into the medium in this year: Jacques Tardi's Adèle Blanc-Sec.[23] Drawn in Tardi's distinctive realist style set against meticulously researched backgrounds of Belle Époque Paris, *Les Aventures extraordinaires d'Adèle Blanc-Sec* remain un-concluded with the last of the nine published albums appearing in 2007. Alongside Bécassine and Barbarella, Adèle, a serial novel writer with a sardonic wit, prone to becoming embroiled in mysteries, is one of the most well-known female principal characters in the history of the *bande dessinée*. She made her leap onto the big screen in 2010 when her 'extraordinary adventures' became a film directed by Luc Besson, with Louise Bourgoin in the role of Adèle. In *Masters of the Ninth Art: Bandes Dessinées and Franco-Belgian Identity*, Matthew Screech notes that the *Aventures extraordinaires d'Adèle Blanc-Sec* had a marked thematic effect on the *bande dessinée* of the late 1970s and 1980s, encouraging the appearance of historically based series and heroes and heroines who 'like Adèle, are frequently overtaken by events' (2005: 152). This impact makes Adèle a rare example of a female primary figure whose characterization has influenced the medium as a whole. One strip that shows evidence of this influence is François Bourgeon's *Les Passagers du vent* which, like *Les Aventures extraordinaires d'Adèle Blanc-Sec*, boasts both a historical setting – in this case the late eighteenth century – and a female principal character with an apparently modern existential outlook. Like Adèle Blanc-Sec, the brave, intelligent, forward-thinking Isabeau is considered by some *bande dessinée* scholars a mould-breaking female figure 'of which there are few in the *bande dessinée*' (Moliterni et al. 2004: 1271)[24]; however, whilst it is true that Isabeau's characterization and her dominant contribution to the development of the series's narrative set her apart from many of her contemporary female figures, it remains the case that a significant part of her introduction is devoted to her sexualization. In the first half of the opening album, for example, in almost all scenes in which Isabeau and her female companion Agnès appear they are either naked, partially undressed or shown in very revealing corseted dresses. On two such occasions, men are shown looking at the women naked, establishing them as objects for a sexualized male gaze. Isabeau's 'mould-breaking' depiction, then, does not preclude her inclusion as yet another example of the long tradition of female sexualization in the medium.

In the 1980s, the structure of the *bande dessinée* industry underwent an important change as journal sales decreased and the commercial importance of the *bande dessinée* album augmented. In *Reading bande dessinée: Critical Approaches to French-language Comic Strip*, Ann Miller notes that '[a]cross the whole sector, as editors became ever more desperate to win back readers, the display of naked women was a frequent tactic in the circulation battle: even *Pilote* was not immune' (2007: 33). This saturation and increased normalization of sexualized female characters within the medium is evidenced in their inclusion across a range of genres and styles (and aimed at a variety of age ranges) from the figure of Aria, the skimpily dressed eponymous focus of a heroic fantasy strip first published in the journal *Tintin* in 1980 to the more openly eroticized Linda of *Linda aime l'art* (*Pilote*, 1983), an 'adult' video maker displayed via an interestingly angular *ligne claire* style. In the same year as *Aria*'s publication, Jill Bioskop appeared in Enki Bilal's *La Femme piège*, the second instalment of the *Nikopol* trilogy, which was serialized in *Pilote* in 1980. This complex narrative, mixing elements of social realism, science-fiction and fantasy, highlighted the eroticized depiction of Jill in its particular manipulation of artist Bilal's signature style, showcasing the specific effects of static *bande dessinée* imagery in the sexualization of female imagery. The contrasting use of colour between the watery greens and drab browns that make up the background of the strip's desolate landscape and the striking 'Bilal blue' of Bioskop's feminine features – hair, lips, nails, nipples – over several scenes that show her naked underline the sexualized subtext of the futuristic narrative.

Although varyingly eroticized women figures emerged in the early 1980s, the medium also showed a certain reaction to this ever-increasing female representation by producing principal women characters that, quite unusually for the *bande dessinée*, were neither beautiful nor young. *Soeur Marie-Thérèse de Batignolles* (created by Maëster), featuring a smoking, swearing nun, and *Carmen Cru* (by Jean-Marc Lelong), a retired, incurable grouch, were both published in *Fluide Glacial* in 1982 and were examples of comic BDs featuring elderly female characters. This pairing of comedy and older women figures provided these strips with a focus lacking from most female-led strips previously found in the francophone *bande dessinée*, particularly in the post-war period. Whilst not an elderly character, Jean-Marc Reiser's Jeanine would carry on this trend for crass comedic depictions of women towards the end of the decade in a one-shot, *Jeanine*, published in 1987, which collected humorous short strips featuring the smoking, child-neglecting, self-obsessed principal character. As Groensteen (2013) has noted, however, such depictions rejecting the idealized, beautified female figure seen elsewhere in the medium remain exceptional in the *bande dessinée*. Another exceptional figure to appear in the 1980s was Marc Wasterlain's Jeanette Pointu (from the strip of the same name), whose adventures were first serialized in *Spirou* from 1982 and went on to be published in album-format until 2005. Hailed by Gaumer as 'one of the great neoclassical series' (2010: 448), this *bande dessinée* features a modern, intelligent and non-sexualized leading figure. Travelling journalist Jeanette Pointu appears to defy the conventions of the *bande dessinée* action narrative – notably dominated elsewhere in the 1980s by male protagonists – by competently leading the narrative forward without falling foul of stereotyped 'feminine' foibles.

From the mid-to-late-1980s, few new female principal characters appear to have emerged within the medium. This is perhaps because the reigning thematic vogue for heroic fantasy favoured the placing of male characters in leading roles, with female figures easier to cast in minor narrative parts. Two figures who did appear, however, did so in strips that continued the pairing of dark, dystopian narratives with the display of attractive women seen most clearly in *La Femme piège*. Aude, the leading lady of Paul Gillon's sexualized, post-apocalyptic *La Survivante* first appeared in *L'Écho des savanes* in April 1985. The eroticized nature of this series, which would tell the story of Aude, the sole female survivor of a nuclear catastrophe, fit well with its parent publication's rather X-rated 1980s re-direction (Miller 2007: 33). *Jessica Blandy*, created by Belgian team Jean Dufaux and Renaud, was published directly in album form without prior serialization and focused on the world of Californian novelist Jessica as she crossed paths with serial killers, satanic sects and corrupt politicians (Moliterni et al. 2004: 1177). Drawn in a colourful, elegantly realist style, this strip to an extent sexualizes the depiction of Blandy (including showing her as the victim of eroticized sexual violence: see, for example, *Jessica Blandy 6: Au loin, la fille d'Ipanema...*), although, fairly unusually, male characters are on occasion displayed too (as seen, for example, in *Jessica Blandy 7, Répondez, mourant...* (1992)). The example of male exhibition in the Jessica Blandy series would not go on to inspire a trend of eroticization of male characters on a par with that of female figures, however. Another, perhaps more notable, element of the Jessica Blandy series is her bisexuality, which progressively appears as the series develops, as do examples of lesbian relationships; see, for example, the last volume of the Jessica Blandy series, *Les Gardiens* (2006).[25] In a postface to this final album, Dufaux indicates that Blandy's 'different sexuality' was a cause for publishing concern and almost censored (2006: 58). As noted below and discussed further in Chapter 10, the representation of lesbian or bisexual women is rare in the *bande dessinée*: Jessica Blandy is an exceptional example.

The 1990s were a revolutionary decade for the *bande dessinée* as a whole as smaller, independent publishing houses appeared, challenging the dominance of the large, commercially driven companies such as Albin Michel and Hachette (Miller 2007: 33) that ruled the often formulaic production of the 1980s.[26] However, although this was an exciting time for the wider medium, with new artists, styles and diverse content coming to the fore, the production of male-created strips featuring female principal characters does not fully reflect this, with few strips emerging that would go on to receive serious critical attention. Unlike other decades examined, in which certain trends and patterns are revealed, the female-led strips of the 1990s appear rather disparate and unconnected, with the futuristic settings and female gun-toting figures of three of the below-noted series proving the principal identifiable link.

Despite the general shift of sales towards albums, some female characters still made their entry into the *bande dessinée* via serialization in periodicals. One such example, Mélusine, from the strip of the same name by Clarke and François Gilson, first appeared in *Spirou* in 1992. Featuring a brightly coloured, slick and modern cartoon style depicting the adventures of a witch in training, this comedic strip for a juvenile audience also serves as a reminder that despite the sexualized, mature focus of female characters for a large part of the post-war era, strips were still produced that were clearly aimed at a young (and sometimes female) audience. The appearance the following year of the straight-to-album *Les Aventures de Charlotte* – drawn by André Taymans and scripted by Rudi Miel – proved to be another example of this and showed via its *ligne claire* style that classic artistic influences continued into 1990s BD despite the more modern draughtsmanship of strips like *Mélusine*.

Another album-launched heroine, Anita Bomba (again, from the strip of the same name), appeared in 1994, but with a very different presence. Created by Eric Gratien (script) and Cromwell (artwork), Anita is a shapely, *Tomb Raider*-style heroine, drawn in a darkly expressive style that would have fit well into the pages of science-fiction journal *Métal Hurlant* in the late 1970s. Two further female figures, whose characterization bears a resemblance to Anita Bomba, were introduced later in the decade. Carmen McCallum, an ex-IRA mercenary, and Yiu, a female contract killer, appeared as eponymous lead characters of new strips in 1996 and 1999 respectively, both *bandes dessinées* featuring futuristic settings. Reflecting the lack of consistent artistic trends in the 1990s, however, these thematically-similar strips displayed very different visual styles. *Carmen McCallum* (the collective creative effort of Fred Duval, Olivier Vatine, Gess and Fred Blanchard) bore a strikingly modern graphic style, while *Yiu* (by artists Téhy, Vee, Renéaume and Guénet), more like the aesthetic approach of Anita Bomba, featured an expressive graphic style bearing the influence of experimental 1970s strips. This appearance of assertive, physically-dangerous female lead characters in the *bande dessinée* of the 1990s appears to have developed from the dystopian *bande dessinée* narratives of the 1980s, but also seems to mirror the wider pop-culture trend that saw women figures such as *Tomb Raider*'s Lara Croft (video games), *Buffy the Vampire Slayer*'s Buffy Summers (television) and *The Matrix*'s Trinity (film) take centre stage at the end of the millennium.

Towards the end of the 1990s, few new *bande dessinée* heroines in male-scripted strips are notable. This is not to say that women primary characters were absent from the medium at this time; rather, the rise of female figures in works created by women (discussed in Section 3) constitutes a most notable evolution of female depiction in the medium and it is possible that the paucity of male-created figures is a reaction to this change. In the final year of the millennium, certain new figures appeared only to quickly disappear again in such strips as *Kegoyo et Klamédia* by Guillaume Bianco and *Ninie Rezergoude* by Yoann and Eric Omond – both only lasting two albums apiece – and the artistic production of female leading figures in the first decade of the new millennium began much as it had concluded in the 1990s, with no real 'star' figures emerging. Strips such as *Atalante*, drawn and scripted by Crisse (*Atalante* bucks the trend identified above in its development over nine albums between 2000 and 2016) and *Princesse Maya* (2003; notable for its design as a 3D album created to be viewed through glasses) by artist and script-writer Jeronaton, exhibited the longevity of the eroticized mythological/fantasy-based female character trend.

Probably the most well-known female leading character of the 2000–10 decade – Aya of Clément Oubrerie and Marguerite Abouet's *Aya de Yopougon* series – made her entrance in 2005. Drawn by a male-female creative team, *Aya de Yopougon* fits into both this history and that of female artists/authors laid out in Chapter 10 (and, as such, is included in both) and constitutes an example of a *bande dessinée* trend seen across the post-millennial medium in its adaptation into a feature film in 2013. *Aya de Yopougon* is unusual, however, in two ways, both as an example of a female-led *bande dessinée* that would receive a prize at the Angoulême festival[27] and as an example of a francophone strip featuring a black female lead character. The exceptional nature of Aya (and the very few characters of colour found elsewhere in the history of the *bande dessinée* such as Aymone or the one-shot *La Voyageuse de Petite Ceinture*'s Naima [drawn by another male-female duo, Pierre Christin and Annie Goetzinger in 1985]) serves as a reminder of the lack of racial diversity amongst women *bande dessinée* characters.

It is towards the end of this first decade of the new millennium that the influence of the independent sector, with its artistic rather than commercial focus, and the subsequent filtering back to the larger publishing houses of its new styles and artistic approaches, is finally seen in strips by male creators featuring female leading figures. From the middle of the decade onwards, a new slew of narratives appeared featuring female figures who eschewed in their characterization both the futuristic, gun-wielding-type somewhat favoured in the 1990s and the mythological beauties of the early 2000s, instead producing introspective, character-led stories whose focus was often the internal – rather than visually external – struggle of the leading figure. *Le Long Voyage de Léna* by Pierre Christin and André Juillard, which mixes introspection with action over the course of two albums of 'political fiction', is one such example from 2006 and is relatively unusual in the history of female figures in the medium as the principal character Léna's story is written in the first person.[28] *Lulu femme nue* (2008) is another notable proponent of this trend. Drawn and written by Etienne Davodeau, again unfolding over two albums, Lulu's decision to 'abandon' her family is told from a range of retrospective viewpoints, displaying a minimalist, rounded graphic style. Lulu is a rare figure in the history of the *bande dessinée* due to her status as a middle-aged female principal character.

A consequence of the medium's general move from periodicals towards albums, instigated in the 1980s and continuing into the next century, appears to be the creation of female principal characters (although this may not be gender specific), like Léna and Lulu, whose longevity is distinctly reduced. The majority of women figures introduced between 2000 and 2010 appear in five or fewer albums from the opening to the conclusion of their BD existence. One final example of a relatively short-lived female figure from this decade, and one whose characterization is a reminder of the artistic and thematic diversity of *bande dessinée* production when the medium is considered as a whole (as it does not seem to stem from the same introspective trend described above) is *Sarah* by Christophe Bec and Stefano Raffaele (2008). Dark in both content and colour, *Sarah* appears, like *Anita Bomba*, *Carmen McCallum* and *Yiu*, to draw on trends established in other media of pop culture, particularly, in this case, on the vogue for female-led horror films (such as *Scream*, *I Know What You Did Last Summer*) established in cinema from the late 1990s.

The depiction of female central figures in the *bande dessinée* has clearly evolved greatly in the 103-year span tracked here. Female characters have generally progressed from young, childish figures to young women, although older adult characters remain few and far between. In accordance with this, general character traits have largely evolved from meddlesome and mischievous (*L'Espiègle Lili*, *Nigaude et Malicette* etc.) to capable and intelligent. One standard that has remained without significant deviation throughout the twentieth century and beyond, amid all the thematic and setting variations, concerns the attractiveness of the female character, who, only in the rarest of instances – Carmen Cru, for example, or the matriarch of BD women, Bécassine – may not be described as cute, pretty or beautiful, depending on age. The sexualization of female characters in the second half of the century is established quickly following its initial inklings in the 1950s and becomes a near-constant, even in strips appearing in publications traditionally directed to younger audiences. There is no principal role undertaken by female primary characters across the medium, although warrior figures in past or future settings appear frequently, as do investigative/detective types in varying incarnations. Female characters are overwhelmingly white, although figures of

African and Asian origin sporadically appear at various points over time, and very little evidence was found of bisexual or lesbian characters drawn by male artists in the mainstream medium.[29]

Considering the studied time period – 1905–2008 – as a whole, certain general observations can now be made. The relative paucity of francophone strips featuring female primary characters prior to the Second World War – particularly when considered alongside their popular and certainly better-remembered American sisters such as Winnie Winkle and Little Orphan Annie – in addition to the reaction of some artists when faced with the 1949 law and their subsequent inclination to remove women characters from strips, is evidence of a historic reluctance to draw the 'problematic' female as a primary character in the Franco-Belgian medium. The uptick in creation of female leading figures following the introduction of sexualization to women's characterization in the medium suggests this to be the principal, defining feature of their presence in the medium since the Second World War and the apparent obtaining 'solution' to the perennial difficulty that depicting women seems to present. The most well-known and well-remembered female primary characters of the BD stand out as Bécassine, Barbarella and Adèle Blanc-Sec. Detailed studies of each figure will be presented in the next three chapters with a view to finding out why these figures have been afforded this exceptional status and how their respective artists manipulate the *bande dessinée* medium to overcome the 'problem' of their representation.

2

Bécassine: The First Lady of *Bande Dessinée*?

The long-running series *Bécassine* occupies a special place in the *bande dessinée* (BD). An early example of the burgeoning medium, beginning in 1905, it was the first French *bande dessinée* series to feature a recurring female principal character and, from its inaugural published album in 1913, provided the first use of 'flashback' narrative in the Franco-Belgian medium (Davreux 2006: 20).[1]

As will be discussed below, Bécassine has, in recent years, been heralded as a pioneering example of an active, emancipated female character in the *bande dessinée*. This chapter will show in contrast that, throughout the series, visual and narrative elements of Bécassine's characterization are employed as de-feminizing tools, defusing the 'threat' posed by the depiction of an adult woman even to the strip's young female readers. A close study of album *Bécassine pendant la Grande Guerre* (1915) will further posit that in specific instances this famous figure is dehumanized and literally alienated, removing her womanhood to the fullest extent.

The Five Lives of Bécassine

The figure of Bécassine first appeared on the back page of the first issue of *La Semaine de Suzette* – an *illustré* for young girls of a bourgeois, Catholic background, financed by the publishing house Editions Gautier. After appearing only sporadically across the first issues of this new publication, Bécassine's popularity soon made her the journal's star attraction and she would remain a principal feature of the *illustré* until its demise in 1960. Initially created by *Semaine de Suzette* editor Jacqueline Rivière and Joseph-Porphyre Pinchon, who respectively wrote and drew each instalment between 1905 and 1913, the principal creative pair behind the series was to be artist J. P. Pinchon alongside Maurice Languereau, better known under the pen-name Caumery.[2] Between 1913 and 1939, this pair produced innumerable *Bécassine* strips for *La Semaine de Suzette* in addition to publishing 25 albums chronicling the Breton maid's adventures.³ Following the war and Caumery's death in 1941, two more *Bécassine* stories were produced and printed in *La Semaine de Suzette*, drawn by Pinchon and bearing Caumery's name – *Les Petits Ennuis de Bécassine* (1948) and *Bécassine au studio* (1950) – however, the real script-writers for these albums remain unconfirmed. Two narratives created by an entirely new team after Pinchon's death in 1953 – *Bécassine revient* drawn by Jean Trubert and written by Camille François and *Bécassine mène l'enquête* by Trubert and Vaubant – were published in 1959 and 1962 respectively.⁴ Unlike their predecessors, these albums showed some evidence of formal modification – notably the introduction of speech bubbles to the series for the first time. However, despite her earlier prowess, Bécassine did not long outlive her original artist, and these more 'experimental' albums seemed to be her last. A new Bécassine narrative, however, *Les Vacances de Bécassine* by Corbeyran et Béja, was published in 2016 by Gautier Languereau, (re)introducing the character to young, modern readers.

A key series in the history of the *bande dessinée*, with a lifespan of more than a century, it is interesting to note that the creation of *Bécassine* was, to an extent, a happy accident. Hélène Davreux recounts in *Bécassine ou l'image d'une femme* (2006) that as the publication date for the first issue of *La Semaine de Suzette* approached in 1905, the back page of this new *illustré* remained empty due to the failure of a writer to submit his promised story. Maurice Languereau, the strip's future script-writer who worked at that time for Editions Gautier, asked editor-in-chief Rivière to improvise a story and at random chose an artist, Pinchon (set to provide sketches for future issues of *La Semaine de Suzette*), to illustrate Rivière's tale. Davreux notes that '[b]ecause [Pinchon] often holidayed in Brittany, he chose this French region for the story's setting whilst Jacqueline Rivière recounted a gaffe made by her young maid. This story was made into a series of images and named "Bécassine's mistake"' (2006: 14).⁵ Following this improvised beginning, the figure of Bécassine was not scheduled to re-appear within *La Semaine de Suzette*, having served her purpose as 'filler'. However, following the positive reception of the hastily created character, more strips were commissioned and Bécassine, like Tintin decades later in *le Petit Vingtième*, soon became the star of her *illustré*.

Despite the sudden and ultimately fortuitous nature of Bécassine's creation as noted by Davreux, other sources suggest that this character's most basic feature – her position as a Breton maid – was influenced by other popular depictions present prior to her 1905 creation. Michelle Zancarini-Fournel (2005) reminds us of the tradition of painted representations of Brittany (notably by the painters of the Pont-Aven school) visible from the latter part of the 1800s.⁶ From the turn of the century, she cites specific artistic examples from the more popular milieu of the illustrated journal (for adults) depicting Breton maids, bearing similarities to Bécassine:

> A February 1905 issue of the satirical paper *Le Rire* included the character of a maid, Yvonne Labrutec (semantically similar to Annaïck Labornez, the real name of Bécassine, born five years later). In October 1903, *L'Assiette au beurre* tackled the religious traditionalism of Breton women: in the background, one of the Breton women wearing the *coiffe* and apron strongly resembles the future character Bécassine.[7]
> (Zancarini-Fournel 2005: 182)

Hence, it seems likely that Bécassine's creation was born both out of chance and necessity, and the general artistic visibility of Brittany and 'traditionally Breton' figures.

Following her creation, Bécassine's considerable *bande dessinée* lifespan can be divided into five stages. The first begins with the inaugural issue of *La Semaine de Suzette* in February 1905 and ends in 1913, when responsibility for scripting the strip passed from Jacqueline Rivière to Caumery. During this period, the heroine of the *bande dessinée* appears significantly different to her later incarnations present in the published album series. Describing the first manifestation of the figure as 'Proto-Bécassine' (a term in turn borrowed from Bernard Lehembre, whose work on the series is discussed below), Davreux notes the figure to be physically stiff and, in terms of character, one-dimensional – more marionette, in fact, than maiden (2006: 20). The second incarnation of Bécassine following the change in creative pairing provided the character with something of a reinvention, however. Pinchon and Caumery constructed her past, family and memories (visible from the first album, *L'Enfance de Bécassine* [1913] and second, *Bécassine en apprentissage* [1914]), conveyed her real name, Annaïck Labornez, to her young readers for the first time, and developed her personality. Moving beyond the previously limited formula of the strip that showed Bécassine solely in her capacity as a maid prone to humorous mistakes and misunderstandings, Pinchon and Caumery's version of the character went on adventures, contributed to the First World War effort, travelled the world and undertook different jobs when not in Parisian employer the Marquise de Grand-Air's service, later returning to become a nanny and mother-figure to Loulotte, a child adopted by the Marquise. This second manifestation of the Breton maid's existence, lasting 28 years from 1913 until the death of Caumery in 1941 (as opposed to 'Proto-Bécassine's' seven and a half) and immortalized in 25 albums (contrasting with the more evanescent existence of the earlier character in strips in *La Semaine de Suzette*) has become the enduring incarnation of the Bécassine character and, thus, will be studied here.

The third general phase of Bécassine's life is considerably more fleeting, consisting only of five albums (including the aforementioned alphabet book

L'Alphabet de Bécassine) made after Caumery's demise (and the final three following the death of Pinchon). The Bécassine of these final albums is not significantly different from the heroine now long-established in the mold cast by Pinchon and Caumery, although, as noted, some stylistic experimentation is seen in the last three publications, breaking the previously precise formal confines of the series. It is not currently clear whether the new addition to the character's lifespan of *Les Vacances de Bécassine* by Corbeyran et Béja in 2016 is intended to develop into a series.

A fourth life of Bécassine comes not from her *La Semaine de Suzette* or album incarnations, but from the pastiches, tributes and adaptations of the character over the twentieth century. *Bécassine* became the first *bande dessinée* series to be transformed into a live-action film, as a celluloid interpretation of the Breton maid's adventures – simply entitled *Bécassine*, directed by René Chateau and starring Paulette Dubost in the eponymous role – was made in 1939. Chateau and Dubost's Bécassine shows herself to be headstrong and cheeky in the film – in one scene she solicits a bribe from a house-guest of Madame de Grand-Air – and thus appears rather different to her much more servile *bande dessinée* incarnation. Decades later, the Bécassine character was again reinterpreted, but in a very different manner – as Charles Forsdick (2005: 25) notes, she became 'the subject of at least two pornographic pastiches'. The figure of Bécassine has also been evoked in songs, notably Georges Brassens's 'Bécassine' (1969) in which the figure is also sexualized (but subtly so), followed by Chantal Goya's more innocent 'Bécassine, c'est ma cousine' in 1979. This wider cultural influence demarcates Bécassine as a truly exceptional female *bande dessinée* character: alongside Barbarella, whose wider popularity, in any case, owes more to her cinematic reinterpretation than to her *bande dessinée* origins, no other woman figure has repeatedly attracted the attention of the pop culture world.[8] It is, however, important to note that the translation of Bécassine into these other forms has consistently altered her depiction, adding elements regarded as traditionally 'womanly' – impulsiveness and, particularly, eroticism – that are not visible in the *bande dessinée* version, this underlining the defeminization of the drawn strip character that will be explained below.

Before moving on to analyse the representation of this exceptional famous female figure, to the 'four lives' of Bécassine it is necessary to add a final fifth, visible in the pages of scholarly works and 'fan-friendly' publications that discuss and define her and have, in recent years, retrospectively reinvented her. In her 2011 article 'Strange Encounters during Wartime: *Bécassine chez les Turcs*', Anabelle Cone suggests that '[a]lthough critical writing on *bande dessinée* has attained respect in academia, writing about *Bécassine* still remains as guarded as the heroine herself' (2001: 181). This is certainly true of English-language academic writing, which is limited in its consideration of this significant *bande dessinée* character, although a more diverse critical picture of the figure is ascertainable from French-language sources. Of the three female principal characters examined in this first section, many more francophone scholarly sources are available which discuss Bécassine than either Adèle Blanc-Sec or Barbarella. Much of the scholarly writing on Bécassine in either language, however, defines the character as a potentially offensive Breton stereotype, and often discusses in connection to this the historical context around the strip's premise that saw large numbers of workers from rural settings in Brittany move to urban spaces such as Paris in search of employment (cf. Forsdick, Zancarini-Fournel, Cone). Some sources, however, such as Forsdick's article 'Exoticising the domestique: Bécassine, Brittany and the beauty of the dead' (which, as the title indicates, focuses largely on the sociogeographical context of the strip), also underline a recent change in the popular reception of Bécassine since the republication of the series around the early 1990s. As Forsdick notes in his introduction:

> Locked away like an embarrassing elderly relative, Bécassine was long subject to unofficial censorship that has only gradually been lifted [...] The recent republication of the whole series of Bécassine albums suggests, however, the beginnings of a radical reassessment. A popular conception of Bécassine – seasoned traveller, adventurer seeming to thrive on regular crises – is that she is Tintin in drag, with a *coiffe* instead of a quiff.
>
> (2005: 23)

This reconfiguring of Bécassine alluded to by Forsdick, identifying her characterization as more than just a negatively exaggerated Breton stereotype but, rather, a successful female interpretation of the dominant *bande dessinée* criteria of the early twentieth century is distinguishable, for example, in Bernard Lehembre's summary of, and tribute to, the series, *Bécassine, une légende du siècle* (2005), albeit in a slightly different formulation. Lehembre defines Bécassine as a pioneer of women's liberation – not only as proof of a positive female principal character early in the developing *bande dessinée*, but, by listing her exploits, a visual narrative example of the progressive 'social and cultural conquests of women in the 20th century' (2005: 53).[9] The following study of the Bécassine character and series as a whole, and in-depth analysis of *Bécassine pendant la Grande Guerre*, closely examines Pinchon and Caumery's Bécassine as a female figure of the *bande dessinée*, looking beyond (but, at times, necessarily crossing paths with) the oft-cited focus on her status as *Bretonne*. Its findings call into question the popular revival of Bécassine's characterization exemplified by Lehembre's work and her crowning therein as the first 'emancipated woman' of the *bande dessinée*.

Looking at Bécassine

The *Bécassine* series displayed throughout its principal almost-60-year run formal characteristics that would anchor it to the era of its creation: three equally sized, unframed 'strips' per page, a lack of outlined panels and no speech bubbles, with all text placed below each image. The stylistic composition within the panels was simple and traditional – Pinchon and Caumery employed little manipulation of perspective, panel layout or shading in the service of their storytelling. As Lise Tannahill notes, the strip, in fact, 'straddles the divide between old-style *histoires illustrées* (illustrated stories) and bona fide BD in their modern form' (2016: 222), but that it was during this era – inhabited by *Bécassine* – of progression from the drawn strip form towards modern *bande dessinée* that the image, for the first time, became the dominant priority over the text (2016: 225). A primary visual analysis of the Bécassine figure shows that recognizing the importance of this shift towards the image, Pinchon and Caumery coded the visual features of their leading character's physical appearance in certain key ways to contribute to her characterization and the narrative of the series – this contention shall now be examined, focusing on what this coding reveals about Bécassine's 'woman-ness'.

The figure of Bécassine, perhaps more so than any other *bande dessinée* character following her in the twentieth century, has become synonymous in popular memory with her outfit – a green dress and white *coiffe*, versions of the traditional sartorial choice of the Breton maid – which the character wears with very few exceptions in every strip or album instalment of her adventures. Due to Bécassine's near-constant donning of this ensemble, the majority of her body is always covered, with only her face – an almost perfectly round circle, minimally decorated with eyes, eyebrows and a half-circle denoting her nose – and her hands visible. She is usually drawn without a mouth, although this feature occasionally appears in the shape of a small circle or line in order to convey emotion, usually surprise (as Forsdick has rightly indicated, Bécassine's lack of a mouth clearly conveys a difficulty with self-expression [2005: 26]). Although Bécassine's dress gathers slightly at the waist and extends into a full skirt, indicating a modicum of traditional 'femininity' (this represents the standard style for dresses in the late nineteenth and early twentieth century and is equally seen in dresses for young girls in the series), her bodily appearance conveys no real semblance of 'femaleness': not a strand of hair is visible underneath her *coiffe*, there is no curve at her chest, her hands and feet appear large (and in the case of the latter, are habitually placed in flat, shapeless brown shoes).

In her article, Cone indicates that the 'invisibility' of Bécassine's body may be a result of her depiction as a maid, noting the following of domestic protagonists: 'either extremely sexual or asexual, but always "denied", the maid's body and head must disappear under a uniform that reduces them to their function' (2001: 182). This is a viable hypothesis, and likely true to a certain extent; however, Bécassine's bodily form is nonetheless distinct from other female domestic staff seen throughout the series, who are variously depicted with more feminine accessories (such as pointed shoes), at least some hair visible and with slight shading on the body to denote breasts. It is also worth noting that as the series progresses, Bécassine takes on many other roles aside from her position as a maid – the first cycle of albums by Pinchon and Caumery sees the figure leave Madame de Grand-Air's employ, travel internationally, try various different jobs and finally, as the series moves on, rejoin the Marquise's service primarily as a nanny for the young Loulotte. Although Bécassine almost always remains firmly within her maid's outfit whatever her activity, her original position as a servant is not the prime focus of the series as it progresses, and Bécassine herself is far from invisible. Bécassine's underdeveloped visual representation would appear to be, rather, employed steadfastly throughout the series in order to distract from her position as physically female – to minimize the visibility of her corporeal difference. Her bodily appearance is but one among several elements of her representation that are coded by Pinchon and Caumery to deny her femininity.

Aside from Bécassine's lack of lips or breasts, a key example of this sexual muting comes from her manner of wearing, and devotion to, her *coiffe*. As an item of clothing ostensibly worn to demarcate Bécassine as Breton, this item of the character's ensemble, when discussed in scholarly texts, is often related to its symbolic regional implications, in accordance with the sociogeographical critical focus often directed towards the strip. However, this critical focus largely overlooks the more general gendered considerations connected to the character's continual wearing of the *coiffe*. As an item of clothing only worn by women, Bécassine's *coiffe* remains (alongside her dress), the only visual indication of the character's femaleness. Bécassine's manner of wearing it also serves to completely cover her hair, however – a traditional marker of femininity. Like her attachment to her dress, Bécassine's insistence on keeping her *coiffe* on at all times during the day is more evident from the first cycle of Pinchon and Caumery's work together onwards as her activities diversify – in the 1923 album *Bécassine alpiniste*, for example, she is forced to take off her headgear but notes as she does so that to remove her *coiffe* and show her hair makes her feel ashamed. In post-1913 strips featuring other Breton women from Bécassine's hometown, it also becomes clear that she is the only *bretonne* character whose *coiffe* entirely, and in every panel, covers her hair – even her mother and cousin, Marie Quillouch, show strands of hair under their headgear. The habit of these latter characters corresponds to Yann Guesdon's historical account of *coiffe*-wearing in Brittany: although originally conceived of as a means of covering a woman's hair in order to conform to religious requirements of modesty (2014: 7), by the mid-nineteenth century, women's attitudes to the *coiffe* had changed – strands of hair were often seen emerging from it as women began to see their heads not as something to be hidden but, rather, highlighted (2014: 14). Bécassine's rigid manner of wearing her *coiffe*, therefore, adds more to her depiction than a simple visual indicator of her geographical origins – it acts also as a largely outdated and, thus, notable physical circumvention of her bodily femininity.

Davreux, author of a rare, detailed study of Bécassine as a woman (but one that restricts itself to a rigorously sociological methodology, comparing the depiction of Bécassine to statistics concerning real-life women in pre–Second World War France) also briefly notes Bécassine's physical asexuality. She first hypothesizes that Bécassine, although adult, is essentially represented as a child in a fully grown body, hence her lack of corporeal indicators of adult female sexual maturity. Such a suggestion, however, does not account for her lack of hair, lips or eyelashes, which are all present in depictions of Bécassine's *bande dessinée* contemporaries, such as the young Lili (from the 1909 strip of the same name). Davreux, however, then goes on to briefly suggest that the physical androgyny of the figure may be due to the age of the intended readership – *La Semaine de Suzette* was directed towards young girls of eight to fourteen years old – and a desire on the part of the creators to restrict the character's femininity in order to avoid implying 'the theme of sexuality which must be kept secret from little girls' (2006: 42).[10] Davreux does not elaborate on this notion beyond the stated supposition. However, its expression in her work supports the notion presented throughout this book that drawing women in the *bande dessinée* (as in visual art more generally) implies difficulties, one of which is the traditional understanding that viewing women is indivisible from viewing sexuality and sexual difference. Although she does not specify beyond her initial proposition, that Davreux suggests this of a female principal character meant to be read by young girls illustrates the rigidity of this traditional understanding and the effect of this rigidity on artistic creation – as noted above, almost every hint of femaleness is removed from Bécassine's depiction.[11]

A narrative example of Bécassine's desexualization, which, as with her physical appearance, both admits and strongly denies her womanhood, is her role as a 'mother'. In the ninth album of her adventures, *Bécassine nourrice*, drawn by Pinchon and Caumery, Bécassine becomes the nanny to a baby taken in by Madame de Grand-Air. With no other maternal figure in the house, Bécassine's role in the young Loulotte's life clearly extends beyond that for which she is paid, and she essentially becomes the girl's mother, even referring to her at times as her daughter. Despite Bécassine's tendency towards misunderstandings (in *Bécassine nourrice*, for example, she temporarily loses Loulotte when she pushes the wrong pram home [2015: 226–28]), she is shown to be very devoted to her charge, referring to her in their first story together, for example, as 'love like all love put together'[12] (2015: 202). It is clear, however, that despite having a 'daughter', Bécassine remains steadfastly asexual: she never once in her fifty-five-year publication span has any kind of romantic relationship with a man, and it is made clear from her introduction onwards that Loulotte is not her biological child. This narrative arrangement allows Bécassine to take on the role so often associated with artistic representations of women (notably religious representations)[13] of the idealized mother – devoted and self-sacrificing – whilst also denying her association with women's reproductive role, described by Jane Ussher as 'feminine excess at its most extreme' (2006: 161).

It might be countered at this juncture that Bécassine is not 'just' a mother-figure during the Pinchon/Caumery years and does, as Lehembre states in his book, undertake an impressive range of activities and jobs, thus leading to his contention that she represents the evolving status of French women during the first half of the twentieth century. The above analysis already posits that Bécassine cannot be considered an example of contemporary *woman*hood as her position as a woman is so visibly denied. It should also be noted, concerning the numerous jobs and tasks she accomplishes – flying a plane, for example, or driving, skiing and travelling – that despite their diverse extent, Bécassine seems, as Forsdick notes, to carry out these activities almost despite herself (2005: 32). In *Bécassine voyage*, for example, in the space of three consecutive pages, Bécassine is unable to work the knobs in her hotel room that control the murphy bed so she has to sleep in an armchair (1921: 17), is later jostled by a crowd while trying to get on to a tram and thus misses it (1921: 18), is then almost immediately hit by another tram and must be rescued by a policeman (1921: 19), misses her stop when she finally does get aboard a tram and, finally, manages to hit a man hard on the head with her umbrella as she brandishes it out of the window trying to get the driver's attention and is consequently fined by a station manager for her behaviour. As this series of misadventures attests, it is precisely her misunderstanding and lack of proficiency throughout the series of often unbidden and unwitting endeavours that she undertakes that proves a key source of amusement for each strip.[14] This comedic narrative trope would seem to undermine the notion that Bécassine represents the 'modern woman' of the early twentieth century, as, in addition to the coding of her appearance to dampen her femaleness, her competence and intelligence are so frequently called in to question.

The (Principal) Secondary 'Women' of Bécassine's World

As indicated, Bécassine is fairly exceptional amongst the other female characters present within her *bande dessinée* series and it is necessary to note that the defeminizing applied to the principal character is not uniformly employed to less permanently visible female figures. Her fellow *bretonne* compatriots show at least some hair under their *coiffe*s and minor female characters such as servants show both more femininity and modernity in their dress. Almost all characters show more intelligence in their actions and conversation. The second-most prominent female character in the series, the Marquise de Grand-Air, clearly differs greatly from Bécassine in her depiction. A classically aristocratic figure whose mode of dress draws more from the nineteenth century than the twentieth (Davreux 2006: 18), Bécassine's employer is intelligent, restrained and dignified. Despite muted references to physical femaleness (hair and a curve at her chest despite an otherwise rather shapeless corpulence), Madame de Grand-Air represents a stereotype – the 'grand dame' or 'lady' – which, according to Mary Ferguson, is (unusually for a female character) dependent more on social class than biology. Special rules for the behaviour of those adhering to this type are prescribed by rigid social systems rather than traditional assumptions regarding male and female roles (1981: 10; female stereotypes will be discussed in detail in Section 2 of this book): as such, the visual and narrative effect of her physical femaleness is lessened.

Loulotte, on the other hand, grows from a baby to a young woman across the narratives (she appears to be the only female figure of the long-running series who truly shows evolution over time) and, as she matures, is shown to be slender and feminine, her clothes typical of young women of her time and her long brown hair rarely covered. As a secondary character, Loulotte is less visible than Bécassine throughout the series; consequently, her depiction as (young) womanly appears to have posed less of a problem to her creators. However, the contrast between the two when she is present also serves to underline the overt defeminization of Bécassine's depiction, emphasizing her nanny as asexual – neither womanly or particularly masculine, but 'Other'.

Bécassine pendant la Grande Guerre

Much can be noted about Bécassine's characterization in general terms, deduced from a consideration of several strips collectively, or the series in its entirety. A study of Bécassine's depiction in a specific narrative will prove useful, however, in order to support the more general findings presented above and to develop in further detail the analysis of her characterization.

Bécassine pendant la Grande Guerre was first published in 1915 under the title *Bécassine pendant la guerre*, but was renamed following its 1974 republication to avoid historical confusion (Vitruve 2001: 19).[15] It has been chosen for analysis here as it is the first of the *Bécassine* strips to show the heroine in her standard characterization – the prior narratives, *L'Enfance de Bécassine* (1913) and *Bécassine en apprentissage* (1914) respectively depict Bécassine as a child, and a younger maid beginning her professional life.[16] *Bécassine pendant la Grande Guerre* constitutes the first of three albums published during the First World War, and the only of these three narratives to be drawn by Pinchon, who was temporarily replaced by another illustrator, Edouard Zier, when called to the Eastern Front in 1916 (Davreux 2006: 20).[17] The following analysis concentrates on the album's characterization of Bécassine, but it is also interesting to note that this narrative constitutes a relatively rare example of French women's experience during the Great War. As Margaret H. Darrow notes: '[d]uring the war, many French men and women wrote about women's wartime activities ... Some French women published diaries or memoirs of their war experiences. But none of these stories "stuck". With the exception of Bécassine's adventures, reissued in 1947 and again recently, French women's stories of the war quickly disappeared' (2000: 1).

As one would expect from a children's tale, *Bécassine pendant la Grande Guerre* follows a linear narrative that is predominantly event-based: there is little extended dialogue or commentary by the characters beyond the events happening around them. The story follows the exploits of the Breton maid during the first phase of the First World War. She attends to injured soldiers in a field hospital set up by the Marquise, spends time in her home town, Clocher-les-Bécasses, helping her uncle with his duties as mayor, becomes a *marraine de guerre* to a soldier from Timbuktu and finally attends the wedding of Bertrand de Grand-Air, nephew to the Marquise, in the contested territory of Alsace-Lorraine.[18]

From the beginning, the humour of this topical strip set against such grave real-world events comes from Bécassine's lack of intelligence. After failing to find 'la Bochie' in an atlas on the first page of the album, she reassures the worried Marquise that '[m]aybe there will be war, but seeing as it'll be against people who don't exist it's not so bad...' (1993: 2).[19] Overleaf, she rushes to find Bertrand de Grand-Air some protective headgear after hearing that he will soon be in danger 'on his front' (1993: 3).[20] This humour stemming from Bécassine's stupidity and over-literal nature – the standard comedic formula for the *Bécassine* stories throughout the series – continues throughout the narrative. However, interestingly, it is made clear in the final sequence of the album that although Bécassine lacks intelligence, she possesses something of an awareness of her status as a character. Meeting young children in Alsace-Lorraine, she is surprised to find that they recognize her, but is moved when they tell her that they too read French journals and love her stories in *La Semaine de Suzette*.

The differentiation of Bécassine's representation from other characters noted previously is clearly visible in *Bécassine pendant la Grande Guerre* and is a trope that occurs on several different levels – physically, intellectually and in terms of personality. During her time in Clocher-les-Bécasses, these differences from her family and neighbours are particularly underlined. Visually, there is very little resemblance between Bécassine and even her immediate relatives, who all have more detailed, expressive faces with full sets of features. This differentiation of Bécassine is also clear in terms of characterization, as she is shown to be notably less intelligent than her regional compatriots: this is particularly clear in the sequence describing Bécassine's brief experience as Deputy Mayor of Clocher-les-Bécasses during her uncle's temporary absence (during which, for example, she announces the end of a market that hasn't begun yet in order to give all the merchants 'the same chance' to sell their wares [1993: 42–43]). It becomes obvious also that she shares few personality traits with other young women from her hometown – in contrast to Bécassine's naive optimism, the latter appear in this narrative to be competitive and malicious, as seen when Marie Quillouch, Bécassine's cousin, is brought to tears by her contemporaries' taunts concerning firstly her unmarried status (1993: 46) and then her subsequent wedding, as the elderly character La Pipe must stand in for her conscripted fiancé, who is unable to leave the front lines.[21]

The differentiation from other Breton characters in *Bécassine pendant la Grande Guerre* highlights two intertwined issues. The first suggests, despite continual criticism of the Bécassine character for being an offensive depiction of the Breton people – Forsdick notes in his article the 'potentially metonymic substitution of character for a whole country or region' (2005: 28) – and the violently hostile reactions towards this perceived ridiculing of Bretons, for example the vandalizing of a museum waxwork of Bécassine in 1939 (2005: 29) – that although she continually wears traditional Breton dress, Bécassine's character appears not to stand for any notion of collective 'Breton-ness'. The second concerns the fact that her difference from other women figures, which appears more generally elsewhere in the series, is further underlined by her alterity from female relatives and neighbours in this album, thus ruling out any consideration that her difference is due to regional or class factors.

It has been contended above that the representation of Bécassine, remembered as one of the longest-running and perhaps the most popular female character in the history of the Franco-Belgian *bande dessinée*, is coded in multiple ways to deny her woman-ness, rendering her neither feminine nor particularly masculine but 'Other'. A close consideration of further elements of *Bécassine pendant la Grande Guerre* reveals another key element of Bécassine's characterization drawing upon this Othering, however: in addition to the character's sexual differentiation, her entire being is repeatedly presented, both visually and narratively, as both sub-human and curiously alien.

The first of these depictions is clear simply from a superficial consideration of Bécassine's physicality. The front cover of this album shows a full-length image of

Bécassine holding the hand of a young girl and boy in traditional Alsatian dress who stand on either side of her. Compared to the more fully drawn features of the children looking directly out towards the reader, Bécassine's lack of facial detail, and in particular here her lack of a mouth, suggests that her illustration is somewhat 'unfinished', rendering the maid a less complete version of the children who appear next to her. On the first page of the narrative, this idea of physical 'underdevelopment' is discretely reinforced by Bécassine's stance as she discusses (and misunderstands) the approaching war with the Marquise and other members of her staff. Three successive images of the maid show her bent significantly forward with her arms hanging in front of her, rather than standing or sitting upright like the other characters present. As a stooped pose is visually associated with lesser stages of human evolution, Bécassine's repeated display in a bent stance in this first page encourages the idea that she is somewhat 'sub-human'.[22]

This implied notion of Bécassine's basic biological deficit in comparison to other characters is more directly addressed in a notable episode from this album. Separated from the Marquise after committing yet another amusing blunder during a journey together, Bécassine and the young Zidore, also in the Marquise's service, find themselves at the home of Mr Proey-Minans, an acquaintance of their employer. Introduced by the narrator as a man fascinated by phrenology (which is, in turn, explained to the readers as 'the study of personalities based on the bumps on people's heads' [1993: 14]),[23] Proey-Minans indicates that Bécassine's reputation as an oddity has preceded her and that he is interested in examining her. The maid obliges and, in a rare gesture, removes her *coiffe*. As Bécassine stoops forward, the phrenologist conducts his investigation of her skull, stating triumphantly: 'Perfect! ... Here we find goodness, devotion, simple-mindedness ... What a source for the work I'm completing!' (1993: 14).[24] Again the suggestion that Bécassine is fundamentally different and less-developed than other characters (her qualities as noted during Proey-Minans' cranial examination are akin to those one might also expect in a Labrador) is presented to the young reader.[25] It is suggested during this episode that Proey-Minans might examine Zidore as well; however, this cranial observation never occurs.

Bécassine's depiction as fundamentally Other continues beyond physical and biological considerations in *Bécassine pendant la Grande Guerre*, to the social implication that she is not merely 'sub-human' but entirely alien. During her time assisting the nurses in Madame de Grand-Air's chateau-turned-hospital, an official comes to inspect the infirmary. The latter is an old friend of Bertrand de Grand-Air (who has been injured in battle and permitted to convalesce with his aunt) and once he has finished his official business is advised by Bertrand to ask to see Bécassine who is 'the most peculiar' aspect of the hospital, to which he replies that he is intrigued to see this 'curiosity' (Caumery and Pinchon 1993: 33).[26] This description of Bécassine as an exotic, abnormal creature is continued when she is joined by several recovering soldiers at the seaside. Upon the arrival of the soldiers, Bécassine is greeted warmly by a man only referred to as 'Le Parisien' who shakes her hand and laughs a lot while looking at her, repeating '[h]ow funny she is!' (1993: 55) while the Marquise and the other soldiers look on.[27]

The most striking example of Bécassine's 'alienation' from all those around her comes later in the same sequence with the injured soldiers. Le Parisien suggests that she become the *marraine de guerre* of a soldier, Boudou, due to join them imminently. When he tells Bécassine that this man is a prince, she is very excited to meet him (Caumery and Pinchon 1993: 55), but she is astounded when he arrives, greeted ceremoniously by the salutes and bows of the other soldiers, as he is black and dressed in the uniform of an Algerian cavalry regiment. This visual surprise is immediately compounded when Boudou dances a welcoming greeting, speaks in a language that she cannot understand, and appears suddenly to suffer from an agitated physical affliction, which the other soldiers, trying not to laugh, explain as a demand for food. Later warned that Boudou has cannibalistic tendencies, she bursts into the office of Madame de Grand-Air as the latter is welcoming the black soldier screaming 'Careful, Madame! The canny ball is going to eat your arm!' (Caumery and Pinchon 1993: 57).[28] Faced with the Marquise's anger, it is explained that Boudou's strange behaviour since his arrival has been the result of a practical joke played on Bécassine by the injured soldiers – he is, in fact, the son of a king from Timbuktu who was raised by missionaries, speaks French fluently and is a decorated soldier in the French army. The purpose of this episode in *Bécassine pendant la Grande Guerre* is clearly to provide a humorous incident again stemming from the protagonist's uninformed naivety, but it is nonetheless significant that even when placed alongside a black prince from Timbuktu, who in the France of 1914 represented a truly 'different' outsider, it is Bécassine who is once again Othered and set apart from her contemporaries. Her continual alienation by those who discuss her as a 'curiosity' and manipulate her lack of mental capacity in order to estrange her from society for comedic gain indirectly indicate throughout this album her status as sub-human and symbolically alien.[29]

Conclusion: From Breton bonne to Sixties Sex-Symbol

Bécassine is often considered the most prominent female character in the history of the *bande dessinée*. The preceding analysis has proposed that, rather than representing an early example of drawn womanhood, she is generally and continually de-feminized throughout the series, particularly during the years of her production by Pinchon and Caumery. It has further gone on to note that in specific instances, such as those examined in *Bécassine pendant la Grande Guerre*, the famous *Bretonne* is even de-humanized and literally alienated and, thus, entirely neutralized as a potentially 'threatening' female representation. Reflecting on the history of the *bande dessinée*, it now seems clear that Bécassine was indeed the first woman character to be defeminized for this purpose. She would not be the last and, due to her unusual prominence as a female figure, is likely to have contributed to this trend.

The next chapter will consider another so-called 'pioneer' of female representation in the *bande dessinée*, but one created in a different era and for a very different audience than that intended for the *Bécassine* series. Despite the visible contrasts between this early strip and the focus of the next case study, Jean-Claude Forest's 1960s sci-fi odyssey *Barbarella*, it will be proposed that the female presence of this latter character is, like Bécassine, essentially denied albeit via a significantly contrasting visual mechanism.

3

Barbarella: Study of a Sex-Symbol

Barbarella: A Multi-Media Icon

In texts discussing the *bande dessinée* (BD), Jean-Claude Forest's Barbarella is often noted alongside Bécassine as a rare example of a female leading figure enjoying popularity and a certain iconic status within the medium.[1] Indeed, the title of Thierry Groensteen's exhibition and accompanying text *Astérix, Barbarella et Cie* (2000), which charted the history of the francophone *bande dessinée* via the collections of the *Musée de la bande dessinée* at Angoulême, places this science-fiction heroine alongside the diminutive Gaul as a shorthand for France's 'Ninth Art' as a whole. Forest is often credited with being a pioneer of popular adult-oriented *bandes dessinées* due to the success of Barbarella's first album of adventures, and the influence of the character on later examples of sexualized female figures (Pravda, Jodelle, Epoxy etc.) is well established. However, despite this recognition and unlike her Breton forebear examined in the previous chapter, few scholarly articles or, indeed, published works of 'fandom' analysing the character of Barbarella closely appear to exist. Anglophone journals *European Comic Art* and *International Journal of Comic Art* do not feature articles on the figure and the French-language *Le Collectionneur de Bandes Dessinées* makes no significant mention of the character of Barbarella in its 35-year print run (although it does discuss Forest's unusual artistic editing techniques in the creation of the *Barbarella* series (see Lefèvre-Vakana 2003; Lefèvre-Vakana's 2004 overview of Forest's career, *L'Art de Jean-Claude Forest*, also contains some useful information regarding *Barbarella*). *9e art: Les Cahiers du musée de la bande dessinée* and its online successor *neuvième art 2.0* in turn primarily reference Barbarella in relation to discussions about censorship in sequential art with some more recent examination of the strip's eroticized visual content (see Joubert 1999; Berthou 2011; Groensteen 2014).

This paucity of studies concerning such a well-known female *bande dessinée* character is surprising, but is likely due to three main factors. The first is simply due to the lifespan of Barbarella in the medium – unlike other celebrated female figures such as Bécassine or, to a lesser extent, Adèle Blanc-Sec, Barbarella's story is relatively short, unfolding and concluding over the course of four albums. A second and likely more decisive factor concerns the eclipsing of Barbarella as a *bande dessinée* character by the success of her incarnation by Jane Fonda in the 1968 film *Barbarella*, directed by Roger Vadim.² Although this Italian-produced English-language film was not wildly successful in France, the influence of its international popularity was felt in the Hexagon as Barbarella, a newly-made cultural icon, was referenced in songs by Serge Gainsbourg, Robert Charlebois and Gilbert Bécaud, became a neologism used on occasion to designate a female 'man-eater', and later attained the status of 'an iconic reference point for anything concerning eroticism and the sixties' (Lefèvre-Vakana 2004: 13).³ The consuming popularity of the celluloid *Barbarella* is evident in later *bande dessinée* publications featuring the figure – in the 1980 Dargaud re-edition of the second album *Le Semble-Lune* (originally published in 1977), nineteen pages after the close of the BD narrative are dedicated to stills of the film, whilst in the final album *Le Miroir aux tempêtes* (1982), Barbarella herself appears to be aware of her cinematic manifestation as she reflects of her first adventure: '[i]t didn't kill me but they made a film about it' (Forest 1982: 4).⁴ Contrastingly, some cinematic considerations of the Barbarella figure, such as that found in Marie Lathers' *Space Oddities: Women and Outer Space in Popular Film and Culture, 1960-2000* (2010), do not refer at all to her *bande dessinée* origins.

In addition to Barbarella's relatively short-lived *bande dessinée* career and its overshadowing by the internationally successful film, a final factor explaining the surprising lack of analysis of the figure in *bande dessinée*-related publications is likely to be the sexualized nature of the character. The first album, simply titled *Barbarella* (1964), was famously censored a year after its publication by the committee responsible for imposing the 1949 law due to its inclusion of nudity and sexual themes.⁵ This censorship ruling banning 'poster campaigns, advertising and sales to minors' of the original album published by Eric Losfeld's imprint Terrain Vague was protested by a group of artists and directors involved in the *Club des bandes dessinées* (of which Forest himself was a founding member), who publicized their cause via a denunciatory article, 'La censure barbare est là',⁶ printed in another of Losfeld's publications, the cinema journal *Midi Minuit Fantastique* (Lefèvre-Vakana 2004: 12). The album would quickly be re-published featuring some minor sartorial adjustments to avoid a similarly censored fate for new editions (the ruling of the *Commission de contrôle et de surveillance* was only applicable to the specific edition on which it was imposed, not the work itself) and the notoriety gained by its initial restriction in fact boosted the sales of *Barbarella* in such subsequent re-prints by Dargaud, Livre de Poche, J'ai Lu and, again, Losfeld (Joubert 2006: 65). However, although this censorship was eventually beneficial for the sales of *Barbarella*, according to Philippe Lefèvre-Vakana in *L'Art de Jean-Claude Forest*, its infamy was detrimental to the artistic credibility of the work and to Forest as a *bande dessinée* creator: [u]nfortunately, the sexual side of this *bande dessinée* – its nudity – has too often been the only thing remembered about it. It's given Forest the diminished reputation of pornographer, or at least of an erotic BD specialist (Lefèvre-Vakana 2004: 13).[7] This popular designation of the strip as a work of pioneering but qualitatively unremarkable visual erotica appears to have influenced the lack of close study of the *bande dessinée* character, the album and wider series as a whole. However, although it is certainly the case that Barbarella frequently appears naked or sparsely-clothed throughout her adventures, and that innuendo and sexual themes are present, this does not render the character a useless focus of study. Fully examining for the first time how Barbarella is represented and sexualized, and how Forest guides the reader to gaze at this famous figure, is not only an intriguing task in itself, it also contributes to understanding more about the artistic manipulation of female representation in the *bande dessinée* in response to the 'women problems' outlined in the Introduction to this book, and how the formal specificity of the medium may play a part therein. The following section will undertake a close study of Barbarella, first considering the progression of the character across her four-album existence, before providing a case study of the first album, with a view to uncovering the intricacies of Barbarella's depiction behind this so-called 'skin strip'.

The Life and Grounding of an Inter-Stellar Wanderer

Barbarella's first set of adventures was pre-published in the trimestral *V-Magazine*, with the heroine making her first appearance in March 1962. Jean-Claude Forest had been an understated figure in the *bande dessinée* industry throughout the 1950s, working sporadically for children's journals including *Vaillant* and *La Semaine de Suzette* (Lefèvre-Vakana 2004: 8).[8] He also contributed to the wider artistic community via illustrations and cover sketches for several publications.[9] The editor of one such periodical, *V-Magazine*'s Georges Hilaire Gallet, wanted to showcase an erotic *bande dessinée* featuring a female leading character in his publication. Forest was chosen for the project and, provided he respected Gallet's basic criteria, was given free rein to create the strip to his own specifications (Lefèvre-Vakana 2004: 12). The serialization of the first narrative took place over a period of almost two years, concluding in January of 1964, but this incrementally-appearing *Barbarella* did not prove to be particularly successful. However, following the popularity of the album and later film, Forest produced over time three more narratives featuring the figure of Barbarella. The second of the series, *Les Colères du Mange-minutes*, was first pre-published in Italian journal *Linus* in October 1967 followed some months later by a serialization in *V-Magazine* and finally published as an album in 1974, whilst *Le Semble-Lune*, the third instalment, was directly published as an album without serialization in 1977. The concluding narrative, *Le Miroir aux tempêtes*, exceptional in that it was written by Forest but drawn by fellow artist Daniel Billon (although Forest is said to have extensively 'retouched' Billon's work prior to publication), was serialized in *L'Écho des Savanes* between 1980 and 1981, and finally published as an album in 1982 (Lefèvre-Vakana 2004: 14). The character of Barbarella also appeared in Forest's 1971 *bande dessinée* adaptation of Jules Verne's *L'Île mystérieuse*, entitled *Mystérieuse matin, midi et soir*, in which she undertakes the role originally held by Captain Nemo.

Across the four principal tales that comprise Barbarella's *bande dessinée* lifespan, there exists no overarching narrative. She is introduced in *Barbarella* with no back-story and no particular path to follow.[10] Each of the first three albums is independent of its precedent and involves an entirely different cast of secondary characters. Barbarella variously occupies across these tales the role of space adventurer, alien circus master, dream invader and time traveller, while frequently finding time to disrobe on a whim or delight in intra-species sexual activity.

In a 1968 interview, Jean-Claude Forest described his media-spanning heroine as 'a free, wild, independent girl. She's neither really a suffragette nor a police officer' (Forest 1994: n.pag.)[11] and it is true, despite her noted reputation, that Barbarella's personality across the albums reveals her to be more than a mere sexual plaything. In each album she proves herself to be courageous, compassionate and willing to put herself in danger to help those in need. She also shows herself on occasion to be both authoritative – most notably in her role as director of the 'Délirium-Circus' in *Les Colères du Mange-minutes* – and cunning (although most of her quick-thinking plans do involve taking her clothes off for various reasons), and is even noted to be university-educated.[12]

Although Barbarella's basic character traits do not change drastically over the course of her four album lifespan, there is a noted progression in her role within the narrative over the course of the stories. In her text discussing cinematic depictions of women in space, Lathers suggests that in any space-faring narrative a female character is likely to be 'grounded'; that is, encouraged to stay 'on earth, in the home, in the kitchen or in the back yard', as '[i]t is understood that something, something residing in the very organs that make up "women", cannot defy gravity, cannot leave home' (2010: 7). Where female characters are shown travelling amongst the stars, their process of 'grounding' must come from other elements in the narrative, which reinforce the woman's essential subservience to a supposedly natural patriarchal system, and hence '"ground" her as a woman, as a body, as linked always already to man and to the earth' (2010: 8).[13] Barbarella, although 'free, wild and independent' as her adventures begin, appears to be progressively grounded over the course of the series. In the first album, she travels alone or with different companions across the planet Lythion. She seems to have no ties or responsibilities, is repeatedly shown in varying states of undress and appears to sleep with several different partners, including an anatomically male robot.[14] The tone of *Les Colères du Mange-minutes*, which charts the exploits of Barbarella as she leads the Délirium-Circus and is repeatedly double-crossed by her mysterious water-dwelling lover Narval on the mysterious planet Spectra, is somewhat darker. Barbarella's position of authority as the circus director is counter-balanced both by a progression of bondage-style outfits – the opening panel, for example, shows her making an announcement about the circus to assembled members of the press whilst wearing a collar and chain round her neck – and her tenure as the most successful prostitute in a sado-masochist-themed brothel run by the ruling 'Frères de la bouche'.[15]

Whereas Barbarella's progression from free and promiscuous to prominent prostitute may suggest a certain constraining of the character to a more contained and male-regimented sexuality, the third album, *Le Semble-Lune*, changes direction entirely and Barbarella's narrative journey is henceforth grounded in a most traditional fashion. Unlike the previous Barbarella tales, the third tome of her adventures features a male character, with whom the eponymous figure shares the spotlight, and who appears on pages independently of her. Browningwell, a cosmic architect into whose dreaming subconscious Barbarella is projected at the opening of the narrative and who quickly becomes her lover, conceives and constructs over the course of the story a giant space sculpture of Barbarella naked. Barbarella, in turn, anxious to prove that women too can create 'masterpieces', sleeps with Browningwell before heading alone to Gyn-Gyn, the planet of fertility, proudly returning with the pair's new-born baby.[16] In addition to the diffusion of narrative focus beyond the single figure of Barbarella, there is a notable reduction in erotic depictions of the character in this story, particularly following the birth of her child, Petit Renard.[17] Over the final third of the narrative, Forest directs the sexualized gaze typically associated with Barbarella away from the new mother and onto her nude interstellar effigy.

The fourth album is the only of Barbarella's tales to retain the same main crop of secondary characters as its previous instalment as Browningwell and Petit Renard again play significant roles in the narrative. As it opens, the reader learns that unlike her previous existence as an interplanetary traveller, Barbarella now lives on Earth (and in a real-life location – by Lake Vassivière in the Limousin region of France) with 'love of her life' Browningwell and their mischievous child. After a gift from Petit Renard on the occasion of the invented 'Saint Barbarella' day proves more dangerous than it looks, Barbarella is pulled between time periods, with the narrative devoted to solving this temporal mystery. The formal construction of this story confirms Forest's progressive stylistic evolution away from image-led narratives to textually-driven strips as seen gradually over the course of the previous albums, as much of this story is conveyed by long passages of dialogue. This turn away from the visual is strongly underlined by the fact that only two small images show Barbarella naked, and both appear as fleeting memories (shown to the heroine by an immortal alien being). This further supports the observation that Barbarella's representation across these four albums is incrementally de-eroticized, and that her previously independent, nomadic and sexually-liberated lifestyle is replaced by her role as wife and mother. This grounding of Barbarella is emphasized in the last sequence of the final album, which sees her preparing a cheese soufflé for her family and some guests. In a strange twist, the oven she attempts to use resembles a life-size statue of Bécassine (and is referred to as 'Bécassine'), thus linking the de-eroticized Barbarella to this ultimate symbol of asexuality and servitude. The final panel of the series reveals that 'Bécassine' has broken down but that Barbarella has still managed to prepare a particularly tasty soufflé. With no further adventures following *Le Miroir aux tempêtes*, this final image of Barbarella – a Bécassine-like figure, settled in France with her partner and child – thoroughly and eternally grounds the character in the eyes of the reader.

Barbarella in Barbarella

Lefèvre-Vakana notes in his overview of the *Barbarella* series that following the success of the first album, each subsequent instalment was notably less successful in terms of sales (2004: 14). This may variously be attributed to poor promotion, reader reaction to Forest's changing style from the first album onwards, the steady decrease in nudity and eroticism over the course of the narratives and popular new developments elsewhere in the medium (2004: 14). In later histories of the *bande dessinée*, brief mentions of Barbarella are largely restricted to her appearance in the first album and when the influence of the figure and Forest's rendering of her is discussed in scholarly texts, this discussion is almost always restricted to *Barbarella* alone. Although a study of the character over the course of the series, as briefly presented above, yields noteworthy results concerning this famous figure, a fuller examination of *Barbarella* in particular is necessary to understand the depiction of this character, and the representational processes in this album that have rendered her iconic within the medium.

Unlike the three albums that follow, the introductory *Barbarella* has no master narrative that structures the story from beginning to end. Instead, this first tome is a collection of four adventures upon which Barbarella embarks in different locations across the planet Lythion, with an unexpected crash-landing ensuring her arrival on the planet, and chance largely dictating her experiences on, and passage between, its mysterious lands. This unpredictable narrative is complemented by

Forest's black-and-white sketchy, expressive style, which is entirely at odds with the precise, clear lines that dominated the *bande dessinée* production of the 1950s immediately prior to Barbarella's conception. In *Drawn and Dangerous: Italian Comics of the 1970s and 1980s*, Simone Castaldi briefly discusses *Barbarella*'s international influence, and notes that in addition to heralding a visually innovative graphic style that encouraged a move away from clear line dominance, '[*Barbarella*] introduced the inversion of hierarchies between plot and visual rendition, between plot and discourse [...] which became the trademark of French and Italian adult comics in the following decade' (2010: 33). Unlike other *bandes dessinées* that relegate visual elements to their role within the narrative, Castaldi suggests, 'in Forest's work the relationship is inverted – it is the visionary surge that demands of the plot the means to come to fruition' (2010: 33). Although this visual dominance would progressively fade over the course of the three following albums, in which Forest increasingly prioritized the transmission of narrative via text and dialogue, in *Barbarella* it is the image, and in particular the erotic image of Barbarella, which is given primacy.[18]

This visual prioritizing of the principal character is established early in the narrative. Barbarella crash-lands on Lythion and finds herself in the Great Greenhouse of Cristallia. Crawling out of the wreckage of her spaceship, she calls out in pain as she is scratched and cut by giant rose thorns (Forest 1994: 2). Then in a double-sized panel on the following third page – the first entirely text-less panel of the narrative – Barbarella suddenly appears with her clothes ripped from the waist up (Figure 1). She is shown from head to knees leaning back with her lips parted and arms raised to expose her breasts entirely, as leaves and branches frame the view of her body. In 'Visual Pleasure and Narrative Cinema', Mulvey describes the presence of woman as an indispensable yet hazardous element of spectacle in film, as 'her visual presence tends to work against the development of a storyline, to freeze the flow of action in moments of erotic contemplation' (1989: 19); a problem that must be counteracted in order to integrate this 'alien presence' in cohesion with the narrative. This early frame of *Barbarella*, however, is crafted precisely to arrest the flow of the narrative and fix the gaze of the reader on the static, exposed view of Barbarella. The size of the panel, its placement as the first on the page, the lack of text, the dark shading of the plants encircling Barbarella's body and, finally, the character's pose, all suggest Forest's intention to subjugate narrative progression to this arresting image.

Such 'frozen' views of Barbarella stilt the flow of the story throughout this first album. A further notable example comes as, following Barbarella's departure from Cristallia, her newly-acquired rocket is boarded by aliens who insist she and her companions aboard must disrobe. A fully-dressed Barbarella is shown at the bottom of the relevant page warming to the thought of obeying this command as the ship's captain protests behind her (Forest 1994: 13). As the reader turns the page, however, they are suddenly confronted with another page-opening, double-sized panel showing Barbarella entirely naked in the foreground being sprayed with a vaporized substance from a hose (apparently to 'protect her Earthling skin') as her male companions look on, fully clothed (Figure 2). Again in this striking image, Forest plays with shading to draw in further the reader's gaze already distracted by the suddenly naked vision of the buxom Barbarella. Against a background of darkest black, the ejaculatory spray of the vapour appears as a bright light shining against the figure's white skin. This blinding erotic image suddenly presented to the viewer following a strategic page-turn once more freezes the rhythm of their reading and cuts the flow of the story in static, sexual contemplation. As indicated, Forest continues this visual manipulation until the end of the story.

Forest's foregrounding of erotic visuality over narrative cohesion is certainly a factor in the establishment of *Barbarella* as a pioneering work of adult *bande dessinée*. However, a further, but connected, aspect of Forest's depiction of the Barbarella character has no doubt also contributed to her now-iconic status amongst readers of the BD: that of the complete scopophilic control of her eroticized form afforded to the reader.

As discussed in the Introduction to this book, psychoanalytic theory has proven a useful tool in the study of visual narratives. Turning psychoanalytic reflection towards the experience of reading a *bande dessinée* and, in particular, towards how readers are guided to gaze at women across its structured progression of panels, produces the following points. The *bande dessinée*, like other visual narratives, satisfies the basic human desire for 'pleasurable looking' (scopophilia). The series of varyingly-displayed and sexualized female figures denoted in the foregoing historical chronology (and, indeed, the further histories of female representation presented later in this work) indicate also that the *bande dessinée* traditionally respects the sexual division of the gaze, defined by Mulvey in relation to cinema, which is required by the phallocentric culture responsible for its creation – the man looks, but the woman is looked at (1989: 18). The experience of reading a *bande dessinée* promotes a particularly intense sense of private voyeuristic pleasure for the reader as, unlike other visual forms such as painting and visual narratives such as film, which are most often intended to be experienced in a public space, the *bande dessinée* is predominantly read alone and, particularly when produced as an album, is sealed between two covers. The reader opens this private world and gazes, (usually) individually, at the images and figures that inhabit it. The reading of a BD is also a particularly active pleasure. Whereas auditory aspects are provided for patrons of other visual narrative arts such as cinema or theatre, when reading a *bande dessinée* such details are open to interpretation by the individual. The reader must participate in the imaginative processes necessary to 'fill in' this and other un-provided details, thus holding a certain position of control over some narrative aspects.[19] Further, by virtue of, simply, the manner of consuming a *bande dessinée* – the reader must hold the work and turn the pages themselves – the individual is also always in possession of a certain amount of power in regulating the pace of reading and in lingering on certain images (although artistic features such as panel layout can greatly influence this), again ensuring a particularly engaged reading experience. Mulvey describes the basic scopophilic instinct as an active and individual desire from infancy onwards to 'possess', and have a sense of power over, what one sees (1989: 16). The preceding analysis suggests that the formal specificity of the *bande dessinée* seems particularly suited to provide the pleasure associated with this 'active, controlling gaze', perhaps more so than the more distanced voyeuristic gazes associated with other visual media – this, indeed, may be a contributing factor to the extensive presence of sexualized female figures visible across so many examples of the BD. It may be Forest's particular manipulation of the *bande dessinée*'s uniquely controlling look, guided towards the display of Barbarella, that has aided her ascension to 'icon' of the medium.

Rather than mediating the gaze of the *bande dessinée* viewer upon the figure of Barbarella through the eyes of a single, prominent male character who looks at her (a frequent tactic used in traditional Hollywood cinema, identified by Mulvey [2009: 21]), Forest repeatedly structures the sexualized depiction of Barbarella in *Barbarella* to allow the reader a direct scopophilic 'possession' of the character. An early example of this in the work is already outlined above – in the first erotic view of Barbarella in the greenhouse, no other figures mediate the gaze and Forest structures the image to guide the reader to linger over this openly exposed rendering of the character. A more distinct manifestation of this manipulation of a possessive gaze is found later in Barbarella's adventure in Cristallia. Intent on helping end the conflict between the inhabitants of the greenhouse, the Adonides, and their enemies the Orhomrs, Barbarella travels to Orhomr territory but is not welcomed diplomatically by the natives who strip her to the waist and throw her on the ground. Although, somewhat like Bécassine, Barbarella is not a stranger to announcing out loud what is happening to her, the last panel of this page (again, double the standard size) is an exceptional example of this narrative device (Figure 3). Barbarella is shown half naked and on all fours, her angle in the frame emphasizing the shape of her behind, as she looks away from the attacking Orhomrs and towards the reader to ask 'Why have they thrown me on to these sharp stones [...]?' (1994: 6).[20] Via this panel, placed significantly early within the narrative, not only is the reader directly invited to gaze at this sexualized view of Barbarella, but he becomes a participant in her narrative plight.[21] A direct connection between the character and the reader now established, in the first panels of the following page, as the still-exposed Barbarella is spirited away from danger by an unknown source (revealed as she lands to be a peaceful Orhomr), the reader may allow himself to briefly assume that he is her rescuer and has power over her helpless, sexualized form.

Although it is argued here that in *Barbarella* images of this eponymous figure are manipulated to allow the reader a sense of direct scopophilic control over her, it is also true that various male characters sporadically gaze upon Barbarella throughout the story, thus potentially threatening the viewer's dominant scopophilic possession of the figure. However, Forest's depiction of Barbarella's interactions with the male characters that flit in and out of the narrative is carefully crafted to allow the reader largely to retain his position of erotic visual power over her. Where male figures are present in frames to gaze upon the displayed form of Barbarella, such as the panel discussed above in which she is sprayed with vapour (Figure 2), the positioning of the characters within the frame is used to assert the visual dominance of the viewer's gaze.[22] Barbarella is repeatedly placed in the foreground, angled to face the reader, while the male figures occupy the background behind or to the side of the female figure.

Barbarella also becomes intimate with male figures on occasion in this inaugural album, although as indicated above, despite its reputation as a 'skin strip', *Barbarella* is not explicit by modern standards. Preludes to Barbarella's intimate encounters largely include a verbal indication via a suggestive comment from the heroine and/or an image showing Barbarella undressing or partially nude, rather than a visual display of physical contact between the character and her chosen male companion. The pictorial trope by which Forest indicates that Barbarella has engaged in sexual activity, established in *Barbarella* and then repeated in *Les Colères du Mange minutes* and *Le Semble-Lune*, consists repeatedly of a single panel depicting her naked and draped over the body of her chosen lover, who in turn is always clothed (see, for example, page 7 of *Barbarella* as the heroine submits to 'her curiosity to know the tenderness of an Orhomr').[23] Although the suggestion that Barbarella has been intimate with a man is clearly made, she is still presented erotically to the reader – naked, reclining and suggestively posed to emphasize her curves.[24] The non-visualization of the supposed act and the systematic presence of this erotic display on each occasion combine to leave unthreatened the reader's scopophilic possession of Barbarella.

Two 'adult' male characters appear in *Barbarella* during whose interactions with the heroine Forest does not employ his standard visual strategies to ensure the dominance of the reader's gaze, relying instead on the characterization of these figures to annul any potential scopophilic threat. The first is a robot named Viktor who saves Barbarella as she is attacked by royal guards in the city of Sogo during her last and longest adventure in the album. The pair's brief encounter lasts only two pages; however, in this brief time Barbarella is able to ascertain that Viktor is anatomically equipped and able to do 'everything [...] and very attentively' (1994: 53),²⁵ before the narrative jumps forward to show a frame of the pair in bed, apparently post-coitus (Figure 4). This panel is unusual amongst those hinting at Barbarella's recent sexual activity in that it is particularly large – four times the size of a standard panel – and that it shows the heroine's partner by her side rather than hidden behind her displayed form. It is also the most explicitly sexually suggestive of any image of its kind throughout the series – Barbarella is seen lying back with her legs apart, a thin sheet covering her body below her hips, as she clasps her breast exclaiming 'You have style, Viktor!'.²⁶ By choosing a robot as the heroine's partner in this sequence – Viktor is humanoid, eloquent but visually mechanical and apparently metallic – Forest is able to go further in the pictorial expression of Barbarella's sexual encounter than he has elsewhere without alienating the reader. Needless to say, this robotic erotic experience also adds to the mounting impression of promiscuity attributed to the character, a risqué narrative aspect designed to titillate the early 1960s reader.

Pygar – the 'last Ornithantrope', condemned to wander the labyrinth of Sogo – is the second male figure whose particular characterization allows him to be placed unthreateningly alongside Barbarella. He appears intermittently across the final story of *Barbarella*, and is the most prominent male figure of the album. Tall and well-muscled with strong features, Pygar variously embraces, carries and rescues Barbarella at points during her attempts to free the labyrinth prisoners from Sogo's evil queen. The fact that he is blind, however, and the outward visual emphasis of this by the consistent presence of cloth wrapped around his eyes, serves symbolically to castrate the character, and eliminates the possibility of his altering the scopophilic hierarchy established in the work.²⁷ Pygar's winged, angelic presence also helps to feminize his representation, thus neutralizing the potentially troubling effect of his corporeal display to the reader – unlike any other male character in the album, the sculpted frame of this gigantesque figure is exhibited as he helps Barbarella on her mission dressed only in a short, feathered skirt. That the oft-rescued Barbarella must, in turn, save Pygar following his capture and crucifixion-like display by the queen of Sogo during which he is restrained against a structure by huge nails driven through his wings, furthers the feminization of this figure and helps to neutralize his display in this final adventure.²⁸

As now clearly shown, numerous elements of visuality, layout and characterization are manipulated by Forest to give the *bande dessinée* reader unfettered ocular access to the figure he described as 'the girl I've always dreamed of meeting [...]' (1994: n.pag.).²⁹ Further examples of Barbarella posing or pouting provocatively whilst favourably angled towards an exterior viewpoint are too numerous to list. As explained in the Introduction to this book, Mulvey suggests in her work that such fetishizing of the female form is undertaken to counteract the 'deeper problem' posed by the womanly body: that, ultimately, she represents absence and distress to the masculine viewer. The excessive display and overvaluation of the female form may be used as a way to escape the castration anxiety posed by her presence, as turning the woman herself into a fetish (normally a tool used to displace the sight of woman's imaginary castration onto something else) renders her reassuring more than dangerous (1989: 21).[30]

Forest in fact underlines the castration anxiety inspired by woman in several ways in *Barbarella*. Strikingly, the first real adversary that Barbarella comes across in the narrative, in the second of her four adventures, is a Medusa figure who may take on the form of any woman with whom she comes into contact (including Barbarella), and who wears a mask over her face with snakes protruding from it. This character serves to suggest that not just Barbarella, but all women are beings that may inspire fear in the male subject, and is a particularly symbolic choice of figure as Freud himself used the example of the mythological Medusa to illustrate his theory that 'a multiplication of penis symbols signifies castration' (see Wilk 2000: 98).[31] Correspondingly, the myriad of towers that make up the city of Sogo, oppressed by the rule of its despotic queen, are unmistakeably phallic (see particularly Forest, 1994, 37).

Despite other visual manifestations, however, it is, simply by her continual presence, Barbarella who poses the most consistent threat of castration anxiety, and by her endless fetishized display and eroticization, the most visible response to it. Her sexualized exposure continues regardless of changes within the narrative. On occasion she appears undressed for no apparent reason consistent with the progressing storyline and when she is clothed, her standard outfit – a seamless jumpsuit – is so skin-tight that it is at points unclear whether she is dressed or not. That Barbarella's eroticization is, across the album, the most noteworthy element of her depiction reveals an essential final element concerning her characterization. Barbarella is continually undressed, posed, angled and displayed for the dominant gaze of the reader. She is introduced with no back-story and almost no information is given concerning her life before the narrative's beginning, thus allowing the reader to complete her characterization mentally using his imagination. Almost every part of her depiction is coded to pique the desire of the individual reader, to the extent that she, as a female character, is not truly present beyond her physical outline. Although she displays, on occasion, traits of bravery or compassion, or delivers witty one-liners (although usually innuendo-laden) from time to time, the overwhelmingly exposed and sexualized nature of her depiction in this album mean that essentially Barbarella represents fetishized eroticism, the reader's desire and little else. Whilst Bécassine's asexualization restricted her development as a female character as seen in the last chapter, here it is clear that Barbarella's over-sexualization has all but erased her real female presence from *Barbarella*.

4

Solving the Mystery of Adèle Blanc-Sec

Les Aventures extraordinaires d'Adèle Blanc-Sec

In early 2010, the newly re-housed *bande dessinée* museum at the *Centre national de la bande dessinée et de l'image* (CNBDI) presented its first exhibition, *Cent pour cent bande dessinée*, which featured pages from 100 'masterpieces' of the form, reinterpreted by other artists. Of these 100 celebrated œuvres, very few featured a female principal character, with the most notable amongst this small selection being Jacques Tardi's *Aventures extraordinaires d'Adèle Blanc-Sec*. Tardi and his work as a whole have received considerable attention in studies of the *bande dessinée* (BD) – Groensteen's first monograph, *Tardi* (1980), was devoted to the artist and a chapter of Matt Screech's 2005 book *Masters of the Ninth Art* designates him as such. Additionally, in 2000, the 173-page *Tardi: Interviews with Numa Sadoul* added the artist to Sadoul's already impressive collection of BD interviews.[1] Much attention in these works is given to Tardi's distinctive style, a *ligne-claire*-inspired combination of realism and caricature, and to his documentary accuracy in geographical and historical detail.[2]

Les Aventures extraordinaires d'Adèle Blanc-Sec is Tardi's longest-running *bande dessinée*, spanning nine albums between 1976 and 2007, with the series currently unfinished.[3] The strip begins in the final years of the *Belle Époque* in 1911 – jumping forward a few years to reach 1918 at the start of the sixth album – and follows the exploits of serial-novel writer Adèle Blanc-Sec as she becomes repeatedly embroiled in mysterious happenings across Paris. Faithful to his style established in earlier *bandes dessinées* such as *Adieu Brindavoine* and *Le Démon des glaces* (both 1974), in *Les Aventures extraordinaires d'Adèle Blanc-Sec* Tardi presents with minimal exceptions a meticulously researched and historically accurate visual representation of pre–First World War Paris, with even the structure of the series – which takes the form of a serialized novel – faithful to his chosen era.

Much of the current scholarship available concerning the *Blanc-Sec* story focuses on its formal construction: Screech's chapter dives into an investigation of the serialized fiction tradition and considers Adèle's characterization within this framework, while a 2007 article by Géraldine Molina considers the detective novel aspect of the mystery series. Useful observations of the figure of Adèle Blanc-Sec certainly exist in these and other sources (noted below); however, a full study of the figure and her characterization throughout the series has thus far been unavailable. This is perhaps because the series remains unfinished, so the destiny of the figure is, as yet, unclear. It may also be due to the character's opaque nature, as despite appearing as the eponymous principal character in nine album episodes, the combination of Adèle's lack of emotion and the complicated twists and turns of Tardi's plots significantly obscure insights into the nature of the character. As an exceptional figure in the history of the *bande dessinée*, however – a female principal figure of a series deemed a masterpiece of the form – a full investigation of this mysterious mystery-writer and her representation by Tardi is needed. The following chapter undertakes this task, examining the character's indefinable, fluctuating characterization and ambiguous gender performance before analysing Tardi's alternating narrative 'monstering' and visual idealization of this female, and, thus, problematic, figure.

A Sketch of Adèle

Like Barbarella, the figure of Adèle is presented by Tardi with very little back-story. All the details the reader gathers about her personal circumstances are presented visually as part of the narrative, over the course of the series. The first album, *Adèle et la bête*, provides little information on the series's heroine, with Adèle's first appearance not until the tenth page, and no mention of her prior to her entrance in the story. Assuming a false identity in her opening scenes, her real name is not known until the thirtieth page. The second instalment, *Le Démon de la Tour Eiffel*, allows more details about Tardi's character to become clear. The reader learns that she is a writer of serial novels, and her home is seen for the first time – a small but typically bourgeois apartment in a Haussmannian building in Paris – which confirms her place as comfortably middle-class, a fact already suggested by her style of dress. Physically, Adèle appears to be a woman of her era. In the first four albums (published between 1976 and 1978) her typical outfit consists of a feathered hat, a blouse and long skirt supported by a petticoat, and a fur-trimmed, empire-line coat in a dark green hue, this colour apparently chosen by Tardi in homage to Bécassine, as one of the rare notable female characters of the *bande dessinée* (Finet and Tardi 2010: 12). Adèle dies at the climax of the fourth album *Momies en folie* and 'sleeps' through the First World War. When she is brought back to life on Armistice Day, 1918, she is quick to change her style of clothing, opting for a more shapeless, androgynous style, complete with a *garçonne*-esque bob.

Beyond her physical presence, however, Adèle's personality and way of life are far from the standard, stereotypical representation of the early-twentieth-century *Parisienne* and appear to defy any attempt at categorization. She is single, lives alone, writes mystery stories (based on her own adventures, as we see most clearly in the seventh album, *Tous des monstres!* (1994), when she is shown arguing with her editor about the cover of her serial novel, named, as in the first album, *Adèle et la bête*), goes out alone at night, smokes, drinks and swears. Tardi notes of the figure in *Le Livre d'Adèle* – a light-hearted survey of the series, and the fullest examination of the character of Adèle Blanc-Sec currently available – that 'the character certainly doesn't have the mentality of a woman from the strip's time-period. Adèle is more like a modern female figure' (Finet and Tardi 2010: 34).[4] The artist goes on to state that the feminist political context at the time of Adèle's 1970s creation certainly influenced her characterization (2010: 34). Adèle, however, despite Nicolas Finet's assertion that she behaves as a feminist and wouldn't be out of place as a suffragette (2010: 34), utters only one phrase throughout the nine-album narrative that suggests an interest in feminist issues, and shows little affinity with, or support for, the few other female characters who filter in and out of the series.[5] It is interesting to note that Tardi was to a small extent involved in the creation of feminist *bandes dessinées* in the 1970s – for the first issue of the female-led *illustré Ah! Nana* (1976) he illustrated a strip scripted by a woman – however, he also notes as an influence in the development of his *bande dessinée* career the series of works published over the 1960s by Eric Losfeld, such as *Barbarella*, *Pravda la survivreuse* and *Les Aventures de Jodelle*, which popularized eroticized depictions of women directed towards male readers.

Returning to specific considerations of Adèle as a character, in addition to her ostensibly anachronistic independence (a notion that will be considered more fully below), Adèle is also fairly anti-authoritarian – mistrusting the intentions of both police and state – endlessly dry-witted, and consistently unemotional. The latter is evident, for example, in the third album, *Le Savant fou*, when she simply wonders following the second attempt on her life that day: 'This is the second time tonight that someone's tried to kill me [...] I wonder if I should stay up or go back to bed?' (2007c: 18).[6] She appears to maintain no social relations with others and is often caustic in her interactions with the sizeable cast of minor characters she encounters in the course of the series's mysteries. She quickly tires even of Brindavoine, a character Tardi has borrowed from his earlier First World War narrative *Adieu Brindavoine* to bring Adèle back to life following her six-year preservation and feature alongside her in her *Aventures extraordinaires*. Rather than falling hopelessly in love with her 'prince', as the fairytale version of this story might unfold, Adèle accuses Brindavoine of being annoying (2007b: 9) as he accompanies her back to her home following her awakening. Adèle also shows herself to be increasingly pessimistic as the series develops and is progressively less interested in the mysteries surrounding her: a notable example of this comes in *Tous des monstres!* when, as the story reaches its climax, Adèle repeats four times over two pages her desire simply to go home to bed (1976: 40–41). Despite the serial-novel structuring of the Adèle Blanc-Sec narratives, this lack of action disassociates Adèle's characterization from that of notable serial-novel figures such as Maurice Leblanc's Arsène Lupin, described by Karen Taylor as 'like a Robin Hood of modern times, infinitely appealing in his sense of justice and gallantry' (2007: 223).

Tardi bases *Les Aventures extraordinaires d'Adèle Blanc-Sec* on an endless circuit of uncertainties. Each episode presents a complex, sometimes indecipherable plot, whose conclusion is only momentary, with the end of each album outlining the mysteries of the next. The Paris drawn by Tardi is historically and geographically accurate, but full of monsters, mummies and figures who rise from the dead. Most of the action across the nine albums takes place at night, with the liminal spaces of bridges and the Seine below featuring heavily.[7] In amongst this uncertain environment, the figure of Adèle too, unlike many other female *bande dessinée* characters (as shall be particularly seen in Section 2 of this book), defies classification. Her personality, as the above outline indicates, does not easily fit into any particular character 'type', and her place in the series is thoroughly ambiguous. It is to this ambiguity that this study will now turn, in order to decipher as far as is possible the representation of this very liminal figure. To present a more concentrated examination of the long-running character, the following section will favour examples emanating from Adèle's introductory adventure, *Adèle et la bête*, with reference to other of the eight narratives included when relevant.

Adèle, La Bête and the Art of Ambiguity

It is suggested above that possible reasons for the paucity of character studies examining Adèle Blanc-Sec, in spite of her exceptional place in *bande dessinée* history, are the unfinished status of her 'extraordinary adventures', and the impenetrable nature of her personality. A further reason, on closer examination of the figure, might also concern the uncertain nature of Adèle as 'principal character'. Although her name adorns the cover of each album adventure, Adèle's presence amongst the sizeable cast of mad scientists and bumbling policemen who also populate each 48-page tale is rarely dominant. Her introduction to the series in *Adèle et la bête* is exemplary of the lack of principal focus directed towards the character throughout the nine-album series.

In *Adèle et la bête*, Tardi introduces the reader to his newly created world in relative confusion, as several different narrative strands are immediately begun without explanatory context. As the story unfolds, it gradually becomes clear that a pterodactyl, hatched from an egg kept in Paris's natural history museum by the psychic powers of an old scientist, has broken free and is terrorizing Paris. Adèle Blanc-Sec enters the story as a kidnapper, holding Edith Rabatjoie – the daughter of a man who has built a mechanical flying copy of the pterodactyl – to ransom over her desire to borrow his contraption to rescue her lover, Ripol, from his death sentence for a murder he did not commit. Adèle is unsuccessful in her rescue attempt, as she is betrayed by the men she hired to kidnap Rabatjoie; however, in a complicated twist it is the latter who rescues Ripol with the mechanical pterodactyl in order to later obtain information from him. Reunited with Adèle after the flying rescue, the two go to collect some ill-gotten gains hidden for safety in the natural history museum. Ripol (like the pterodactyl elsewhere in the complex narrative web) is killed at the story's close by one of Adèle's ex-accomplices and the last page, featuring a large question mark in the centre, summarizes the questions remaining unsolved from this story and ominously introduces the mystery of the next album, *Le Démon de la Tour Eiffel*.

As noted above, Adèle does not appear in this story until the tenth page, as Tardi opens the narrative with a focus on the hatching pterodactyl and the introduction of a pre-kidnap Edith Rabatjoie. Although delaying the protagonist's entry into the story may simply be a narrative choice, in *Le Livre d'Adèle* Finet suggests that the relatively late introduction of Adèle to the strip reflects a certain hesitation on the part of Tardi over his choice of heroine (2010: 8). He goes on to note briefly (as does Groensteen in *Tardi*) that when originally commissioned by Casterman to create a series, Tardi's initial decision was to create *Les Aventures extraordinaires d'Edith Rabatjoie*, with Adèle as a secondary character.[8] In fact, Groensteen further states that, even following the decision to make Adèle the lead character in the first album, Tardi, 'unsure of his heroine's future', was preparing for a potential last-minute character swap by introducing the character of Simon Flageolet (who appears on the last page of *Adèle et la bête*) (1980: 34). This indecision over the principal figure of the series – Casterman's outline for the commission requiring a series built around a single leading character (Finet and Tardi 2010: 7) – makes clear the fact that, unlike Bécassine, for example, Adèle's character is not the key element of the series. This is supported by Tardi's assertion that his conceptual process for the creation of each album begins firstly with the choice of physical place he would most like to draw, with the narrative (and therefore Adèle's place within it) secondary to this principal artistic concern (Groensteen 1980: 55). Historical accuracy also takes precedence over diegetic and characterization concerns; Tardi explains in his work with Finet that he abandoned a prospective Adèle adventure set to take place at Paris's wax museum, the musée Grévin, that he had already begun working on because he couldn't find documentation showing what the entrance to the museum looked like during the time period concerned (2010: 23). Adèle, then, although the eponymous heroine of the series, is secondary to a host of artistic considerations in the creation and development in the series.

The lack of predominant focus on the figure of Adèle in her first adventure – in total, she features in only 24 out of the 46 pages that make up the album – also casts doubt on her position as the principal figure of the narrative. This continues throughout the series, and is most clearly noticeable in *Le Secret de la Salamandre* (1981) when, following her 'death' in the previous tome, Lucien Brindavoine leads the narrative throughout the album, with Adèle only re-appearing, awakened, on the penultimate page. Following this episode, Brindavoine appears often throughout the remainder of the albums, the frequency of his presence at certain points seeming to rival that of Adèle. More generally in the series Tardi presents a host of secondary characters, to the extent that the reader is taxed to recall their names, who share the spotlight with Adèle, the latter sometimes disappearing for multiple pages at a time.

The ambiguous nature of Adèle's character status in the long-running *bande dessinée* springs from several sources. However, this ephemeral existence between a traditional 'principal figure' such as Bécassine or Barbarella, who appears in the majority of pages and whose presence is essential to the overarching narrative, and a secondary character, who moves in and out of the story amongst other minor figures, is not the only uncertain aspect of her depiction by Tardi. In *Masters of the Ninth Art*, Screech discusses the narrative tool used by Tardi in strips such as *La Véritable Histoire du soldat inconnu* (1974) of casting doubt within the story over the identity of the narrator (2005: 140). This narrative uncertainty is also occasionally apparent in *Les Aventures extraordinaires d'Adèle Blanc-Sec*, as Tardi sporadically hints that Adèle might be the narrating voice of the series, in addition to her position as its eponymous character.[9] The *mise en abyme* of Adèle as both Tardi's character and her own in the self-featuring serial novels she writes is progressively apparent from the second album (in which we discover Adèle's profession) but almost always remains a very subtle aspect of the diegesis. The suspicion concerning Adèle's dual identity as narrator and character is first aroused near the beginning of the fourth album, *Momies en folie*, however, when Tardi very briefly underlines the overlapping nature of his narrative series with that of his character. Adèle is shown at her desk reading aloud an instalment of her novel: '[o]ur young and beautiful heroine disarmed the two bandits, then ripped off the hideous masks hiding their faces' (2007d: 6).[10] Adèle's third-person description of herself in her own novel is similar to that found in the caption of the *bande dessinée* series. Indeed, four pages after this scene, as night falls and Adèle goes to sleep, the caption informs the reader that '[a]ll is calm in our young and beautiful heroine's apartment' (2007d: 10).[11] Very subtly, the notion that Adèle may be the narrator of the series is suggested here to the observant reader. This suspicion appears to be dashed, however, at the beginning of the fifth album, *Le Secret de la salamandre*, which opens with an unnamed elderly character talking directly to the reader. This man explains briefly what has happened in the time between the closing of the last album with Adèle's death in 1913, and the beginning of this narrative in 1916. Progressively over the course of four pages his speech-bubble-encased words die away to become incorporated into the caption, suggesting that he is the narrator of the tale. He re-appears on the final page of this album, however, and for the first and last time in the series the caption concludes the story without posing questions to lead the reader into the following instalment, this isolating the narrative style of *Le Secret de la salamandre* significantly from the rest of the series and, thus, casting doubt once more on the identity of the narrator in other albums. Adèle's undefined position between character and 'creator' of the series of tales is then again briefly emphasized in the seventh album, *Tous des monstres!*, as on its final page she, in turn, appears to speak directly to the reader, holding up a copy of *Adèle et la bête* as she talks. This uncertainty concerning the identity of the narrator remains unresolved by Tardi in *Les Aventures extraordinaires d'Adèle Blanc-Sec*, as it does in other of his works as indicated by Screech. Although always remaining an understated element of the series, these brief moments of doubt concerning Adèle's position in the structure of the narrative add to the building picture of the figure as ultimately indefinable and ambiguous.

Progressing from considerations of Adèle's status within the overarching narrative, a final aspect of uncertainty in her representation – particularly intriguing for the focus of this book – concerns the complexly-ambiguous gendered portrayal of the character. For Judith Butler, '[g]ender is the repeated stylization of the body, a set of repeated acts within a highly rigid regulatory framework that congeal over time to produce the appearance of substance, of a natural sort of being' (quoted in Ussher 2006: 3), or as Jane Ussher explains the theory, 'gender is a performance […] something one does rather than what one is' (2006: 3). Adèle, on multiple occasions throughout the series, abstains from performing 'woman'. An example of this intimated above concerns the fact that she displays none of the emotional traits stereotypically connected to 'femininity' as she remains steadfastly unemotional and unsympathetic. Some more tangible manifestations of this ambiguous gender performativity may be linked to expectations of womanhood in the time of the series' setting – she smokes (smoking remaining until the mid-1920s 'largely a male habit' [Hannah et al. 2004: 239]), wears trousers on occasion and walks the streets of Paris unaccompanied after dark.[12] Other examples are less open to temporal interpretation. In *Adèle et la bête*, Adèle spends nine out of the twenty-four pages in which she is present dressed as a man. After reuniting with Ripol following his rescue from the guillotine moments before his planned execution, Adèle and the fugitive prisoner disguise themselves with fake moustaches, suits and bowler hats and head to Paris's *Jardin des plantes* to recover the spoils of a robbery. This sequence triggers the conclusion of the narrative and prior to this point in the story, Adèle has been absent for eight pages. In her last appearance before this suit-attired showdown in the *Muséum d'Histoire naturelle*, Adèle is shown taking a bath and then answering the phone partly covered in a towel. Judith Butler notes 'drag' to be a gendered transgression that highlights the performativity of 'standard' gender roles (Ussher 2006: 3). Here, towards the close of *Adèle et la bête*, Tardi plays with the gendered representation of his character as Adèle is depicted first naked, her bodily femininity highlighted (this image of Adèle in the bath is more fully analysed below), and then dressed as a man, unrecognizable at first before removing her bearded mask.[13] Later in the sequence, this mixing of gender positions continues as she is shown leaving the scene, in her three-piece suit and tie, walking dejectedly with her hands in her pockets, the typically masculine pose complementing her male attire. Only her face and hair indicate that she is female.

Beyond the first album, Tardi's desire to play with the gendered portrayal of his character continues. One interesting instance of this comes near the opening of *Le Savant fou*. Invited alongside a group of scientists to view the results of a new experiment in which a *pithecanthropus erectus* has been brought to life, the group is addressed on multiple occasions as 'Messieurs', ignoring the presence of a woman amongst them (2007c: 9). This disregard for her 'difference' is replaced later in the same sequence, however, by a concentrated focus on her status as female when the *pithécanthrope*, reacting to his surroundings, is suddenly horrified upon realizing a woman is present before him. Tardi thus plays with Adèle's presence amongst the sizeable cast of mostly male secondary characters to destabilize further her female status.

K. A. Laity states in 'Construction of a "Female Hero": Iconography in *Les Aventures extraordinaires d'Adèle Blanc-Sec*' regarding this cast of male figures that 'Adèle seems at times to be surrounded by the great crowd of bowler-hatted men, as if to verify her female status [...] She is not only feminine, but attractive (hence the constant phalanx of men surrounding her)' (2002: 165). However, despite occasional romantically fuelled reactions towards Adèle, she is not always popular with individual male figures, and sometimes provokes violently negative reactions (the young scientist Zborowsky swoons on sight of her in *Momies en folie*, for example [2007d: 20], but two pages later Flageolet vehemently refuses Adèle's call for help), casting doubt on the theory that the male characters are, in part, present in order to underline her femaleness.

Another notable way in which Adèle's gendered characterization is rendered ambiguous is via Tardi's representation of the character as both 'rescued' and 'rescuer'. The trope of the 'damsel in distress' is well-established to the point of cliché in the narrative representation of women across various media. This gender-dependent type serves to uphold the phallocentric paradigm by placing the female character in a relation to her male saviour of weakness and dependence. Over the *Adèle Blanc-Sec* series, the eponymous character is frequently saved by male characters (never by female figures), with even the *pithécantrope* in *Le Savant fou* liberating Adèle from kidnappers. Her series of rescues begins in *Adèle et la bête* over a short sequence of panels, a close examination of which yields noteworthy results. Mid-way through this first narrative, when she is invited to a mysterious meeting at the natural history museum by Zborowsky who claims to have information concerning the pterodactyl, Adèle is suddenly thrown by an unknown assailant into a watery crocodile enclosure. The first panel of this sequence shows a man, his face hidden from view, pushing Adèle from behind as a speech bubble containing a large question mark conveys her shocked confusion (2007a: 26). The next panel, on the following page, shows her dramatic, almost vertical, fall (Figure 5). Her head is cut out of sight by the lower border of the panel, with the effect that this image, clearly displaying Adèle's heeled boots, fitted coat and fur stole, reduces her identity to that of any helpless, bourgeois woman. Adèle re-appears two panels later, during which Esperandieu, a character involved in the re-animation of the pterodactyl, has seized Adèle's umbrella to use as a weapon, and leapt into the enclosure. In a symbolically significant scene, Adèle appears on all fours as she apparently rises from her fall, her arched back showing the curve of her behind, and her head raised in the bottom half of the panel (Figure 5). Heightening this sexualized pose, she is shown with her eyes closed and mouth open as drops of water fall from her face, not unlike beads of sweat. Esperandieu, brandishing Adèle's umbrella and ordering her not to move, stands aloft behind her. Although only constituting a small panel amongst a page of ten, the phallic imagery of the horizontally poised umbrella in this frame powerfully corresponds with Adèle's sexually evocative pose, surreptitiously reminding the reader that Adèle, as female, remains subject to the phallus, even in this world where she appears to have autonomy. The gendered division of the rescuer-rescued roles is repeated as the page continues when Adèle is pulled over the enclosure railings by a group of male passers-by while Esperandieu keeps three crocodiles at bay using the umbrella. He is then commended by a male bystander for his heroic act and Adèle is comforted by an older woman who refers to her as '[m]y poor child' – a compassionate appellation that nonetheless highlights the former's status as weak and in need of rescue.[14]

As seen in this example from the first album, then, Adèle at times inhabits the classic female narrative role of 'damsel in distress', appearing in a stereotypically weak and dependent relation to her male rescuer. It is, however, also true that Adèle occasionally appears as the rescuer of others in the series – although this occurs less frequently and mostly when it is in Adèle's interest to act. She in fact saves the life of Esperandieu in *Le Savant fou* when the pair is shot at while travelling in a car by assailants in another vehicle (2007c: 14). Despite being injured in the head and then thrown from her car, Adèle still manages to stop the attack by shooting the pursuing vehicle's fuel tank with a gun she suddenly produces from somewhere on her person (2007c: 15). On returning home, she disinfects and bandages her own head wound before simply smoking a cigarette and going to sleep (2007c: 17).[15]

Adèle's fluctuating role as both rescuer and rescued is a final way in which Tardi plays with the gendered representation of his character. As a rescuer she once again does not 'perform' stereotypical, passive femininity; however, as a female figure frequently saved by male characters the traditional role of 'woman' is imposed upon her, as it is occasionally elsewhere in the series by the amorous or hateful reactions of male characters to her presence.

The liminality of Adèle's gendered depiction may be the reason behind Tardi's choice to 'kill' the character in 1913 and have her re-awaken on the day of the Armistice. The First World War demanded a definite division of roles between men and women into which Adèle's characterization does not fit; thus, depicting Adèle's experience of the war whilst maintaining historical accuracy may have proven difficult for Tardi. The artist appears to concur with this conjecture in a quotation appearing in Laity's article in which he states that the war would have been 'no place' for Adèle as 'she would not have been allowed to fight, and could no more have settled for being a nurse, than she could have remained home rolling bandages' (2002: 168).[16]

As stated above, Tardi has indicated elsewhere that the feminist political context of the era of Adèle's conception influenced, to an extent, her design. Although more specific indications of where these influences lie within the depiction of Adèle have not been noted by the artist, it is possible that the feminist challenge to traditional gender roles in the 1970s contributed to Tardi's manipulation of the character's gender position discussed here. It is also interesting to note, however, that Tardi does suggest in *Le Livre d'Adèle* that, as posited more generally in the Introduction to this book, the depiction of women in the *bande dessinée* medium previously – or, rather, the lack thereof – complicated the creation of Adèle and influenced the way he imagined her characterization, despite his determination to create a female leading character: '[f]rom a female point of view, the *bande dessinée* was practically a desert. There had been Bécassine and then Barbarella and almost nothing in between. I decided that I was going to create a sort of female Brindavoine' (Finet and Tardi 2010: 8).¹⁷ He later notes that much of Adèle's character as it develops over the series is based on his own personality, as he utters the Flaubert-inspired 'Adèle Blanc-Sec, c'est moi' (2010: 16). In addition to the sociopolitical context of Adèle's creation, then, the lack of preceding *bande dessinée* heroines and consequent male inspiration behind the figure may partly also inform her lack of 'female' gender performativity.

It appears after examining several aspects of Adèle's representation by Tardi – her uncertain position as principal character, her possible place as the series's narrator in addition to her overlapping identities as character and writer, and, most prominently, the ambiguity of her gendered representation in terms of personality, behaviour and treatment by other characters – that Adèle remains an uncategorizable and indefinable figure throughout her series of 'extraordinary adventures'. In Sécheret and Schlesser's article 'Tardi, un carnaval des monstres', the writers discuss the fantastical and 'monstrous' focus of Tardi's œuvre, particularly within the pages of the *Adèle Blanc-Sec* series, first taking care to define the notion of 'monster': 'that which the collective imaginary automatically recognises as such: a creature which is contrary to that which is (rightly or wrongly) perceived as the natural order' (2010: 79–80).¹⁸ Sécheret and Schlesser include in their definition of 'monster' the spirits, mummies, dinosaurs and giant sea creatures that appear in the series, but also the progression of deformed, handicapped and mutilated human characters that increasingly file through the narrative. One possible 'monster' that the authors of this article do not identify as such, however, is Adèle herself. The following, final section of this study of Adèle Blanc-Sec will suggest the depiction of the character to be not just indefinable and ambiguous, but, in fact, monstrous.

Adèle est la bête

Adèle fits in several ways Sécheret and Schlesser's criterion of being 'contrary to that which is considered natural'. The blurred boundaries of her gendered portrayal as described above certainly contradict the perceived 'natural' distinction between masculine and feminine so entrenched in society and in *bande dessinée* history. Even when this is disregarded, however, and she is examined as a female and feminine figure (as, for example, in Laity's estimation), certain aspects of her representation seem to conform to the defined notion of 'monstrosity'.

One such aspect is Adèle's position as single and childless. The brief liaison between Adèle and Ripol in *Adèle et la bête* indicates that she is heterosexual, but thereafter Adèle shows no romantic interest in any of the plethora of male characters who flit in and out of the story, and she clearly lives alone. In 'The Spinster Detective', Mary Jane Jones writes of unmarried female characters:

'[o]ccasionally, some book appears which presents a woman successfully living alone, but only in special circumstances – in extreme youth or old age, during wars, between marriages. That she would choose to do so for a lifetime relegates her to the literature of the grotesque (without, however, elevating her to the status of the maimed hero)' (1975: 106).[19] Simply by virtue of being female and unmarried, then, Adèle lives outside the 'natural order' noted by Sécheret and Schlesser, and thus may be considered grotesque or monstrous. Laura Mulvey notes that within patriarchal narratives, to compensate for woman's 'lack' – which itself is considered 'monstrous' within the phallocentric paradigm – female characters are deemed 'guilty', and then 'saved' (usually in the form of marriage) or 'punished' (often in the form of death) (1989: 21). Adèle's 'guilt' is never explicitly evoked in Tardi's narrative; however, in place of a marriage, or a less formalized relationship that would see her symbolically subject to a male figure, Adèle is continually punished throughout the series. She is knocked unconscious on multiple occasions, kidnapped and wounded several times, and, most notably, fatally stabbed by another woman wielding a phallic weapon. The monstrousness of her single, independent status appears to push the narrative to confront Adèle's femaleness in violent ways.

Adèle, unlike Bécassine (an ersatz adoptive mother) and Barbarella, also remains childless throughout the series. Tardi has stated that the choice not to make Adèle a mother was made for practical narrative reasons in order to maintain her freedom, wryly noting that '[i]t would be hard to imagine Sherlock homes going to pick up the kids from school' (Finet and Tardi 2010: 14).[20] However, as an adult female figure without a child, Adèle is automatically placed on the outskirts of 'normal' patriarchal society. Bernadette Jacobs notes that to varying extents over time, the childless woman has cross-culturally been regarded as 'unnatural' and even as a figure to be feared (2007: 68). Adèle's childlessness, despite Tardi's narrative justification, subtly adds to the depiction of his eponymous character as 'contrary to the natural order' further rendering her 'monstrous'.

In keeping with Tardi's depiction of 'other' monsters throughout the series such as the pterodactyl or *pithécanthrope*, Adèle too is an exceptional and isolated figure. As Groensteen notes, following the first album and the loss of Ripol, Adèle appears to have no social contact with male figures beyond her interactions with those involved in the current mystery (1980: 34). She also appears to have no amicable connections with any other female characters and develops hostile relations with all women figures who enter the narrative, even her latterly appearing long-lost sister, Mireille Pain-Sec.[21] The only being towards whom Adèle shows any warmth is the Egyptian mummy who stands motionless in a glass case in her apartment until his re-awakening in *Momies en folie*. Adèle is sporadically shown talking to the mummy over the first four albums, expressing her feelings to the static figure. When the pair are briefly reunited after his re-animation at the end of *Le Labyrinthe infernal* (the mummy tells her he has returned to Paris for a conference), she confesses that she misses his company. With the exception of this supernatural sounding board, however, Adèle appears friendless and alone.

Also, simply by virtue of being a female figure, Adèle is exceptional and isolated over the course of the extended narrative. The large cast of characters assembled by Tardi is overwhelmingly male and often these male characters appear and disappear in groups. The introduction of a female character is rare in comparison, and minor women figures are never shown together. The gender disproportion amongst these secondary characters is visible throughout the series, but particularly in certain albums such as *Le Savant fou*, a standard 48-page story in which only three panels feature a female character other than Adèle. The few women who do appear as part of the narrative may all in addition be described in certain ways as 'monstrous' – they are exceptional and isolated like Adèle, but also murderous and hysterical. Indeed, Clara Bernhardt, an actress-turned-nemesis of Adèle who appears throughout the first half of the series, becomes an almost literal monster when she assumes the identity and dons the disguise of the demon Pazuzu in *Le Démon de la Tour Eiffel*.[22] She is later horribly disfigured in a fire and '[t]urned half-crazy by the loss of her beauty'[23] (Tardi 2007d: 42), dresses in bandages, and identifies with the figure of a mummy. It is Bernhardt who, disfigured and insane, kills Adèle at the end of the fourth album.

Adèle, then, in several ways seems to fit Sécheret and Schlesser's definition of 'monster' and appears, like Tardi's other monstrous creatures, to be isolated and exceptional. It is notable that much of what relates Adèle's depiction to the monstrous depends on the fact that she is, at least in body, female. The equation of the female body with notions of monstrosity is well-established in theoretical considerations of phallocentrism, with Rosi Braidotti noting that '[w]oman, as sign of difference, is monstrous. If we define the monster as a bodily entity that is anomalous and deviant vis-à-vis the norm, then we can argue that the female body shares with the monster the privilege of bringing out a unique blend of fascination and horror' (quoted in Ussher 2006: 1). Jane M. Ussher discusses this notion in *Managing the Monstrous Feminine: Regulating the Reproductive Body* and suggests that the incidence of the female nude in artistic representations is an attempt to contain the bodily monstrosity of the female – an equivalent to the perceived necessity of neutralizing the 'problematic' female lack, as discussed in the Introduction to this book – by idealizing and objectifying it (2006: 2).[24] It is possible to consider the *Adèle Blanc-Sec* series in light of Ussher's theory, as Adèle, not in keeping with Tardi's chaste style elsewhere in his œuvre, appears nude in five out of nine albums.[25]

This display of Adèle's body begins soon after the series does, with two separate instances appearing in *Adèle et la bête*. The first occurs five pages after the character's brief introductory sequence in the train alongside Zborowsky (2007a: 21). The latter, who believes Adèle to be Edith Rabatjoie, falls asleep after a night of pterodactyl-scouting and dreams that he is in a prehistoric land populated by fearsome dinosaurs. The first image of Zborowsky's subconscious vision shows him dressed in animal pelts standing before a row of cactus-like upright stalks (Figure 6). In the following panel, he suddenly sees the silhouette of a naked woman, standing in front of the sun and posing provocatively with her arms behind her head. He identifies her as 'Edith' and calls out to her, his positioning in front of the phallic desert plants symbolizing his desire. Adèle says nothing, but turns to the side, her profile pose emphasizing her curved silhouette against the sun. Suddenly, a roar interrupts Zborowsky's contemplation of Adèle and he must flee a herd of dinosaurs that chase him off a cliff and into a lake below. Emerging from the water, Zborowsky again calls out to the shadow of Adèle above him, now surrounded by dinosaurs (2007a: 22). Again she does not respond but after the next panel, in which a giant sea monster emerges from the lake to swallow Zborowsky, she is finally shown in the light where she stands naked, but carefully positioned to avoid entirely revealing her body, laughing amongst a herd of pterodactyls that appear to croak their amused agreement (Figure 7). Here, in only the second sequence featuring Adèle in the series, she appears explicitly linked to monstrous creatures, their shared laughter indicating their complicity. Her precisely posed nudity, however – showing off the curves of her breasts and hips, but concealing her nipples and lower intimate body parts – serves to neutralize the monstrosity of her representation in this scene. She appears, as Ussher describes the female nude in art, as an idealized naked figure – 'all abhorrent reminders of her fecund corporeality removed – secretions, pubic hair, genitals, and disfiguring veins or blemishes all left out of the frame' (2006: 2) – a displayed beauty amongst winged beasts.

Later in *Adèle et la bête*, after she returns from her dangerous tumble into the crocodile enclosure, Adèle, in a scene that has become iconic of the series as a whole, is shown taking a bath.[26] Her hair, always knotted in a chignon atop her head, is shown loose around her shoulders. The water sits just in line with Adèle's breasts, again obscuring any clear view of the character's 'fecund corporeality', but nonetheless drawing the reader's eye to her chest. Here the monstrosity of Adèle's femaleness is not only neutralized by this idealized, carefully arranged nude image, it is also cleansed and purified by the symbolic act of bathing, a trope common to depictions of women in other visual media, particularly painting.[27]

The view of Adèle in, or preparing to take, a bath is repeated in the *bande dessinée* series, re-appearing in *Le Noyé à deux têtes* (the image of Adèle holding a towel against her naked body after emerging from the bath actually appears on the cover of this album), and again in *Le Labyrinthe infernal*.[28] As Lynda Nead states of the female nude, the 'magical regulation' of the feared female body performed by showing woman as an idealized nude works only fleetingly, and must be repeated to effectively 'contain' the subconscious horror inspired by female bodily difference (Ussher 2006: 2). Tardi repeats the vision of Adèle naked, particularly bathing, throughout the *Adèle Blanc-Sec* series in an attempt, perhaps, to 'contain' her monstrosity.

A Final Word on Adèle Blanc-Sec

As indicated above, Tardi created the character of Adèle Blanc-Sec in a conscious attempt to extend the presence of female figures in the *bande dessinée* beyond that of Bécassine and Barbarella. The artist's chosen alternative to the sexual extremes represented by these polarized women characters – one asexualized to the point of dehumanization and the other over-sexualized to the point of symbolic invisibility – manifests itself in the complex and conflicted figure of Adèle Blanc-Sec. Adèle is treated as a woman at times by aspects of the narrative: she is rescued, punished and occasionally shown to be dangerously seductive. However, she herself does not always perform 'woman'. Her difference to the stereotypical depiction of women characters in traditional narratives (she is unmarried, independent and childless) only serves to add further to the 'monstrosity' with which the female form is already symbolically viewed, and she must be displayed nude on several occasions to neutralize the unease subtly provoked by her problematic female monstrousness. *Les Aventures extraordinaires d'Adèle Blanc-Sec* is a serial mystery narrative in which a fiend, beast or evil foe must be uncovered and defeated in each instalment. It is perhaps also an ongoing attempt to decipher the key to representing a female character in the *bande dessinée* that is neither a- nor over-sexualized. The endless uncertainty of Adèle's depiction in addition to the recurring cycle of monstrous 'purification' seen across Tardi's *Adèle Blanc-Sec* series attests to the difficulty of this task, even for a master of the Ninth Art.

SECTION 2

SECONDARY WOMEN CHARACTERS

Preface: A Brief Consideration of the Minor

In the preface to her 2002 work *All About Thelma and Eve: Sidekicks and Third Wheels*, Judith Roof notes a significant theoretical concern regarding her examination of secondary female comic characters in film: '[w]riting about the minor and the middle threatens to deform it by making it the centre of focus' (2002: x). Certainly, an academic concentration on those female figures not positioned at the centre of the dominant narrative of a *bande dessinée*, carries the same potential pitfall. However, as the rest of Roof's text continually attests, a careful analysis of such marginalized figures may unveil previously invisible facets of a text seemingly rigidly adherent to the structuring ideologies of phallocentric narrative.

A very simple point, but one worth making nonetheless, is this: in the *bande dessinée*, as in any medium, the reader looks where (s)he is told. The narrative is tailored to guide the reader from a structured beginning to middle to end, whilst the layout, the colouring and the artistic style collude to bolster the viewer's focus on the central characters of the tale. Secondary or minor figures, where they exist in a story, are present but easily ignored by readers whose eyes follow the trajectory laid out for them by the dominant narrative. Such, more often than not, is the fate of the female character in the BD, who largely occupies a secondary role behind one or more male principal figures. Her narratively unremarkable and structurally minor depiction in many (if not most) strips explains to an extent her general absence from both historical and theoretical texts examining the medium, as previously noted. However, when the gaze is conscientiously repositioned to include, and then focus on, this marginalized female figure, her liminal position between presence and invisibility opens up possibilities and alternatives for textual analysis adding to the comprehension of the medium as a whole, and its representation of women in particular.

Of course, male characters too find themselves occupying minor roles and marginalized positions in the *bande dessinée*. Nevertheless, narrative, shaped to reflect the dominant phallocentric ideals of its surrounding society, frequently positions male and female characters in different roles according to gender and, thus, minor figures of opposing sexes may be considered separately. Furthermore, whilst male characters do fill a significant percentage of secondary roles within the medium, this marginal positioning within strips is not necessarily a dominant feature of male depiction in the *bande dessinée* as it is with female representation. Considering modern *bande dessinée* publications as a whole, women have been placed in a secondary role, as Pilloy observes, nine times out of ten (1994: 16).

A qualification must be made at this juncture concerning the interchangeability presupposed between the categories of 'secondary' and 'minor' henceforth in this chapter, and the range of character types that may be seen to be part of such categories. Whilst it is true that there may exist within a *bande dessinée* a truly 'secondary' character – that is, one who does not occupy the most prominent role, such as Obélix in *Astérix le Gaulois* (or any perennially present sidekick), but who nonetheless plays a very central role in the narrative – the use of the term 'secondary' throughout the following case studies does not refer to the female figure's immediate following of the main character(s) in any descending hierarchy of personages. It indicates, rather, the notion that these figures are 'secondary' in narrative importance – or perhaps even 'tertiary', as no such distinctions as to the rankings of various non-primary characters within specific *bandes dessinées* will be made here. As the term 'secondary' will be used in this manner, its equivalence to the category of the 'minor' seems apparent and appropriate.

The distinction of what will be referred to henceforth as a 'secondary' female character now clarified, it must further be noted that this category still incorporates many different sub-divisions of minor figures. It may conceivably refer to identity-less 'extras' in background and crowd scenes, 'negligible' characters insignificant to the narrative who appear briefly with little or no dialogue (for example waitresses or minor male characters' girlfriends) as well as recurring, identifiable secondary characters who, whilst not protagonists of the narrative, are nonetheless significant in some way to the story. Although analysis of the first two groups of minor figures may still yield interesting findings (particularly for a feminist study, as a significant proportion of *bandes dessinées* only present female characters in these inconsequential roles), in order to avoid the theoretical dilemma posed by Roof of distorting aspects of the minor beyond a useful or realistic limit, in the following case studies only those secondary characters with some significance in the chosen narratives will be considered.

Although the categorical parameters of the following section have now been clarified, the analysis itself remains far from straightforward. Whilst a tangible element of their respective texts, these secondary figures nevertheless occupy the analytically ambiguous 'middle'. Out of the reader's eye-line as (s)he obligingly follows the progression of the dominant storyline but still making up part of the narrative, these characters exist in a complex, dual relationship with the text – one which is at once vital to consider and, also, rather unimportant. In elucidating various ways to theorize her chosen cinematic 'sidekicks and third wheels', Roof cites Deleuze and Guattari's conception of the minor as self-contradictory: '[o]n the one hand, [the minor] rambles, multiplies, evades, and wanders, and on the other, like the psychoanalytical symptom, it is the site where unconscious meaning opens up and becomes visible' (2002: 5). The relativity of the minor further adds to its complexity – it can only be theorized alongside a concurrent consideration of the 'major'. This means, for the purposes of this study, that female secondary characters may be considered separately, but their relationship to male primary characters must also be examined. However, it is within these presented difficulties that lies the motivation for studying the minor. Faced, as the theorist of the *bande dessinée* often is, with the ideological construction of traditional patriarchal narratives which largely steer the reader's attention towards the protagonists' journeys from beginning, middle, to end, an investigation of the minor may prove a hidden access point to aspects of the text submerged beneath the dominant diegesis.

Prior to beginning the following close analyses of female secondary characters in the *bande dessinée*, however, it is, as in the last chapter, necessary to present a historical account of the progression of the minor woman figure in the medium as a whole. This chronology is important in reclaiming the forgotten history of these previously overlooked figures within the *bande dessinée* and for charting how evolving styles, trends and changing political and legal contexts influenced their depictions, in addition to providing the reader of this study with adequate historical contextualization for the following case-study chapters. It is to this chronology that attention will now be turned.

5

Beyond Bonemine: An Introductory History of Female Secondary Characters in the Francophone *Bande Dessinée*

In the previous historical chapter outlining the progression of female principal characters, the difficulty of compiling a historical chronology specific to female representation in the *bande dessinée* (BD) was noted. The complexity of this challenge is further increased, however, when a history of the female secondary character in the medium is attempted. Cover-to-cover consultation of expansive historical tomes such as Gaumer and Moliterni's *Dictionnaire mondial de la bande dessinée* leave one with little information on the existence of female secondary characters in even the most famous of strips; a considerable problem, as the overwhelming majority of female BD characters figure in secondary roles.

In *Les Compagnes des héros de B.D: des femmes et des bulles*, Annie Pilloy divides her analysis of female secondary representation in Lombard and Dupuis-published children's strips from 1948 to 1990 by genre and concludes her work with several noteworthy general findings. She explains that most secondary heroines are relatively young, whether adolescents or young women, with little girls appearing rarely and older women even less. These youthful female characters are mostly pretty and, although sometimes seductive are rarely overtly so, due no doubt to the age of the intended audience. Interestingly, Pilloy further states that although the physique of the female character is widely and consistently stereotyped, there is one parameter that varies according to the character's temperament or role: that of hair colour. Those female figures with blonde hair (a category that encompasses most of the female BD characters Pilloy's research encounters) seem sweet and fragile, whilst their brunette counterparts often show determination and capability. Red-headed women are strong, often stubborn, characters, whilst jet-black hair symbolizes 'treachery, deceit' (1994: 258).[1]

Moving away from physical attributes, Pilloy notes of the female characters in these children's strips that their range of occupations is limited, whilst the association of women with motherhood and domesticity is present in *every* series she considers. Within the strips it goes without saying that the female characters know how to cook and do housework, and when it comes to dealing with the 'everyday details' within the narrative, it is the women who attend to such things, whatever their profession or social position (1994: 259). Concerning personality, Pilloy claims that no matter their importance to the overall narrative, female characters in the children's strips published by Lombard and Dupuis all have more or less the same communal traits: 'sensitivity, fragility, vanity, intuition and [...] the art of attracting trouble' (1994: 259).[2] Significantly, she closes her study with the observation that sexism and gender stereotypes are more present in the *bande dessinée* than she had realized before beginning her work but that, despite her choice to structure her research by genre, variations in female representation are more likely to be due to artistic choice than required by the codes associated with specific genres (1994: 260–61).

Pilloy's study takes a first important step in analysing the minor female character in the *bande dessinée*. However, in addition to narrowing her field by choice of publisher, her work, as indicated, focuses largely on children's strips and series from the late twentieth century, which leaves unexamined both the early representation of female secondary characters in pre-war publications (largely destined for children, in keeping with the medium's juvenile status at this time), and their depiction amongst the pages of adult-directed strips from the 1950s and 1960s onwards. In what follows, an overview of the female secondary character throughout the twentieth century will be presented in order to chart for the first time a more wide-ranging chronological progression of this 'minor' figure. Unlike the place of the primary female figure in the *bande dessinée*, however, the category of 'secondary character' covers the extensive majority of women figures in the *bande dessinée*. Thus, owing to the size of the task at hand and to the dearth of pre-existing research on this topic, the proceeding historical consideration must, particularly out of the three history chapters of this book, be intended as an abridged chronology only.

As previously indicated, throughout the first years of the twentieth century the *bande dessinée* tentatively developed its talents within the pages of *illustrés* aimed at gender-specific juvenile readerships. Although a female character, Bécassine, proved to be a prominent recurring lead figure of the nascent medium (the female secondary characters of this strip are examined in Chapter 2), it quickly became the case across the range of *illustrés* as a whole that more strips were produced featuring male characters than female – a trend contributing early on to the perceived idea that the *bande dessinée* is 'for boys' (see pp. 4-5 of this book) – one which would continue throughout the century (as previously stated, Pilloy notes in her study that some 90% of the strips she consulted were led by male protagonists). At this developmental stage, female figures were not absent from strips, but appeared much less regularly and often only as minor narrative players, usually in the role of wives or mothers. In three of the most notable strips of the early twentieth century, for example – Louis Forton's *Les Pieds Nickelés* (introduced in *L'Epatant* in 1908), Alain Saint-Ogan's *Zig et Puce* (*Le Dimanche illustré*, 1925) and Hergé's *Tintin* (*Le Petit Vingtième*, 1929) women are markedly sidelined, supporting the contention made in the primary characters history that the pre-war *bande dessinée* showed itself reluctant to depict women. Female figures did appear infrequently in *Les Pieds Nickelés* – Ribouldingue and Filochard marry in episodes from, respectively, 1909 and 1952; however, such female figures appear very sporadically and do not become regular characters in the series. Correspondingly, Zig and Puce do make the acquaintance of the charming American heiress Dolly in 1927 when their trans-Atlantic ships collide, and they subsequently strike up a firm friendship with her. Dolly, who later re-appears as 'Sheila' in a 1966 strip drawn after the series' revival by artist Greg, is rather exceptional within the strip, however, which remains very male-led throughout its 45-year publication span. More notably, of the 350 secondary characters whom Tintin encounters throughout this most popular of *bande dessinée* series (the official *Tintin* website cited in 2017 album sales of over 230 million worldwide [Anon. 2017]), only eight figures are identifiable as female (Parris 2009). In contrast to Pilloy's findings taken from more recent children's strips, none of these women are young or noticeably attractive. Bianca Castafiore is the only memorable female character to appear throughout the series, variously displaying the gambit of negative traits archaically associated with women, such as hysteria, vanity and narcissism alongside dramatic physical and emotional fragility. Aside from this operatic diva, the only other female character re-appearing throughout Tintin's adventures is General Alcazar's wife Peggy, this figure hardly improving the young journalist's experience of women with her sniping, bullying and hard-drinking persona (Parris 2009) – her hair-colour conforming to Pilloy's theory of the *bande dessinée*'s classically 'strong-willed' redhead.

However, although, as noted thus far, the developing Franco-Belgian tradition of the *bande dessinée* tended towards a very notable lack of female presence in the majority of its most popular strips, the importation of action-adventure strips from the United States was to illustrate an altogether different attitude to the appearance of women. The noble-born but jungle-living Tarzan, first portrayed in a novel by Edgar Rice Burroughs in 1912, was adapted some seventeen years later into comic strip format, drawn by Harold Foster (who would later cede artistic control of the series to a succession of different artists), the translation appearing in French-language publications soon after. Tarzan, the tall, well-built opposite of the slight, diminutive Tintin and his noted forebears, was accompanied in his adventures, of course, by the beautiful Jane Porter. Jane appeared in varying states of undress throughout the publication of the series (as did various other scantily-clad women, appearing and disappearing as the narrative required) and occupied the classic role of damsel in distress repeatedly over the course of Tarzan's exploits.

While *Tarzan* added images of near-naked jungle-inhabiting females to the very proper, male-centric landscape inhabited by the likes of *Zig et Puce* and *Tintin*, *Flash Gordon* (sometimes known as *Guy l'Éclair* on the French-language market), scripted by Alex Raymond and drawn by Edwin Balmer, travelled with this trend into outer-space.[3] Appearing in France from 1936 in various publications including *Robinson*, *Bravo!* and Winkler's era-defining *Journal de Mickey* (Gaumer and Moliterni 1994: 247), *Flash Gordon*'s cast of supporting characters boasted many well-proportioned beauties with the striking Dale Arden the most frequently recurring female figure. Dale is present in the story from the first strip, although in this episode she has neither dialogue nor back-story, her role as another damsel in distress apparently requiring neither. Dale's femininely fragile example is not followed by all the women encountered by Flash on his travels, however. Several powerful female figures flit in and out of the story, usually immediately and obsessively enamoured with the handsome Flash whilst dangerously jealous of Dale. Queen Azura, leader of the Magic Men, is so taken with the strip's hero that she uses drugs to wipe his memory and convince him that he is her consort; underwater ruler Queen Undina transforms Flash into a water-breather in an attempt to keep him submerged with her forever; whilst Sonja, sister of rebel leader Count Bulok, conspires to help Emperor Ming regain his throne when she is rejected by Flash in favour of Dale. With such clearly contrasting roles for its female characters, this popular imported strip presented to the French-language audience an early example of the classic binary good girl/bad girl split that would remain very much part of female representation in American comics – notably DC and Marvel-published strips – into the late twentieth century and arguably beyond.

Although American series such as *Tarzan* and *Flash Gordon* were very popular on the Franco-Belgian market in the 1930s, this largely due to the success of *Le Journal de Mickey*, production of new home-grown strips continued alongside this foreign invasion. Whilst many of the most popular strips created across the Atlantic allowed a certain visual focus on the female figure, the most celebrated francophone *bandes dessinées* of the 1930s and 1940s still hugely concentrated on male characters, with female figures occupying far smaller or non-existent roles. It was not unusual for strips to be created and run for years with an all-male cast, with a tentative first female character added as an afterthought much later. The star strip of *Spirou* in its early years of publication, *Spirou et Fantasio*, for example, first created in 1938 by Rob Vel and his wife Davine (Gaumer and Moliterni 1994: 590), did not see its first female character until 1955. Drawn by André Franquin in an episode entitled *La Corne de rhinocéros*,

Seccotine, when she finally appeared, was a strong, intelligent and competent woman, although this combination was unusual for female secondary characters in the 1950s adventure BD (Screech 2005: 56). Several other best-selling strips, such as *Les Schtroumpfs* (known in English as *The Smurfs*) and *Astérix*, later followed the example set by *Spirou et Fantasio*, only adding female characters after the successful establishment of the series.

Post-war, one of the first emerging and highly successful strips was to be Edgar Pierre Jacobs's *Blake et Mortimer*, which debuted in the first issue of the new *Tintin* journal in 1946. Although Jacobs had not shied away from drawing women characters in the past, three years after *Blake et Mortimer* debuted, the 1949 *Loi du 16 juillet 1949 sur les publications destinées à la jeunesse* would be passed, reducing the already minimal appearance of secondary women in the *bande dessinée* (see Chapter 1 for further discussion of the impact of this law). The legal prohibition of certain negative influences (banditry, lying, theft, laziness, cowardice, hatred, debauchery) was, as previously noted, easily applicable to American adventure strips, with the subsidiary consequence for the category of secondary female figures that the Jane Porters and Dale Ardens of US creation were suddenly unwelcome on the francophone market.[4] The legal restriction against suggestive or 'debauched' content also contained in the 1949 law had a further effect on the representation of minor women characters in francophone strips, however, as the looming fear of censorship encouraged certain creators to avoid depicting women figures altogether (see pp. 22–23 of this book). That some artists and publishers found it easier to remove any female representation from their strips rather than endeavour to create women characters without a sexual presence indicative of 'debauchery' seems highly indicative of the rather unremarkable and disposable place of the secondary female in the medium up to this point and quite in keeping with the notion, explained in the Introduction to this book, that representing women is inherently 'problematic'. However, it is undeniable that the pre- and post-publication scrutiny of women characters following the introduction of the 1949 law was intense, as experienced by Edgar Pierre Jacobs and a seemingly innocent panel for the *Blake et Mortimer* tale *La Marque Jaune*. As noted by Pilloy, this episode of the classic series caused a minor scandal following its 1953 serialization in *Tintin* magazine due to Jacobs' drawing of Dr Septimus carrying a magazine sporting a ballerina on the cover. The dancer merely appeared sitting on a box of costumes, whilst the drawing of the magazine measured just 2.5 cm by 1.5 cm, but still the reviews of the strip all exclaimed the same thing: 'Jacobs is an old lech' (1994: 12).[5] The drawing was almost immediately removed from the strip by *Tintin*'s publisher and subsequently did not appear in *La Marque Jaune*'s 1956 album release. Perhaps unsurprisingly following such an occurrence, Jacobs would henceforth almost entirely remove any notable female presence from the lives of his stars Blake and

Mortimer, the pair only having real contact with the opposite sex after Benoît and Van Hamme's revival of their adventures in the much more liberal 1990s.

One means of depicting female figures seemingly deemed appropriate in this time of heightened censorship was through the portrayal of historical personages. Lonesome cowboy *Lucky Luke*, whose strip is now considered one of the 'essential classics of the 9th art' (Gaumer and Moliterni 1994: 404),[6] had very little contact with women, but did make the acquaintance of Calamity Jane. Similarly, Jacques Martin's strikingly clear-line strip *Alix*, featuring the fearless Gaul-turned-Roman of the same name, was to feature Cleopatra long before Goscinny and Uderzo's band of warriors would meet her. Although during the early episodes of the *Alix* series women figures were few and far between – the first story, *Alix l'intrépide*, features a female character in only six panels of its 64 pages, and the face of this woman is almost entirely masked throughout her appearance – it should be noted that, over time, female figures began to be included in this strip as the culture of censorship in the BD industry relaxed to a certain extent. These characters never lasted, however, as despite apparently enjoying their attentions, the brave Alix's unwavering pursuit of social justice continually moved the story from place to place. The ephemeral nature of female presence in *Alix* coincides with Miller's observation that this *bande dessinée* displays a homosexual subtext, although one that may have been invisible to its original readers (2007: 35).

Jacques Martin's strip was not alone in its evolving attitude to female characters as the initial reactions to the 1949 law began to soften. André Franquin's *Gaston Lagaffe*, for example, which first appeared in *Spirou* in 1957, began, like many other strips, as an overwhelmingly male affair. Progressively, however, secondary female characters began to filter into the narrative. M'oiselle Jeanne, who would become the most prominent female figure of the strip, appeared at first as small in stature and rather ugly; however, she was to become more attractive, well-dressed and well-groomed as the story moved forward, an example of the lessening of artists' self-censorship of female characters.

However, whilst some artists took advantage of the slight loosening of the censor's grip to portray more female secondary characters in their strips, *bandes dessinées* still emerged at this time with few or no women characters amongst their cast, a reminder of the important point that the prohibitive 1949 law had merely exacerbated the dearth of female figures in a medium that was already reluctant to represent them. One example of this was Peyo's *Les Schtroumpfs*, which made its debut in a 1958 edition of *Spirou*. Originally an all-male community of little blue men, the *Schtroumpfs* first encounter with the opposite sex came with the introduction of La Schtroumpfette in the 1966 strip of the same name. Despite this apparent nod by Peyo towards the gender-diversification of his little troop, it is established from the beginning that this long-haired, eyelash-batting addition is not really a Schtroumpf. She has been magically created by the evil Gargamel in a plot to cause the heroes' downfall by the simple introduction of a woman into their midst. Her title, Schtroumpfette, continues the assertion of her difference long after the conclusion of this introductory episode and her acceptance into the village. She is not the 'Schtroumpf femme',[7] thus following the pattern shown in names of other inhabitants of Peyo's hamlet such as 'Grand Schtroumpf', 'Schtroumpf paresseux', and 'Schtroumpf bricoleur',[8] but the Schtroumpf-*ette*, the simple addition of this diminutive suffix suggesting her presence as an inferior or insignificant incarnation of a 'real', or male, Schtroumpf. Even following her eventual settlement in the Schtroumpf village, the Schtroumpfette does not seem to gain a definitive role aside from her place as a desirable female.

A year following the introduction of Peyo's little band of blue men, a strip appeared in journal *Pilote* whose popularity would eclipse even the notable success of *Les Schtroumpfs*: Goscinny and Uderzo's *Astérix*. A fuller account of the presence of women in this strip will be given in Chapter 6. It is, however, interesting to note here that this most popular and iconic of *bandes dessinées* – the collection of *Astérix* albums is to date the most successful francophone book series of all time, with more than 300 million copies sold worldwide (Beaty 2007: 171) and counting – constitutes yet another example of a BD that began by featuring only male characters, with female figures added to the story only after some time. Certainly more numerous, but fairly similar in status to the female presence in Peyo's troop, the women of *Astérix* remain, for the most part, secondary and troublesome. The high-profile examples of *Astérix* and *Les Schtroumpfs* indicate that the gradual reintroduction of the secondary female following the lessening of certain artists' post-1949 self-censorship did not necessarily result in a positive or particularly remarkable progression of female representation in the medium.

Whilst by no means revolutionary in its portrayal of female characters, Goscinny and Uderzo's strip was, however, to become a catalyst for perhaps the most major upheaval in the history of the Franco-Belgian *bande dessinée*. Despite appearing in a journal originally created for younger readers, *Pilote*, *Astérix*'s combination of juvenile slapstick humour and much more sophisticated satire made the strip a major success in both the children's and adults' markets. Whilst the *bande dessinée* had, up until this point, been considered predominantly as a medium for children, the exceptional 'crossover appeal' of *Astérix* was to become a first step towards the re-direction of the BD to an adult audience (Sabin 1993: 189). With *Pilote* initially at the forefront, gradually adding increasingly sophisticated *bandes dessinées*, soon strips were created exclusively for an over-16s market (1993: 189) and the boundaries of the 1949 law began to be more seriously tested.[9] A notable change in the place of the female secondary character, most significantly resulting in her sexualization, started to manifest itself within the Franco-Belgian medium.

A particularly successful strip created by Pierre Christin and Jean-Claude Mézières that debuted in *Pilote* in this era was *Valérian* (first serialized in 1967; also variously known as *Valérian: Agent Spatio-Temporel* and *Valérian et Laureline*). Considered a gem of the francophone medium (Gaumer and Moliterni 1994: 646), Christin and Mézières' creation followed the exploits of the spatio-temporal agent Valérian and his companion Laureline, whom he meets in the inaugural story *Les Mauvais Rêves* during a voyage to the Middle Ages. Initially created uniquely for this first episode, the character of Laureline proved popular with readers and so was incorporated as a permanent fixture of the series (Pomerleau 1989: 63). Although in early strips Laureline remained a typical feminine sidekick and onlooker to Valérian's heroics, the sexy medieval red-head became more active as the series progressed. Far from being a simple foil or damsel in distress in this sci-fi odyssey, with her intelligence and numerous charms Laureline overcame her secondary status to become the star of more than one time-travelling exploit. Whilst the depiction of Laureline was undeniably positive and vastly different to the vapid, troublesome women of previous strips, she did not escape female stereotyping in all respects, with her seductiveness often used to manipulate men to her advantage during missions. Not afraid of skimpy clothing, in addition to appearing nude in some episodes, Laureline's image was even to grace the pages of French *Playboy* in a spread that was re-printed for the 1995 publication *Extras de Mézières*. The sexualization of female primary characters begun in the 1960s most notably with the creation of *Barbarella* also, then, clearly extended to the domain of secondary women figures – even those such as Laureline whose characterization appeared, in many other respects, as unclichéd and progressive.

A similar evaluation to that of Laureline can also be made for some of the secondary female figures of another *bande dessinée* 'classic': Hugo Pratt's *Corto Maltese* series (first serialized in Italy in the same year as *Valérian*'s introduction, 1967, and then in *France-Soir* between 1973 and 1974). Groensteen (2013) deems Pratt 'one of the first *bande dessinée* authors whose work allowed a prominent place for women',[10] an assertion somewhat mitigated by certain numerical observations: the companion tome to the Hugo Pratt series, *Corto Maltese: Memoires*, for example, includes just 23 female figures amongst its 120 character portraits laid out at the start of the book. Furthermore, despite the various roles attributed to the female figures who cross paths with Corto Maltese in the strip series (sorcerer, philosopher, spy), a common notable feature across the women remains their aesthetic appeal, an observation interestingly borne out by another companion book, *Les Femmes de Corto Maltese*, created by Hugo Pratt and Michel Pierre. This book features 'letters from' and sketches and watercolours of 22 female Corto Maltese characters, with a clear focus on the physical features of the women, the image-heavy content ranging from full-page, full-length sketches, to large facial close-ups, and to topless and nude sketches of several characters. The similarity in style between fellow Italian artist, Crepax – more commonly-known for his angular, sexualized images of female figures than Maltese's inventor – and Hugo Pratt is clear here.[11]

Although mapping the concurrent development of the drawn strip outside of the Franco-Belgian market is not imperative to the understanding of the francophone *bande dessinée*'s evolution, towards the end of the 1960s a movement gaining popularity across the Atlantic would have a sizeable impact on the nascent adult-oriented BD, and thus, it is important to discuss briefly here. The American underground comics scene that emerged in the late 1960s was not entirely unprecedented in the United States. Between the 1920s and the late 1940s, so-called 'Eight-Pagers' – pornographic comic books often featuring well-known public figures – enjoyed a certain amount of alternative success (Filippini 2006: 14). However, towards the end of the 1960s, in response to the staid content of mainstream comics and the restrictive censorship imposed by the Comics Code (a 1949-law-style code of ethics for the American industry widely self-imposed by creators and publishers in order to avoid government regulation), an underground drawn strip movement developed with a more diverse subject-matter related to the politically, sexually and narcotically active counter-culture.[12] Led by such artists as Robert Crumb and Gilbert Shelton, American underground comics made a big impression on the corresponding European alternative movement and were imported and translated on a regular basis from 1968 (Sabin 1993: 191). Although the arrival of such strips from the United States undeniably stoked the fires of an adult re-direction that was already gaining speed in France and Belgium and contributed to the evolution of female depiction that moved alongside this evolution, the representation of women in these influential American underground strips certainly did not reflect a positive development in the history of female depiction in the wider drawn strip medium. Women characters were noticeably present in the works of Crumb, Shelton and their contemporaries, mostly as secondary, rather than primary, figures, and indeed often no longer occupied the stereotypical roles of mothers, wives or the typical damsel in distress, but instead often became the object of misogynistic, fetishistic and frequently violent strips. Trina Robbins, the foremost comics 'herstorian' of the American industry, goes so far as to state of this era that: '[e]ntrails, usually female, were scattered over the landscape in a phenomenon of violence to women that I believe has never been equalled in any other medium' (quoted in Lemke-Santangelo 2009: 26).

The influence of the American underground generally and its misogynistic vogue to a lesser, but nonetheless apparent, extent manifested itself in the Franco-Belgian industry not only in the strips of specific artists, such as Georges

Wolinski (discussed in the previous historical chapter as the artist responsible for *Paulette*), but also in the creation of new journal publications. *L'Écho des Savanes* was founded in 1972 as a breakaway from the still fairly family-friendly *Pilote*. Bearing the words '[a]dults only' on the cover,[13] its production was largely influenced by the US underground movement (Sabin 1993: 192) with the early journal 'dominated by explicitly sexual, or generally taboo, humour' (Grove 2010: 144). Women secondary characters were once again mainly relegated to sexual objectification and stereotyped minor roles; in this case for the sake of humour.[14] The influence of the US underground and its explicitly sexual depiction of female figures was further felt in the Franco-Belgian market in 1975 with the launch of another new adult journal, *Fluide Glacial*, which emphasised the 'raunchier aspects' of its American alternative influence (Grove 2010: 146).

Not all of the *bandes dessinées* of the late 1960s and 1970s were influenced by the imported American underground movement in their depiction of women, however. Whilst journals for younger audiences began, to an extent, to embrace more fully the idea of capable female heroines – *Spirou*, as noted, launched *Yoko Tsuno* in 1970 – many adult strips simply carried on the trend of largely ignoring the existence of the female sex. In *Le Garage Hermétique*, for example, Moebius's celebrated sci-fi *bande dessinée* that debuted in *Métal Hurlant* in 1979, only one of the seven principally recurring characters seems to have been female (Major Grubert's elegant wife Dame Malvina). Frank Margerin's *Lucien*, which appeared in *Métal Hurlant* in the same year, also predominantly focused on male characters. Centring upon the exploits of the band *Ricky Banlieue et ses riverains*, women figures were again relegated to secondary roles as female relatives or desired, but usually disinterested, acquaintances. *Le Garage Hermétique* and *Lucien*'s parent publication, *Métal Hurlant* – a journal that first appeared in 1975 and whose popularity rapidly provoked its progression from tri-monthly to monthly issues – certainly did not shy away from depicting female figures in strips, however, as its 1976 censorship due to 'degrading' representations of women attests (Delaborde 2005: 41). This financially restrictive ban was eventually overturned in 1978, and *Métal Hurlant* continued publication until 2006.

As indicated in Chapter 1, the *bande dessinée* industry changed dramatically in the 1980s as the economic climate of the decade saw a deterioration of the journal's popularity and a corresponding rise in the importance of album production and sales. Strips continued to make their debuts in periodicals, however, as shown by the first appearance in journal *Circus* of several popular strips following the major thematic trend of the decade for historically-based *bandes dessinées*. Medieval drama series *Les Chemins de Malefosse*, written by Daniel Bardet and drawn by François Dermaut, and *Les Sept Vies de l'Épervier*, scripted by Patrick Cothias and illustrated by André Juillard, made their inaugural appearances in the same issue of *Circus*, in October of 1982 (Moliterni et al. 2004: 1044). *Les Tours de Bois-Maury*, created by Hermann and set in the eleventh century, followed in May of 1984. All three series depict male-centred heroic adventures in the Middle Ages, with female characters, perhaps unsurprisingly, minor in importance. *Les Chemins de Malefosse* attributed to the female figure the most importance of the three series; however, her role was overwhelmingly sexualized as female nudity, sex scenes and, occasionally, depictions of rape appeared across its episodes. Miller notes that although historical realism in the *bande dessinée* already existed prior to the 1980s – notably associated with *Alix* – in this decade, the genre 'was taken to mean the inclusion of sex and violence, and moral ambiguity reigned' (2007: 36). This is evident to varying extents in each of the three series noted here, with *Les Chemins de Malefosse* constituting the most striking example.

The other principal thematic trend of the 1980s *bande dessinée*, heroic fantasy, appears largely to attribute to women characters the same secondary roles. *Balade au bout du monde*, a dramatic, realist-drawn narrative by Pierre Makyo and Laurent Vicomte, which moved between locations and time periods, limited its depiction of female characters. Although women who did appear in this series were not always displayed erotically or shown in sexual situations, this nonetheless made up a large part of their representation. *Les Compagnons du crépuscule*, by *Les Passagers du vent*'s François Bourgeon, allowed women characters a larger role – one of the three main figures was a young blonde woman named Mariotte.[15] Despite her regular appearance in the narrative, however, Mariotte was repeatedly shown naked and in a sexualized manner. Both *Balade au bout du monde* and *Les Compagnons du crépuscule* contained scenes of women subjected to sexual violence, indicating, alongside the example of *Les Chemins de Malfosse* noted above, this to be something of a corollary to the dominant genres of the 1980s.

Jean Van Hamme and Grzegorz Roskinski's series *Thorgal* first appeared in 1977 in *Tintin* magazine, but would continue throughout the 1980s to become one of the decade's most popular strips. *Thorgal*, an adventure series based on a mix of Norse mythology, science fiction and fantasy, presented female secondary characters with, to an extent, less sexualized and more active roles than other 1980s series discussed thus far, proving the existence of at least some diversity of female representation in the dominant heroic fantasy trend. The first episode, for example, introduced both Thorgal's love-interest, Aaricia – a wide-eyed, blonde-haired figure, visually similar to Forest's Barbarella, who is frequently in need of rescue throughout the tale – and Slive, 'the queen of the island of frozen seas', who is strong and active from the start, and who, in contrast, saves the life of the hero Thorgal as the narrative opens.[16]

Secondary women characters of colour appear only very sporadically up to this point in the history of the *bande dessinée*. However, as Mark McKinney notes in his article 'The Representation of Ethnic Minority Women in Comic Books' (2000: 86), the frequency of strips featuring minority women noticeably increased during the mid-to-late 1980s, due to both the influence of political activism by ethnic minority groups (particularly of Maghrebi origin) and the increased appearance of minority artists in the BD industry. The most popular artist featuring characters of non-European origin in his strips in the 1980s and onwards into the 1990s was Farid Boudjellal. McKinney describes Boudjellal as an artist who has single-handedly produced 'many of the comics in which minority women and girl characters appear' (2000: 87). This is a telling fact concerning the position of ethnic minority female figures in the medium following their increased presence in the 1980s, as Boudjellal's œuvre focuses largely on male characters throughout. In his series *L'Oud* and *Petit Polio*, women characters occupy minor roles and mostly appear as relatives. However, in the comedic *Juifs-Arabes* women figures are drawn to give a humorous female perspective on Jewish and Muslim religions, and on tensions arising between the two faiths.

Boudjellal's production of *bandes dessinées* was prolific over the 1980s and beyond, but he was not the only artist to portray ethnic minority women figures as the century drew to a close. German-Belgian pair Warnauts and Raives began a long-term creative collaboration in 1985 that was to result in the production of numerous strips, such as *Congo 40* (1988), *Equatoriales* (1992) and *Lettres d'Outremer* (1996), set in exotic locations and featuring exoticized female secondary figures (see case study in Chapter 8). The ethnic-minority women of Warnauts and Raives's work are given more visual attention than the female figures appearing in Boudjellal's œuvre; however, their role is overwhelmingly restricted to providing sexual thrills to (normally white) male characters.

While the dominant genres of the 1980s and their largely formulaic depiction of female secondary characters allow for a general summation of minor female representation in the decade, the same cannot be said of the more thematically diverse 1990s and on into the new millennium. Historical realism and heroic fantasy did continue into the 1990s (Miller 2007: 57), leaving this strand of female depiction mostly unchanged. Beyond these genres, the arrival of the phenomenally popular *Titeuf* allowed a classic role related to the secondary woman in the *bande dessinée* – that of a distractive force whose presence invariably causes comedic trouble for the principal character – to come back to the forefront of the medium. *Titeuf*, by Swiss artist Zep, first appeared in France amongst the pages of fanzine *Sauve qui peut* in 1992 before quickly being noticed by publishing house Glénat, who commissioned the strip's first album, *Dieu, le sexe, et les bretelles*, published in 1993 (Gaumer 2010: 852). The series, which by 2004 had already sold over eleven million albums (Schofield 2004), follows the comic antics of the young pre-adolescent Titeuf as he plays pranks with his friends and tries to understand the mysteries of the opposite sex. The role of female characters in this strip – the most prominent being the object of Titeuf's affections, Nadia – may to an extent be considered a modernized version of that inhabited by the secondary figures of *Gaston Lagaffe* or *Astérix* in the 1950s and 1960s. Female figures are often attractive but largely unsexualized; in *Titeuf*'s case due to the age range of the characters (although cheeky references and innuendo appear within the strips as the young comedic protagonist begins to understand the notion of sex). They are also clearly distinguished as 'different' from the male characters of the story and largely act as disruptive agents (much like Peyo's Schtroumpfette), providing (often comic) narrative direction to the strip. This updated but familiar depiction of the secondary female in the 1990s was bolstered by the continued (and bestselling) publication of new *Astérix* albums in this decade and into the new millennium.

Other appearances of female secondary characters in the 1990s and beyond allow little comparison with past examples of the *bande dessinée*. Strips emerging from the independent sector by artists such as Lewis Trondheim or Manu Larcenet certainly relegate women characters to minor positions within the narrative, but these women appear neither to be particularly sexualized nor troublesome, instead often occupying wise, parental roles in relation to prominent male characters whose immaturity often provides a comic focus for the narratives (see analysis of Larcenet's *Le Combat ordinaire* in Chapter 9).

Strips issuing from artists like Trondheim and Larcenet, associated with independent publishers such as L'Association, popularized the genre of the 'everyday' within the *bande dessinée*. This depiction of aspects of everyday life – noted by Miller (2007: 40) to have first tentatively emerged in the *bande dessinée* during the 1980s – rather than elements of adventure or fantasy traditionally associated with the medium, may be interpreted as evidence of the *bande dessinée*'s growing maturity as an art-form. The development of this new 'everyday' strand within the medium also appears to allow a diversification of roles for female secondary figures. Whereas the depiction of the female character as passive and sexualized is to an extent stereotypically pre-determined within a genre such as heroic fantasy, there is arguably less established placement for the female character in the modern 'everyday' as interpreted by differing artists with varying life experiences. A similar claim may be made for other new genres appearing in the diverse 1990s and 2000s in the *bande dessinée*, particularly autobiography and biography, which by their personalized natures are less likely to include formulaic, typed versions of female figures that are comparable between strips (see Chapters 10 and 13 for a discussion of women's autobiographical representations of women).

A tendency in the new millennium towards realist fictional narratives (and sometimes non-fictional narratives, in the form of reportage *bandes dessinées*, for example) shows secondary women as victims of violence without the corresponding erotic overtones often present in aggressive scenes featuring women in the historical realism or heroic fantasy genres. This is seen to differing extremes in *La Vie de ma mère* (2003), an adaptation of Thierry Jonquet's novel by artist Jean-Christophe Chauzy and the writer himself, which charts a young boy's experience of life in a poor neighbourhood of Paris (see Chapter 7), and *Déogratias* (2000) by Stassen, which re-lives the Rwandan genocide and, to an extent, the sexual violence perpetrated during this massacre, through the eyes of the young eponymous male character. Contrastingly, elsewhere in the still expanding and diversifying medium, humorous, fictional series such as the prolific *Donjon* – created by Joann Sfar and Lewis Trondheim in 1998 but drawn by a host of different artists before its conclusion in 2014 – recall the *bande dessinée*'s earlier tendency to ignore women figures almost entirely over the course of a series, with only eight minor figures out of the nearly sixty characters identifiable in this multi-strand narrative proving to be female.

Reflecting on the development of female secondary representation in the *bande dessinée* throughout the twentieth and into the twenty-first centuries as now laid out, it would seem that the evolution of the woman secondary character in the *bande dessinée* since its modern beginnings is less marked than that of the primary character previously discussed. Female minor figures do appear to be progressively more visible in strips, particularly in the latter half of the twentieth century when the culture of censorship ushered in by the 1949 law began to relax. However, the majority of such characters tend to fall into one of two categories throughout the century – they are likely either agents of chaos (due either to their attractiveness or, simply, their being troublesome in various ways) or passive, often sexualized victims in need of rescue by a prominent male character (and in some cases these categories overlap). It is only from the mid-1990s onwards and the development of trends issuing from the independent sector that this general division of character types appears to diversify.

Although, as McKinney notes, the frequency of secondary women characters of colour increases from the 1980s onwards, the overwhelming majority of minor female figures throughout the history of the *bande dessinée* are white. Most are young women, although there is a greater tendency to see middle-aged females as secondary figures than was seen amongst primary characters, due to the presence of female relatives of male central characters – particularly mothers – in certain strips. The majority of secondary women are attractive, although rotund, red-faced battle-axes are present in some comic *bandes dessinées*, such as *Astérix* or *Gaston Lagaffe*. As also indicated in Chapter 1 concerning female primary characters, little clear evidence of the presence of lesbian secondary characters in strips by male creators has been found, with most of the (still very) limited examples of gay women figures found in strips created by women (see Chapter 10).

A rather invisible presence in many strips, almost entirely ignored or only notable due to their eroticization in many others, the female secondary character is a particularly understudied aspect of the *bande dessinée*. However, examining this minor figure does, as shall be seen, provide new insights into the nature of the *bande dessinée* as a visual narrative form and, particularly, into how artists have used this form in specific ways to overcome the 'problem' of representing and viewing women. The following four chapters undertake this task.

6

A Study of Stereotypes: The Secondary Female Characters of *Astérix*

Astérix le Gaulois

Goscinny and Uderzo's *Astérix le Gaulois* began its long and incomparably successful history in *Pilote* against the backdrop of the late 1950s. Both celebrating and mocking the locus of French identity found in the history of their Gaulish ancestors, the riotous adventures of Astérix and company as they resisted the might of the Roman Empire grew quickly in popularity, its appeal to an unusually wide demographic generating incredible commercial success. Historical accounts of the *bande dessinée*'s (BD's) evolution frequently credit the appearance of Goscinny and Uderzo's series as a turning point for the medium (see, for example, Sabin 1993: 187–88), not only as a catalyst for the adult re-direction of the form, as previously noted, but also in the acceptance of the *bande dessinée* by bookshops as a financially viable product. This recognized impact on the medium has prompted considerable theoretical discussion of Goscinny and Uderzo's creation by both Anglophone academics (see Grove 2010; Steel 2005) and francophone scholars (see particularly Rouvière 2006, 2008). Frequent anachronistic allusions to contemporary France and a perceived liberal political slant (Sabin 1996: 219) have facilitated differing hypotheses in such texts concerning the strip's possible allegorical connections to the French Resistance during the Second World War or support for de Gaulle's international political strategy (Steel 2005). Little critical attention, however, has been directed towards its representation of women. In Nicolas Rouvière's 2006 close study of the world of Astérix, for example, only four of its 220 pages contain any real discussion of female figures. In 'Astérix. Un mythe et ses figures', a special issue of *Ethnologie française* (1998), the place of women in the Astérix myth remains undiscussed. Lipani-Vaissade's 'Les femmes dans Astérix: uniquement des emmerdeuses?' (2011) is a relatively rare example of an article that does directly study female representation in the series.[1] This work produces a useful introductory survey of female participation across the narratives, but does not go on to analyse the depiction of recurring women characters in great depth, reserving its closest analysis for the historical figure of Cleopatra (who features in only one *Astérix* story). Despite the general lack of in-depth critical analysis, the stereotyped depiction of female figures in the strips has on occasion garnered non-academic attention, however. In 1983, for example, the London Borough of Brent threatened to remove all *Astérix* albums from its libraries due to its 'insulting' representation of women (Rouvière 2006: 200). In what follows, women's representation in *Astérix* will be analysed closely in order to understand the role they play in this great patriarch of the modern medium and to consider how the Astérix creators use the *bande dessinée* form to mediate the 'problematic' status of these characters as women in a very masculine-centred narrative context.

The Women of Astérix

As noted in the preceding history of secondary women figures, the imaginary world of the unbeatable Gauls is initially populated solely with male characters. The first album, simply named *Astérix le Gaulois* (1961), establishes the familiar setting of the Gaulish village without so much as the shadow of a female figure in the background. However, the lives of the peasant warriors do not remain unisex for long, with female characters slowly starting to filter into the strips. The first named female figure appears in the fifth album – *Le Tour de Gaule d'Astérix* – published in 1965. Eponine, the jolly and culinarily talented wife of Massilian tavern owner César Labeldecadix, does not leave the confines of this single episode to become a recurrent secondary character, but in physique (whilst not in temperament) she is representative of the majority of female figures yet to make their appearance in the series – short, squat, rotund and big-nosed. The following album, *Astérix et Cléopâtre*, features a female figure more prominently, as its title suggests. Cleopatra's historical status, however, renders her an exceptional woman character in the *Astérix* series and hence her depiction may be discounted when analysing the standard representation of women over the course of the narratives.[2]

From this tentative beginning, female characters begin sporadically to emerge throughout the strips. Although not a figure who will go on to appear regularly in the albums, Falbala is the first female inhabitant of the Gaulish village to be named, making her debut in 1967's *Astérix legionnaire*.[3] She is followed quickly in the next album, *Le Bouclier arverne*, by Bonemine, the 'First Lady' of the village and the most frequently depicted of female figures in Astérix's world. Initially, as these characters are incrementally introduced to the strips, their appearances are fleeting and restricted in terms of dialogue. However, whilst the female characters will remain largely inconsequential throughout the entirety of the series, an augmentation in the presence of these Gaulish women is visible to an extent as the albums progress. *La Zizanie* (1970) sees the women take an active role in the creation of dramas that drive the narrative, although they are restricted to scenes at the beginning and end of the story. *Le Devin*, published in 1972, affords a greater role to the female characters – Bonemine in particular – in the main development of the diegesis, and shows the women of the village imbibing the druid's magic potion and going into battle with the Romans for the first time, although they are notably still excluded from the traditional victory feast at the album's conclusion. The honour of partaking in the symbolic re-establishment of the status quo that is the closing victory festivity is finally accorded to the women villagers in 1974's *Le Cadeau de César*. Following this implicit acknowledgement of the female characters' developed place in the grand narrative, however, few further progressions in the representation of women figures are notably apparent in subsequent albums. The *Gauloises* (female Gauls) largely remain a distinct group of minor characters throughout the series, although it has been suggested that in the albums written and drawn exclusively by Uderzo following his partner's death there is more interaction between male and female figures inside the village, the depiction of the two sexes remaining fairly separate throughout the strips scripted by the late Goscinny (Haederli 2008). Considering the long-running series in total, however, one thing is clear throughout: far fewer female than male characters inhabit Astérix's world. The 'encyclopaedia' of the official *Astérix* site online, which claims to provide 'nothing less than an exhaustive dictionary of Astérix characters', names and describes eighteen female characters out of a total of 183 (Anon. 2017).[4] This quantitative inequality of representation between the sexes no doubt stems partly from the initial creation of the strip during a time of apparent censorship of female characters (see Chapters 1 and 5) but also from René Goscinny's concerns about including women in comical *bandes dessinées* more generally, as noted in the Introduction to this book, which he explains thus:

> We've often been criticised for the lack of women in Astérix's adventures. But it's important to see that our characters are mostly farcical. They're caricatures. We have too much respect for women to put them in ludicrous situations and draw them in distorted ways.
>
> (quoted in Andrieu 1999: 58)[5]

How, then, is this 'un-distorted' but under-represented essence of womankind depicted in the best-selling strips of the *Astérix* series? Physically, the female characters can be divided into two general categories. Most, like Bonemine and Ielosubmarine (the fishmonger's wife), are decidedly desexualized – they are short, heavy and unattractive with permanently tied-back hair and wear a traditional long-skirted peasant dress accompanied by an ever-present apron. A small percentage of the female characters, however, are tall, beautiful, slender and long-haired. These women, like Falbala and Madame Agecanonix, wear fitted fishtail dresses emphasizing their feminine figures. With the notable exception of Falbala, however, who appears gentle and dainty (as her very name suggests), the *Gauloises*, whatever their physical depiction, collectively display a number of unpleasant personality traits traditionally associated with femininity, as Rouvière also briefly notes, namely vanity, jealousy and petty competitiveness (2006: 200).

In her extensive study of traditional images of women in literature, Mary Ferguson identifies six principal character types very often attributed to female figures. These stereotypes – the 'mother', the 'submissive wife', the 'dominating wife', the 'woman on a pedestal', the 'sex object' and the 'woman alone' – associate women primarily with, and confine women to, their biological roles and their narrative positions in relation to men. Nearly all of the recurring female figures in the *Astérix* series correspond to one of these traditional types. The Gaulish housewives collectively reflect 'the dominating wife' stereotype. The dominating wife (also more widely known as 'the bitch' or 'the shrew') takes on the role of disciplinarian towards her husband: she scolds and nags, pushing him to react negatively as a child (Ferguson 1981: 7). Bonemine, for example, is quick to anger and frequently verbally or physically violent. Married to the village chief, her narcissistic pride in being the 'first lady of the village' does not stop her scolding or belittling her husband, Abraracourcix (in *La Zizanie*, for example, she bellows ironically at her spouse: 'if one day some idiots write our village history, they won't be calling it the adventures of Abraracourcix the Gaul!!!') (Goscinny and Uderzo 1970: 14).[6] Ielosubmarine and Madame Cétautomatix, two other visible wives within the village, are very similar to Bonemine as classic examples of this type.

Madame Agecanonix, who first appears in *La Zizanie* and whose first name is never revealed, also represents the type of the dominating wife, but in a different way. Married to a man three times her age and the most salacious (and the least domestically focused) of the female characters,[7] her domination of her husband comes not from her temper but her beauty, although the infantilizing result is comparable (in *Le Domaine des dieux*, for example, when asked a question as the 'elder of the village', Madame Agecanonix [modelling a new dress] answers for her husband while patting him on his head and referring to him with childish nicknames [Goscinny and Uderzo 1975: 35]).

All the *Gauloises* inhabit almost unfalteringly uniform spaces within the narrative. In their roles as wives they are restricted to the village and, within its imaginary walls, to scenes taking place in domestic locales: mostly in the homes they share with their spouses or, sometimes, in places associated with the fulfilment of household tasks, such as Ordralfabetix's fish stand. The action of this fast-paced adventure strip does not often occur in such domestic spaces and this fact accounts in part for the restricted representation of the female characters who inhabit them. Interestingly, however, it is through the minor scenes set in these typical spaces of subordination that the power of the female characters in this decidedly patriarchal society is seen. The *Gauloises* may be restricted to managing their domicile whilst their husbands work around the village, but within the home, the women rule. Quick to criticize or explode in frustration at their partners, the Gaulish wives often reduce the men of the village to cowardly shadows of their former selves in the home – one scene in *La Zizanie*, for example, sees Bonemine bark at her village-chief husband Abraracourcix as he prepares a speech for an upcoming banquet that instead of spouting 'poppycock' he should help her prepare dinner (Goscinny and Uderzo 1970: 1970).[8] Instances such as these illustrate the contradiction inherent in the 'dominating wife' stereotype, and hence inherent in the characterization of the women of *Astérix*, between the spaces to which representatives of this traditional role are restricted, which often indicate their subordination to men, and the power they exert over men within these spaces: from their confinement to the domestic domain, the women are, to an extent, able temporarily to topple the obtaining patriarchal hierarchy. Goscinny and Uderzo illustrate this contradiction visually by frequently depicting women ferociously wielding domestic objects. Whereas the male characters are frequently depicted with swords, tools or, in the case of Obélix, giant menhirs, the *Gauloises* are more likely to be seen with baskets, rolling pins or foodstuffs. Although clearly domestic accoutrements, these objects often become instruments through which the women express their 'inner power' as they – fish particularly – are used as weapons against their husbands and, sometimes, one another. The dual symbolism of the domestic accessory is clear in an iconic image of Bonemine from *Le Devin*. In this album, historic for the female characters as they are allowed to ingest the magic potion and partake in battle for the first time, Bonemine proves herself worthy of this honour in her vigour for combat. She triumphantly defeats the trouble-making soothsayer and chief of the Roman garrison and, as the male Gauls declare their victory over the Roman soldiers, she is shown standing on their vanquished backs, with her rolling pin held aloft phallically. Her physical subjugation of these prominent male characters with her rolling pin is a symbol of the power the wives yield through active engagement with the traditionally passive domestic sphere.[9]

In Ferguson's work, she explains that '[i]mages of women in literature have always been ambivalent; for every biological role there has been both a negative and a positive view' (1981: 6); this results in her further sub-division of the traditional types she identifies (the 'wife' type already divided into 'dominating' and 'submissive') into opposite extremes. The mothers of Astérix and Obélix, much less frequently depicted in the series than the wives (their principal appearance in the series occurs in the 2001 album *Latraviata*) are both examples of one extreme of the 'mother' stereotype that Ferguson dubs 'the all-powerful "Mom"' (which she contrasts with the romanticized, selfless mother). A category very close in characterization to the dominating wife type – both can be described as 'castrating' – the behaviour of both Gaulish mothers in line with this type is evident in their narrative representations in *Latraviata* as both infantilize their adult sons, immediately chastising them on entering their homes for their lack of cleanliness or poor diet before picking up brooms and ladles to rectify this situation. They further fixate throughout the story on the idea of finding their sons wives to take care of them, organizing social gatherings and dances to push the disinterested Astérix and Obélix towards various young female villagers.

The character of Latraviata who makes her entrance in this album of the same name – a Roman actress who is charged with impersonating Falbala to convince the heroes of the strip to part with valuable weapons – is an undeniable example of the 'woman on a pedestal' type. The 'woman on a pedestal' may be divided between the seductress (known also as the femme fatale) – the effect of whose beauty is disastrous – or the goddess, whose angelic beauty ennobles the men who love her (Ferguson 1981: 7). Latraviata, an Italian term that means 'the fallen woman',[10] represents the seductress side of this type, a form of female depiction present in the oldest of narratives and across every medium. Embodying the archaic fear of female sexuality and its effects on men – even the usually unresponsive Astérix is rendered gormless and gullible faced with the actress's wiles – the character of Latraviata is used as a destabilizing 'weapon' by one group of men to the detriment of another, in a similar way to the creation of La Schtroumpfette. However, unlike many representations of the femme fatale where this figure is finally punished in some way for her actions, the conclusion of Latraviata's role in this album sees her immediately forgiven by the Gauls and presented with gifts instead.

Across these traditional types, the women of Astérix largely play one common role: they are cast as disruptive agents – a very common trope seen throughout narrative history, most famously used in the biblical Genesis story – with the Gaulish housewives, in particular, appearing in several albums primarily to incite the unrest or discord necessary to kick-start the main narrative. In *La Zizanie*, for example, although prompted by a crafty outsider in the employ of their Roman enemies, it is the vindictive, hot-tempered and violent behaviour of the gossiping *Gauloises* that very nearly reduces the village to ruins. Likewise, in *Le Devin*, it is the superstition and vanity of the Gaulish women that lead the little band of usually fearless warriors to flee their homes in terror.

It is now clear that the most prominent women of Uderzo and Goscinny's creation seem to be interpretations of the negative extremes of various long-standing traditional female types. It is important to note, however, that the decidedly negative personalities and actions of the female characters in *Astérix* are not entirely out of step with other figures in the strips. The hot-headed temperament of the women is a frequently-used comic trope and tool of diegetic development intrinsic to several albums, but the male characters of the village are no strangers to negative behaviour either, variously showing themselves to be petulant or quick to anger. However, the male characters also inhabit a variety of roles – village chief, bard, fishmonger, blacksmith – and a range of heroic types – Panoramix is the wise man, Obélix the loyal side-kick – which allow them, equally, to display commendable qualities over the series. The female characters, contrastingly, show in general very little evidence of positive personality traits and are restricted to a much more limited range of roles and character types that are almost always dependent on their relation to the male characters, this lack of variation reducing them mostly to an indistinguishable and disagreeable rabble. In this gendered split of character roles, Goscinny and Uderzo's series exemplify an essential difference identified by Ferguson between traditional uses of male and female typing, namely that female types contain and limit the characterization of women considerably more than their male counterparts: '[m]an has been defined by his relationship to the outside world – to nature, to society, indeed, to God – whereas woman has been defined in relationship to man. The word *defined* means "having a limit around", "fenced in". Women have been fenced into a small place in the world' (1981: 5). Susan L. Robertson agrees in her text *Matriarchy and the Rhetoric of Domesticity*, positing that there exists a common underlying function uniting the use of female stereotypes: '[s]tereotypes do indeed do the work of their (patriarchal) culture. They provide a reassuring framework for human relations. But they also contribute to a reading that reinforces the notion that female characters and the women they represent lack depth, fluidity or individuality […] stereotypes participate in managing and limiting rather than liberating female behaviour' (1994: 130). The use of typing, then, may be a way used in text and image to contain the 'problematic' female presence – not, as noted of the 'regulating' trope of the female nude in *Les Aventures extraordinaires d'Adèle Blanc-Sec*, by presenting an idealized picture of womanhood – but by restricting it to a familiar, patriarchally defined and un-nuanced caricature, which depends principally on the woman's (often biological or marital) role in relation to at least one male figure. Such appears to be the case for almost all recurring female characters in the *Astérix* universe.

More will be said in the following chapter about the structural use of stereotypes and their commonality in the *bande dessinée*. However, before progressing to a close analysis of the album *La Rose et le glaive*, one further, general point is useful to note regarding the very traditional female stereotypes used by Goscinny and Uderzo: the presence of these secondary women in domestic locales and roles plays an undeniably important part in the maintenance of the basic sub-structure of the *Astérix* narrative. The women and the spaces they inhabit remain very much a secondary element of the diegesis but, once introduced, constitute a fairly constant minor fixture of the strips. To borrow a phrase from Judith Roof, the *Gauloises* 'people the background fabric' of the text (2002: 2), their scenic presence and domestic activity to an extent humanizing the Gauls and life in the village, bringing an aspect of normalcy to the narrative that allows the reader to maintain a level of identification with this world of druids and magic potions. The presence of the female characters also helps to extend the narrative beyond the confines of the individual episodes. Their presence and accompanied association with aspects of the domestic and the every-day lends a sense of permanence to the imaginary universe, extending the lives of the main characters and their surroundings beyond the last page of each album. As elements of the minor allowing the extension and delimitation of the text as suggested by Deleuze and Guattari (see p.80), the sense of permanence and realism they add is perhaps the reason for the female secondary characters' inclusion in the series. These women are not a necessary component of the episodic, adventurous nature of the strip – as made clear by the first albums, which appear without female characters – and are certainly not introduced to provide any sustained romantic interest for the principal male characters. The structural and diegetic value of the insertion of women into *Astérix*'s world seems to be, precisely, their minor-ity: the infinite extension of the narrative they enable via their often 'invisible' and, more frequently unremarkable, presence.

La Rose et le glaive

The 1990 album *La Rose et le glaive* constitutes a unique and extreme break with the established, structurally gendered narratives of the *Astérix* series outlined above. Written and drawn by Uderzo, this relatively recent album takes as its satirical subject matter the emergence of feminism and the changing roles of women in society, pushing by narrative necessity the minor figure of the *Gauloise* into the spotlight for the album's 48 pages.[11] In what follows, a brief consideration of this episode and its unusual focus on the serially secondary female will be presented.

The story begins when, unhappy with the bard Assurancetourix's instruction of their children in the village school, the *Gauloises* fetch a woman, Maestria, from Lutèce to take his place. Outraged that a female is summoned to replace him, Assurancetourix leaves the village in self-imposed exile. Maestria, outspoken from the moment of her arrival, incites the women of the village to rebel against their domestic roles in the ancient society, a fact that eventually drives all of the male Gauls to join Assurancetourix in the woods until the women return to normal. Meanwhile, unaware of the feminist coup in the homes of their last Gaulish rivals, the Romans summon a legion of women to attack the village, on the premise that the Gauls, with their unwavering gallantry, will never raise their fists against females. Upon overhearing this, Astérix devises a plan both to save the unprotected Gaulish women from the Roman women centurions and prevent his band of warriors from being ungentlemanly by fighting back themselves: the village is turned into a makeshift shopping mall. The Roman women are sufficiently distracted from their orders, leaving the village happily with new clothes, and order is restored amongst the Gaulish society as the men are welcomed back to their previous positions with open arms by their wives, and Maestria returns to Lutèce.

Whilst the general subordination of the female characters to the patriarchal power structure of the village (domestic disputes notwithstanding) constitutes an underlying, often largely invisible, discourse throughout most of the *Astérix* series, *La Rose et le glaive* consciously illustrates throughout its dominant narrative the chaotic consequences of defying this structure. To the contemporary reader, Maestria is cast as the clichéd militant feminist so successfully ridiculed in the 1970s and 1980s media – much to Obélix's amusement she dresses in a typically masculine manner wearing breeches, refers to women around her as her 'sisters' and exhorts them loudly at every possible opportunity to stand against 'male tyranny'. Her characterization also draws from a more traditional source, however, as she appears a combination of two older and particularly negative types associated with female characters – the 'woman alone' (also known as the 'old maid' or the 'spinster') and the 'educated woman' (an interesting type in that it depends less on women's relationship to men than most others, being linked to both married and unmarried women). These types pair well within a single character as their root (like that of their late-twentieth-century derivative, the 'man-hating feminist') is based on the same key element: fear of the independent woman who is not beholden to a man for company, protection or knowledge. Maestria, as a single woman, is a particularly exceptional figure amongst the Gaulish women of the village, all of whom (unlike a variety of male characters) are married. This difference is emphasized as important upon her first meeting with the *Gauloises* early in the narrative when Bonemine introduces herself as the 'chief's wife' and presents 'Madame Ordralfabétix, Madame Cétautomatix and Madame Agecanonix', to which clear indications of married identification the newcomer responds 'just call me Maestria' (1990: 9). Maestria is also underlined from the beginning of the narrative as an 'educated woman'. She is hired as the new school teacher for the village, chastises Obélix at their first meeting on his lack of arithmetic understanding and is described by Bonemine as being 'learned'. Both of these types, the 'woman alone' and the 'educated woman', differ from the standard division of female stereotypes, as noted above, into opposing idealized and vilified extremes and, instead, appear quite unambivalent in their negative narrative depiction.

Ferguson (1981: 8, 10) notes that the 'woman alone' has, traditionally, often been a figure of pity – Laura L. Doan agrees, stating in her study of the 'spinster' that such figures are deemed pathetic in order to mask the patriarchal fear of the unmarried woman (1991: 1) – and explains that both types are subject to ridicule as an effective means of diffusing the threat they imply.[12] Maestria, a combination of these established character outlines, is roundly mocked from her arrival in the village: her clothes, her manner of speaking, her musical ability and her temperament all become comic elements.[13] Her narrative effect quickly becomes less humorous, however: as she gains power over the women in the village, she becomes a symbol of utter destruction in *La Rose et le glaive*. She pushes the male characters to abandon their homes, thus leaving the stronghold vulnerable to the Roman enemy and allows the children of the village to run amok as she uses it to stage a fashion show for the Gaulish housewives. Most significantly, she suggests that the village finally surrenders to their would-be invaders in order to enjoy the 'benefits of Roman peace'. A shocking proposition both for the fictional community whose way of life is based upon resistance of Roman assimilation – each Astérix album begins with the assertion that 'one small village of indomitable Gauls still holds out against the invaders' – and, indeed, for the faithful Astérix reader (the primary narrative focus of the series as a whole is the continued fight against the Romans), agreeing with Maestria's request for surrender would signal both defeat and an end to Astérix's adventures. Progressively, then, Maestria, not only depicted as single, childless and educated but increasingly as a powerful and influential woman, comes to signify within *La Rose et le glaive* the potentially destructive disorder of 'perverse' alternatives to the established patriarchal system of the Gaulish village. Uderzo's development of Maestria in this extreme way also, like her initial depiction in the familiar 'educated woman' and 'spinster' roles, continues a tradition of female representation well-established in visual media. As Linda Nochlin notes in her work on feminist art history: 'the most potent natural signifier possible for folly and chaos was woman unleashed, self-determined, definitely on top: this was the only image [...] rich enough in negative significations, to indicate the destruction of value itself' (1996: 35). Maestria's characterization, although often lighthearted and comically exaggerated, likens her symbolically to the examples of the 'destructive woman' that Nochlin provides from both sixteenth- and nineteenth-century art, from Flemish artist Peter Brueghel's 1562 *Dulle Griet* (which shows a shrewish woman, Dulle Griet [also known as Mad Meg], leading a band of women to ransack Hell) to French government-sanctioned caricatures showing women participating in the Paris Commune of 1871 as 'demons of destruction intent on literally destroying the very fabric of the social order' (1996: 35).

Predictably, whereas the reversal of the power structure in the Gaulish village is accompanied by an almost unprecedented level of threat, the restoration of the patriarchal hierarchy coincides with the elimination of the danger. Although outsider Maestria retains her feminist stance until her departure, support for the return of 'natural' order within the society seems to come from the Gaulish women themselves, who, throughout their tenure as sole inhabitants of the village, seem unable and unwilling to shake off their traditional roles. Their longing to relinquish power and return to homemaking is most clearly shown in a double page that is heavy with domestic symbolism. Astérix and Obélix briefly visit the village to warn the unprotected women of the new Roman threat. In the left-hand page, the women are featured prominently in each panel (except one, which shows Astérix removing his cap to bow to them) as they discuss the threat to their stronghold, Bonemine seated in the chief's chair (1990: 32). On the opposite page, however, once Maestria is occupied elsewhere and Astérix and Obélix make to leave the settlement, the women's focus changes to that of worry for their husbands' comfort in the forest. The symbolic reversion back to domesticity is underlined visually as the women are progressively removed from sight throughout the page (1990: 33). Bonemine descends from her chieftain's chair in the first panel and by the second is shown half-hidden behind a curtain as she fetches warm clothes to be taken to her husband in the woods. In every panel of the next two strips, Astérix and Obélix are shown standing clearly in frame whilst the hands of the village women emerge from dwellings to their left and right, visually restricted to the edges of the panels, holding blankets, pots and pans and pillows to be taken to their spouses, their visual identities replaced by these symbols of their traditional roles. The aforementioned strength of the female characters in domestic spaces is not visible here, seemingly inextricably linked to their subordination to the male in wider society. To complete this return to 'normal', despite none of their earlier feminist demands inspired by Maestria's explosive arrival being addressed or even remembered, after the defeat of the Roman danger following Astérix's successful and terribly clichéd plan, the men are welcomed back to the village as heroes by their wives who wear their traditional dresses once more, rather than breeches. Even the strong-willed 'shrew', Bonemine, in the last page blushingly returns her husband's shield, the symbol of his chiefdom, and is appeased with flowers.

Whilst the female characters in almost all *Astérix* albums are secondary in depiction and roles, in *La Rose et le glaive* they are temporarily repositioned as 'major': the position of women in the society forms the master narrative and the explicitly patriarchal discourse illustrates the chaotic effects of inverting established gender roles. The album's publication in 1990 places the story some twenty years after the 1970s publicizing of the feminist cause in France and after a certain progression in women's roles in private and political life. Uderzo may be responding in *La Rose et le glaive*, to an extent, to the politicization of feminism in contemporary France, although beyond this speculative contextual explanation the representation of women in this album appears rather outdated and excessively typed. The usefulness of this narrative to the Astérix universe is clear, however, as by showing the distinctly destructive force of the powerful female, the continued place of the woman as minor in the wider series is addressed and defended.

Conclusion

The *Astérix* series is often lauded as a pioneering force in the history of the *bande dessinée*; however, its representation of female characters, almost always secondary, largely remains limited and contained by resolutely traditional and negative stereotyping. Women are presented as distinctive, usually unpleasant, character types, are restricted to domestic spaces, and do not occupy roles beyond those of wives and mothers. They wield some power in domestic settings, although the danger of extending this power beyond these locales is shown with near-catastrophic effect in La Rose et le glaive. The women of *Astérix* are nonetheless useful within the series, however. Their general non-involvement in the magical elements of the strip, staying behind as the male characters imbibe the magic potion and battle the Roman Empire, provides a sense of normality to the fantastical series. Similarly, their often unremarkable presence as the 'background fabric' of the strip as they perform the menial tasks associated with everyday life lends a certain permanence to the series, extending the world of the indomitable Gauls beyond the confines of the individual narratives.

An influential series in the *bande dessinée*, *Astérix*'s depiction of secondary women characters provides an example of the use of traditional typing in the modern medium. The following chapter turns its repositioned gaze to minor female figures in a very different example of the BD, but one that equally resorts to restrictive stereotyping, and shows how features specific to the *bande dessinée* are used to contribute to such character definition.

7

Secondary Women in Urban Realism: *La Vie de ma mère*

La Vie de ma mère[1] is a modern urban *bande dessinée* (BD) narrative divided into two volumes, both published in 2003. Adapted by Jean-Christophe Chauzy and Thierry Jonquet from the latter's 1994 novel of the same name, it follows the first-person narrative of twelve-year-old French boy Kevin as he stumbles via his new gang of friends into a life of crime in and around Paris. Another example of a largely male-led strip, the secondary women of this *bande dessinée* inhabit a very different world to that of the *Astérix* series' Gaulish women, as *La Vie de ma mère* presents an un-comedic, gritty view of modern-day city life.

In what follows, the representation of the roles played, and types inhabited, by secondary female characters from different class backgrounds in this realist narrative will be analysed. *La Vie de ma mère* is unique amongst the strips chosen in this book in its status as an adaptation of a work first appearing in another medium; as such, the opportunity will also be taken to analyse briefly the differences visible between the representation of secondary women between the source text and the later drawn strip version, with a view to uncovering potential specificities of *bande dessinée* representations of minor women figures.

The Major Impact of Minor Women

La Vie de ma mère is an example of a narrative trend that became particularly visible across various media in the 1980s and 1990s, which focused on the social, economic and political realities of working-class urban life. As with many examples of this genre, the women that figure in *La Vie de ma mère* are, in terms of physical presence, largely secondary throughout the *bande dessinée*. However, despite their limited appearance in panels, in Chauzy and Jonquet's work they nonetheless play a pivotal causal role throughout the narrative. It is on returning from visiting his sister that principal character Kevin first encounters the gang who will involve him in their criminal activities, and it is after he prevents a security guard from stopping their assault on a young woman that they readily accept him. The absence of his exhausted and downtrodden mother after she takes a night job at the local hospital allows Kevin to continue his involvement in the gang's plans in secret, whilst his verbal defence of the young teacher Miss Dambre in the classroom incites his young school mates to exclude him, pushing him further towards his new acquaintances. The rape of an anonymous housewife by a gang member in front of Kevin during one of their racketeering excursions proves a turning point for the young boy and his opinion of the gang. Finally, it is their violent attack of Clarisse's mother – Kevin's schoolyard crush on the intelligent, upper-middle-class Clarisse accounts for much of his personal narrative – which closes his story, as the reader learns that he has been arrested and is recounting his tale to a judge via a tape recorder.

Secondary Women: Mothers, Virgins and Whores

The women are, then, central to the development of the diegesis, despite quite notably lacking a corresponding centrality in terms of their direct textual and artistic representation. Unlike many *bandes dessinées* featuring narratively significant secondary female characters, the women of *La Vie de ma mère* are neither problematic nor prone to sowing discord (as in the case of the Gaulish women noted above), nor are they merely pawns to be rescued by, and hence prove the prowess of, male protagonists. The women of Kevin's world are mostly kind and intelligent (although there are exceptions, such as Kevin's sister, who shall be discussed below), promoting the values of education, progress and the importance of supervision in the young man's otherwise difficult and largely ignored existence.

Several women in Kevin's life adopt a positive motherly role towards him. In addition to his own world-weary mother, Kevin's teacher Miss Dambre refers to him as 'dear'[2] and goes to his home to discuss his progress with his family, whilst Clarisse's mother encourages Kevin in his school-work and walks him home at night. An underlying catalytic force in the narrative of *La Vie de ma mère* is Kevin's attempt to fill the maternal role his own mother is too over-worked and exhausted to fulfil effectively; a lack that leads him to gravitate towards the gang whose dealings will ultimately land him in jail.[3]

La Vie de ma mère contains a racially diverse cast of male characters, most of whom inhabit Kevin's very working-class Parisian neighbourhood. All the women of *La Vie de ma mère* are white, and most are attacked, sexually objectified, victimized or disappointed by men (of all ethnicities). As this information suggests, there exists in this two-part *bande dessinée* a distinctive polarization of secondary characters according to gender. Whilst the female figures are mostly caring and gentle, the male secondary characters (with the exception of the grandfatherly neighbour, Mr Hardouin) are negatively portrayed as variously violent, dishonest, disrespectful, abandoning (in the case of Kevin's absent father and brother) or judgemental. Their reproachable behaviour ranges from the pretentious stand-offishness of Clarisse's father to the extreme sexual violence and abusiveness of the gang members.

The secondary male and female figures of Kevin's narrated existence rarely interact and on the infrequent occasions that they do, verbal or physical violence against the women characters almost always ensues. However, their opposing influence on Kevin's life is clearly illustrated at various points in the *bande dessinée*. A notable page appearing mid-way through the second album, for example, visually opposes two strips that show Miss Dambre coming to Kevin's home to discuss with his mother how to help him progress at school with the final strip showing Kevin's educational prospects mocked by the gang, before they set off across Paris in the last image to rob underground car parks (2003b: 24).

Interestingly, the diametrical opposition between genders found in the *bande dessinée* is not so clearly apparent in the source novel. A more ambiguous portrayal of male characters is seen in several instances than their almost entirely negative depiction in the *bande dessinée* version. Mr Belaïche, the director of the special needs section of the school attended by Kevin, for example, is supportive of Kevin's academic progress in the novel and offers him his congratulations; however, the strip version shows him to be aggressive and doubtful of Kevin's potential. Furthermore, in Jonquet's novel during the scene describing the rape of the housewife as the gang raids her house, Kevin describes Djamel, the unofficial leader of the group, as being shocked by the actions of the rapist, Laurent (2001: 112). In the corresponding scene in Jonquet and artist Chauzy's *bande dessinée* adaptation of the text, however, Djamel does not react to what he sees, merely stating once the attack is over: 'Right, let's go! I got the dosh'[4] (2003b: 19). Similarly, the female figures of the 1994 novel are not presented in entirely positive terms. Kevin's mother, for example, is noted early on in his narrative to be racist, disappointed that her daughter is publically dating a black man (Jonquet 2001: 20). However, in the *bande dessinée* Kevin merely notes when his school friends accuse him of racism: '[m]e and my lot aren't racist. Nathalie went out with a black guy once, that proves it'[5] (2003a: 12). This clear division between male and female characters, which appears as the story is translated between media, has the effect of simplifying the characters of the *bande dessinée* adaptation and pushing them into easily recognizable types, as will be discussed further below.

Although the representation of the female secondary characters in the strip is predominantly positive, there exists nonetheless a divisive sub-current in the *bande dessinée*'s portrayal of women. This sub-current takes on the form of a polarizing division between extreme female types: the 'virgin' and the 'sex object'.[6] Doris Tishkoff describes the contrast of these types, a patriarchal sexual division of women visible throughout the history of narrative, as the 'Madonna/Whore' dichotomy, explaining that '[i]n simplest terms it means the ancient split between nice girls vs. bad girls [...] In sociological terms it describes society's age-old custom of putting women into two categories, one legitimate and honoured, the other marginal and debased' (2005: 1). As one would expect following the inter-gender analysis of *La Vie de ma mère* presented above, almost all the named female characters in the *bande dessinée* fall into the former category. However, beyond the representation of these 'angelic' figures, the presence of the 'sex-object' is also strongly felt in the *bande dessinée*, both literally and figuratively. The first indication of the Madonna/whore distinction is suggested in the cover art for the opening album, subtitled *Face A*. The front cover shows Kevin passing by a sex shop on a Paris street at night surrounded by the gang, his blue tracksuit a brightly coloured contrast to the red-tinged backdrop. Standing slightly in the background, but clearly visible, watching the foursome go by are two unidentified women, their skimpy clothing denoting them as prostitutes. The back cover again shows Kevin and the three gang members in the darkened foreground. Kevin looks from his place in the shadows towards Clarisse, who is positioned in the background like the women on the front cover but is walking in the sunlight and depicted as a childlike figure carrying a school bag, completely contrasted to the prostitutes in the opposing image. In his discussion of album paratext, Benoît Mitaine (2013) indicates the importance of cover images to the *bande dessinée*, an art that 'focuses more on image than language (in contrast to novels)',[7] noting that the cover illustration must contain a snapshot of the essential elements of the work. Introducing the 'Madonna/Whore' dichotomy so clearly on the cover, then, indicates its key importance within the pages of the strip.

The contrast between Clarisse, the innocent, pretty, middle-class girl, and various personifications of the 'whore' type is indeed seen from this exterior introduction throughout both albums. Early in Kevin's narrative introduction to his surroundings and family, his sister Nathalie is shown in three separate panels on distinct pages, each image presenting her more progressively as a 'whore' figure. The first image is innocuous, merely showing her at work in a local hairdressing salon (2003a: 7). The second panel, however, shows her at home in a disorderly bedroom with posters of near-naked supermodels on the walls, painting her toenails bright red whilst wearing skimpy flesh-coloured clothing (2003b: 9). The third image cements her representation as belonging to the 'whore' category of the dichotomy Kevin's narrative unwittingly represents – she is shown almost completely naked, lying back on her bed in a pose explicitly displaying her body, engaged in an intimate act with her aforementioned Franco-African boyfriend (2003a: 12). Immediately below this image, a panel shows Nathalie realize Kevin is watching her as she screams for him to get out, before Kevin's narrative in the last frame of the page tells us that 'Nathalie dumped her black guy pretty quick. Now she lives with a Puerto-Rican, Antonio!'.[8] Some pages later, as Kevin's friendship with the young, virginal Clarisse begins to develop, he notes the difference between his school-mate and his sister. As Clarisse kisses her new companion on the cheek, he reflects in his narration on how much 'classier' her perfume smells to that of Nathalie (2003a: 31). This comparison also indicates the social class distinction which frequently accompanies the sexual division of women in *La Vie de ma mère* and, indeed, in countless other narratives across media: the equation of the 'whore' figure with a woman of low socio-economic status is, Tishkoff reminds us, a classic feature of the 'Madonna/Whore' dichotomy (2005: 2). As *Face A* moves towards its conclusion, Kevin again voices the contrast he perceives between Clarisse and Nathalie, deciding that the former would never suggest the sexual acts he knew his sister engaged in (2003a: 44), before reflecting in the next frame about how he, in turn, would treat Clarisse in a different way to the neighbourhood prostitute, Zora.

The representation of Clarisse as the chaste, saintly half of the long-standing Madonna/whore dyad continues into *Face B*, not only through Kevin's narration but in subtler manipulations of the *bande dessinée* form. Between the second and third pages, visible simultaneously in their recto-verso placing, two contrasting scenes of male behaviour towards women are played out. In the first, Kevin is shown copying out a love poem for Clarisse, signing it with a drop of his blood, before she responds by giving him a lock of her hair. The opposite page shows an explicit scene of the gang enjoying the services of Zora, before joking about their experiences with their 'little brother' Kevin (2003b: 5). The possibility offered by the *bande dessinée* to visually oppose two static images adds here to the depiction of the age-old contrast of women between virgin and sex-object.

However, although the diametrical opposition of the Madonna/whore dyad is well-established in the work, there are certain instances in the *bande dessinée* which suggest that the division between these contrasting categories can be easily crossed. The clearest example of this comes in *Face B* during an un-chaperoned evening Kevin spends at Clarisse's house with three of her young male friends (Figure 8). The first strip of this page shows Clarisse dance closely with three of her well-to-do young friends Arthur, Sylvain and Romauld in turn, her face shown in profile in the middle scene, whilst obscured in the panels on either side. Kevin's face is clear in each frame, and his expression darkens with every panel as his narrative exclaims that the way the boys were 'rubbing against' Clarisse reminded him of his sister Nathalie. The middle strip depicts Kevin's flashback of seeing Nathalie in her room dancing with the Puerto-Rican Antonio, the connection between the two dancing scenes in Kevin's mind clear by their similar structuring. Interrupting this memory of his sister and her burgeoning sexual relationship with another boyfriend, the following, bottom strip of this page comprises of one long panel depicting Clarisse inviting a shocked-looking Kevin to dance. The full view of the young woman's face in this panel, following the two strips above mostly obscuring the expressions of both females, imprints the mnemonic reference to the 'whore' divisionary category onto the previously exemplary figure of virginity, Clarisse. Her crossing of the dyadic boundary is brief: overleaf, in the following panel, Kevin reinstates Clarisse's perceived virginal status by dancing with her at a more respectful distance than her friends had adopted – 'so that she didn't think I wanted to do gross things to her'[9] (2003b: 12). However, the liminality of the Madonna/whore division for women in Kevin's world, even in spite of the habitual class-based associations of these types, remains clear from the structuring of the panels in this page, this again showing how Chauzy and Jonquet use the specificity of the *bande dessinée* to manipulate this traditional typed distinction.

Mothers, Angels and Whores: From Page to Strip

Interestingly, as with the exaggeration of male/female difference noted above, the Madonna/whore division of female secondary characters found in the *bande dessinée* is also less overtly present in Jonquet's source novel. The character of Kevin's sister Nathalie in particular, who grounds his understanding of the 'whore' image in the *bande dessinée*, is decidedly more ambiguous in her literary portrayal. Minor details, such as Kevin's passing comments about birthday presents she has given him, or that she leaves him her television when she moves in with Antonio, serve to diversify her character in the novel beyond that of the vain, 'man-obsessed' figure that is presented in the *bande dessinée*. The recounting of the intimate act Kevin witnesses between Nathalie and her partner Steve does occur in the novel, but, differing from the adapted strip, it is neither noted that Nathalie notices Kevin's presence and screams in fury at him to leave as noted above, nor is this incident followed in the novel by Kevin's comments of 'Nathalie dumped her black guy pretty quick [...]' (2003a: 12).

With the absence of Nathalie's untempered depiction as a 'whore' in the novel, the figure of Clarisse is correspondingly less interpretable as her virginal counterpart. Certainly, in the original text there is still little to suggest that this young, innocent school girl is not what she seems, and the above-described incident of Kevin recalling his sister and Antonio when seeing Clarisse dance with her friends is present in the novel (Jonquet 2001: 101); however, the contrast between the two women is much less clear. As noted above in the case of Nathalie, details about Clarisse's behaviour serving to diversify her character and her relationship with Kevin are not present in the *bande dessinée*. Clarisse's defence of her new acquaintance in front of her mocking friends as he dances with her is depicted in the drawn strip adaptation; however, incidental information such as the fact that she loses the love poem Kevin painstakingly writes out for her or that although he spends time at Clarisse's house doing his homework, his main contact there is her mother, is not translated between media. As a result, Clarisse's characterization as presented in Chauzy and Jonquet's *bande dessinée* is less detailed and more dependent on the virginal, angelic stereotype she represents than her more ambivalent literary counterpart.

In an interview printed at the end of *Face B*, artist Chauzy notes the importance of creating something new when working on an adaptation 'in order to avoid the pitfall of simply repeating the original story through images' (2003b: 52)[10] and it is clear that the creators have reinterpreted aspects of the source text to this end. The consistency with which the adaptations of the secondary female characters noted above render their depiction less ambivalent and more sexually-stereotyped, however, may explain something about the nature of *bande dessinée* storytelling, particularly in its traditional format. In *A Theory of Adaptation*, Linda Hutcheon notes the 'condensing' effect of some forms of trans-media adaptation, stating of literature-to-theatre transpositions that 'a novel, in order to be dramatized, has to be distilled, reduced in size, and thus, inevitably, complexity' (2013: 36). This does not reflect on the quality of the adapted work, she continues, as 'when plots are condensed and concentrated, they can sometimes become more powerful' (2013: 36). The same proposition may arguably be made in reference to the adaptation of *La Vie de ma mère* and, thus, to other similar strip adaptations. Although a two-part *bande dessinée*, this work sticks to the traditional format of 48 pages per album, with each page almost always made up of six large panels. This particular formal configuration may provide less artistic 'space' than 140 pages of continuous prose through which small details, off-hand comments or internalized emotional expression can be portrayed, thus, perhaps, encouraging the use of typing as a functional shorthand.

A related consideration concerns the process of graphic storytelling itself. In a 2009 article, Harry Morgan notes the importance of the drawn strip's evolution from caricature to its narratological processes and its character construction, stating that 'graphic literatures [...] preserve the tradition of heavily-stereotyped character, precisely as a result of drawing upon caricature' (2009: 38). This does not mean that the medium is less capable of producing complex characters – as Morgan explains, 'at the same time, graphic storytelling is capable of expressing a character's interiority, in particular in the narrative structure that combines *interior perspective* with *narrator*' (2009: 38; emphasis in original) – and, it is important to note, as Ferguson does, that despite the often pejorative understanding of typing, stereotypes can be 'useful and necessary' narrative tools (1981: 5). The inherent tendency towards typing that Morgan suggests – he cites the traditional importance of recurring characters and character-recognition to graphic narratology (2009: 35) – perhaps contributes to explaining, however, the higher recourse to typing in the *bande dessinée* adaptation of *La Vie de ma mère* than in its source text: as Stam explains of literary to cinematic adaptations, new works must interpret the 'dense network of verbal cues' of the source text through the 'protocols of a distinct medium' (2013: 180). Stam further suggests that adaptations are mediated in their transposition to the new medium by 'a series of filters: reigning ideologies, ambient discourses, studio style [...] and so forth' (2013: 180). As Tardi noted of the importance of previous artistic influence in his creation of Adèle Blanc-Sec (see p.70 of this book), the tendency of previous depictions of secondary female characters in the *bande dessinée* towards sexualized stereotyping may have also played a role in determining Chauzy and Jonquet's characterization choices in *La Vie de ma mère*.

Female stereotypes, as Ferguson and Robertson have noted (see p. 102 of this book), are particularly limiting and, unlike male types, largely restrict women to their biological roles and their relationships to men. Following on from the above analysis, it is perhaps not too bold a claim to make that the underdeveloped, bodily-focused nature of female figures in relation to their male counterparts throughout the twentieth century medium (one thinks again of Peeters' lament, cited in the Introduction, that '(i)n most albums, female faces and bodies remain devoid of individual existence due to their constant depiction using the same patterns and clichés of expressionless seduction'[11] (see p. 6 of this book), particularly in relation to secondary figures, may be due to this interrelated combination of the traditional medium's visual and narratological propensity towards typing and of the circular repetition of previous, negative incarnations of female-specific stereotypes in line with this propensity.

Violence and Visuality

The adaptation of *La Vie de ma mère* into the *bande dessinée* does indicate the visual possibilities of the form that remain unavailable to other modes of artistic expression, however. The stationary visuality of the drawn strip, unique to this art form, allows the medium to present and emphasize details that might have less impact when presented via a purely textual form. A simple example of this can be noted in Chauzy's rendering of the gang's hangout in the basement of a block of flats, a pivotal space recurrently portrayed in the narratives of both the novel and the strips. It is noted in both versions of the story that the walls of the hangout are covered in pornographic pictures of women torn from magazines; however, how this is presented in the differing media lends a very different focus to this minor detail. In Jonquet's source text, reference is made to the gang's choice of wallpaper in Kevin's first description of the space and, thereafter, only briefly once or twice more. The stationary visuality of the *bande dessinée*, however, means that in Jonquet and Chauzy's collaboration, the X-rated decorations are clearly visible in the background of every scene taking place at the hangout. The permanence of these graphic images adds to the representation of secondary female characters in the BD as the Madonna/whore dyad is again played out, in this instance between the kindly, innocent and maternal majority of the named female characters and the anonymous, graphically depicted 'whore' figures constantly adorning the walls of the gang's hangout.

A further narrative aspect of the *bande dessinée* enhanced through the visuality of the form is the rape scene and its aftermath. In the two pages in which the victim is present before the attack, the features of the young housewife become progressively more detailed as her terror mounts. In the first panel in which her face is clearly visible, it is minimally drawn with simple black dots used to denote her eyes and mouth; however, as she begins to realize that she is in danger, her features become much more detailed. The final view of her face comes during the attack, the depiction of her distorted and terrorized features rendering her visage almost inhuman. This shocking image of the woman's distress is made all the more intense by the striking red colouring of the scene, in addition to the woman's central position within the panel, the angle a tight close-up on her contorted features as a simply-drawn, shocked Kevin appears at the edge of the frame in the background. In the novel, as the narrative is entirely unfolded through the young man's monologue, the textual 'close-up' focuses almost entirely on Kevin's experience of watching the rape. His account of the attack is short and perfunctory, with the only reference to the woman's experience of the rape presented thus: 'the chick was terrified, she wasn't moving or anything' (Jonquet 2001: 112).[12] The visual representation of the sequence in the *bande dessinée* massively heightens the focus on the female character as the victim of the attack, the direct view of her distorted features presenting a more personalized, violent account of the crime than Kevin's juvenile report of it in the novel.[13]

The graphic visuality of the rape in the *bande dessinée* is echoed throughout *Face B* in a striking manner and one that is unique to the drawn strip adaptation of the story. Following the attack, which takes place on a week-day morning, Kevin returns to school for his afternoon classes. Upon seeing Clarisse smile at him in the playground, however, the sight of the rape is brought to his mind and he imagines, in quick succession, the housewife being attacked by Laurent behind her, her face hidden by a curtain of black hair, followed by the same image with

Clarisse's body replacing that of the woman, her horrified, chaotic features staring straight out of the panel. Overleaf, as Kevin sits in class, this imaginary view of Clarisse being raped is repeated from a different angle as his narrative explains that he can't get the nightmarish image out of his head (2003b: 22). Two pages later, as Miss Dambre tells Kevin that his scholastic progress is sufficient for him to move back to mainstream classes, the flashback image again suddenly appears, in this instance with the features of his kindly teacher distorted in terror as she is raped by Laurent. This shocking visual echo of the sexual attack witnessed by Kevin present in the *bande dessinée* is inspired by Kevin's comments in Jonquet's source novel as he returns to school following the rape: '[i]n the playground, I saw Clarisse. She smiled at me and in my head it all got muddled up with the smile the woman in Livry-Gargan gave me when I rang her bell, I swear. Her face mixed with Clarisse's, it was like a nightmare' (Jonquet 2001: 114).[14] However, as is clear, the focus of Kevin's recollection is altered entirely between media. In the textual version of the narrative, the young man's guilt over his role in the attack is portrayed through his memory of the housewife's kindness towards him. The *bande dessinée*, however, remembers not the woman's compassion, but her shocking violation, and repeats its image with the faces of familiar female characters in place of the suburban victim, this forcing Kevin – and the reader – to personalize the crime against the anonymous housewife. The rape becomes an assault against the 'Madonna' figures of the story, its emphatic visualization and echoing in the *bande dessinée* significantly shifting its focus from that presented in Jonquet's textual interpretation.

Secondary Women in La Vie de ma mère: *Conclusion*

The secondary female figures of *La Vie de ma mère* clearly occupy very different positions within this narrative to the *Gauloises* of Goscinny and Uderzo's famous creation. Whilst the minor female characters of *Astérix* are comic creations, invariably presented as agents of chaos, the secondary women of *La Vie de ma mère* are mostly figures who try to bring order and comfort to the young protagonist's life and are depicted without humour in the bleak, realist portrayal of modern urban existence. However, a certain level of similarity does remain between these two apparently opposing examples of minor female figures in the *bande dessinée* – both sets of women are heavily typed, these types acting to contain the 'problematic' female to reassuringly recognizable, male-centred roles. Chauzy and Jonquet's female characters are confined to particularly traditional, 'biological' roles reserved for women figures as they are seen to be mothers, Madonnas or whores, with a difference in class evident between the women respectively inhabiting the latter polarized roles. Also like *Astérix*, the story distinctly divides the narrative positions of male and female figures – in *La Vie de ma mère* most male characters are presented negatively, as dishonest, self-serving and aggressive, and the female characters, correspondingly, are often depicted as victims of this negative behaviour.

Although not a *bande dessinée* which has achieved notable status within the medium, analysis of *La Vie de ma mère* yields useful results concerning the representation of secondary women in the *bande dessinée*. By redirecting the gaze towards the 'minor' female figures in protagonist Kevin's life, the narrative importance that secondary figures may hold becomes clear, despite their often infrequent depiction. The exceptional position of this *bande dessinée* narrative as an adaptation of what was originally a novel has further allowed a theoretical consideration of the particularities of *bande dessinée* depiction of secondary female figures beyond this specific drawn art example to be undertaken here. The alterations made between Jonquet's prose and Chauzy and Jonquet's *bande dessinée* rendering highlight both the tendency towards caricature-inspired simplification in representing minor characters – and the consequence of this for women secondary figures – as well as the particular expressive abilities of the *bande dessinée* more generally in its static visuality. Male figures, of course, may be subject to character-typing; however, the depiction of female figures in the *bande dessinée* is overwhelmingly secondary, and the range of types established in the representation of women is patriarchally dictated, limiting and often negative. Thus, these factors may impact on the representation of women in the medium as a whole. The depiction of the minor women figures in *La Vie de ma mère* shows examples of positive female-typing; however, the age-old, misogynistic division of Madonna and whore, which polarizes women into two morally pre-defined sexual extremes, makes up a large part of the shorthand characterization of women in the narrative. Nonetheless, through their visual translation from the page to the strip, the shocking reality of the often violent treatment of these women is highlighted in Chauzy and Jonquet's work.

Hutcheon notes briefly when discussing the literature-to-comics adaptation of Paul Auster's *City of Glass* that the comics 'grid' (the medium's standard division into panels and strips), 'like all formal conventions ... both constrains and enables; it both limits and opens up new possibilities' (2013: 35). *La Vie de ma mère* is evidence of this dual nature of adaptation, and within it may reveal an important feature of women's secondary representation in the wider medium.

8

Black Secondary Women in the Works of Warnauts and Raives: The Eroticization of Difference

Although the women characters examined thus far in each of the chapters across Sections 1 and 2 have differed to an extent in their general appearance, occupation and, sometimes, role within narratives, the women chosen for analysis nonetheless conform to a homogenous notion of femaleness that is both heterosexual and white European. Whilst this does reflect the general depiction of women across the *bande dessinée* (BD), some variation from this standardized character conception is visible within the medium, particularly in works created within the last twenty years.[1] Analysis of female figures that do not conform to the homogenous majority is certainly, therefore, necessary in order to examine as fully as possible the depiction of women within the medium.

German-Belgian creative pair Eric Warnauts and Guy Raives has produced more than thirty *bande dessinée* albums since their partnership began in the mid-1980s. Their collective œuvre is fairly distinctive within the *bande dessinée* in its frequent featuring of secondary women of colour, and as such it constitutes an interesting focus of analysis. Below, two narratives by Warnauts and Raives featuring differing spatial and temporal settings will be examined in order to uncover how women of African origin are depicted in their work, how the characterization of these female figures is shaped and constrained to conform to a historic stereotype specific to women of colour, and, particularly, how the formal specificity of the *bande dessinée* is used to contribute to this depiction.

'Congo blanc'

Warnauts and Raives's 1992 album *Equatoriales* consists of five short stories set in different locations along the equator line. The entirety of the collection is drawn in the artists' habitual style, with quasi-realist depictions of the varying landscapes drawn in vibrant tones of red and brown supplementing the narrative and emphasizing the physical exoticism of the chosen settings. The first tale of *Equatoriales*, entitled 'Congo blanc', is particularly illuminating in its depiction of secondary women.

'Congo blanc' is set, as the title suggests, in the pre-1939 colonized Congo and follows the story of white Belgian Louis and his choice between his European wife and Congolese mistress, Baligi. This story consists of only nine pages, but within this short space Warnauts and Raives manipulate the *mise-en-page* to considerable effect to Other, exoticize and sexualize the colonized African figure Baligi.

The story begins, as each tale does in *Equatoriales*, with a tri-partite introductory page (1994: 9). A portion of map denotes the shape of an unmarked country along the equator line, with the title 'Congo blanc' written beneath in calligraphic script. Below both, the illustration of a black woman clutching a bed sheet between her bared breasts is presented, the already marked sensuality of this image increased by her closed eyes and parted lips. In addition to conveying to the reader the general spatial setting of the story, the title indicates textually the relation of colonial domination imposed upon the Congo as a whole, whilst its significant placing above the image of the female figure provides an implication of imperial domination quite specifically over the naked body of the woman. Far from her entirely unremarkable presence as part of the primitive Congolese collective depicted in Tintin's famous visit to this Belgian colony, the black female is immediately exhibited by the structural composition of this striking page. Its place as the first page of *Equatoriales* immediately exhibits this figure and ensures the establishment of her image as a symbol of sexual desire and abjection – a symbol that, as shall be seen, pervades the story to its final page.

As the narrative proper begins, with a two-page sequence of Louis and Baligi in bed together, the device of the manipulated *mise-en-page* is again used by Warnauts and Raives to emphasize aspects of the Congolese mistress's characterization. Examination of the structuring of this first page of the story reveals its use to Other and exoticize Baligi. The opening page introduces the scene with two vertically full-length, narrow panels, one depicting a column of various strewn objects, with the following introducing the bodies of the as-yet anonymous pair, the man above the sleeping woman, his hand touching her shoulder. In the first panel, the foreignness of the strip's Congolese location is immediately emphasized by the khaki clothes, the map, the bananas and the papaya, with, interestingly, the most exotic of these items – the tropical fruits – placed in the lower half of the frame, structurally in line with the black woman's body in the following panel. This spatial connection to symbols of foreignness implicitly denotes Baligi's place as a similar exotic object from the first panels of the story.[2] Furthermore, the clear sexual symbolism of the fruits, with the placing of the phallic objects above the oval papaya, introduces the relation of sexual domination existing between the pair in the following frame.

The final column of the first page is divided into four snapshots showing different portions of the Congolese woman's face and hair. The re-angling of a panel to focus on different physical aspects of the female form is a device also used in *Lettres d'Outremer*, as shall be noted below. Here, the sequencing of these panels presents the images in a quasi-photographic manner, consequently investing the depiction of the displayed female with the impartiality of representation and realism associated with the photographic medium. Each panel presents one view of Baligi's head and face, the pictures highlighting her blackness as they focus on her braids, her lips and her brown skin, this accentuated physical difference from the white 'norm' subtly rendered less relative and more objectively factual by Warnauts and Raives's choice of photographic style.

In addition to the emphatic function performed by the separation of panels, the division of Baligi's features into four distinct frames in place of one larger portrait recalls, to an extent, the colonial ethnographic photography undertaken in the late nineteenth century by French photographers such as Nadar and hence begins her dehumanization in the eyes of the viewer. Variation in the angling of a chosen subject was common practice in such photography, with pictures of black subjects frequently taken from both front and profile angles. This was intended to reduce the specificity of the subject's identity, aiding in the presentation of the sitter as a mere representative of type (Williams and Willis 2002: 11) and further to objectify the subject, a multiplicity of views suggesting to the spectator that he or she is looking at a classifiable object rather than an individual (Williams and Willis 2002: 28). A late twentieth-century reminder of such adopted trends in imperial photographic ethnography seems present in this small portion of *bande dessinée* representing the colonized subject Baligi, the depersonalized fragmentation of her introduction immediately establishing the voyeuristic position of power held by the reader; this position is almost entirely unimpeded by the returned gaze of the fully visible female subject.

The divided, atomized depiction of Baligi remains a consistent factor of her representation throughout 'Congo blanc'. In fact, the only non-fragmented depiction of Baligi present in the first two pages of the story throughout which her naked, sexualized image dominates shows her in a familiar pose: recumbent, holding a bed sheet between her breasts, eyes closed and lips parted.[3] This panel, significantly, forms a larger scene of the de-contextualized image presented in the title page, its re-appearance in this erotic sequence implicitly re-affirming white domination over the body of this exotic, incohesive Other.

Baligi's depiction in 'Congo blanc' does not correspond to the types noted in the representation of white secondary characters in *Astérix* or *La Vie de ma mère*.

It does, however, resemble a mode of depiction associated with black women throughout the history of their representation within the Western world. Evidence exists in literary texts dating as early as the twelfth century of the projection of a sexualized narrative onto the black female (Sharpley-Whiting 1999: 1); this textual mode of representation was adopted and exploited to great effect from the outset of western colonialism both via the written word and the drawn image. Early colonial ethnographic illustrations of semi-naked native women, which provided many young western men with their first experience of the nude female form (Pieterse 1995: 79), became a first step in pictorializing the textually initiated image of 'savage sexuality' attributed to the black woman. Such drawn images, followed later by photography and colonial expositions, were used to support pre-existing assumptions concerning the 'deviance' of the black female subject from the accepted norm.[4] Their frequent depiction without clothes confirmed to the contemporary viewers of these images the wild sexuality of the black female, cementing her place in the public consciousness as a being to be both desired and feared. By the nineteenth century, the mythical image of the 'Black Venus' – the dark-skinned woman of the colonies embodying western imperialism's ultimate 'Other' through her femaleness, her blackness and her perceived unbridled sexuality – was established across media, in literature, sketches and painted art, before appearing in film from the 1920s, notably in works featuring the exoticized figure of Josephine Baker.[5]

In his work on stereotypes in *The Location of Culture* Homi Bhabha posits that the stereotype in colonial discourse is a complex, ambivalent mode of representation, as concerned with counteracting the fear provoked by racial difference as it is a reminder of this difference (2004: 100). The stereotype must, Bhabha suggests, be 'anxiously repeated' in order to be effective – a contention defended by the development and multiplication of representations of the Black Venus type over centuries and various media as noted above (and one that recalls the notion invoked in Chapter 4 concerning the necessary proliferation of nude images of women in the 'containment' of the female body). The narrative of the Black Venus, which acts to contain the 'doubly-problematic' presence of the black woman by its extreme Othering of her racial and sexual alterity through visual and textual exaggeration, appears, like other racialized assumptions and stereotypes, to have outlived the colonial era, and its 'anxious repetition' continues, to an extent, in modern-day artistic forms. It is visible in the late twentieth-century *bande dessinée* – notably within the work of Warnauts and Raives and their depiction of the Congolese character, Baligi.

Although her presence permeates the remaining pages of 'Congo blanc', Baligi is in fact seen only once more after these initial pages before her depiction at the closing of the story, the subsequent pages progressing to depict the interactions of Louis with his Belgian wife Isabelle. The reader's penultimate view of Baligi comes midway through a two-page spread of panels illustrating in striking blues and browns the jungle and river of the Congo (1994: 12–13). This sequence immediately follows the erotic introductory pages, the reader seeing within it the only images of Louis and Baligi together and fully clothed. Via the division and juxtaposition of two panels, each focusing on the seated form of the male and then female character, the reader sees for the first and only time the comparative cultural differences between Louis and Baligi. As he sits in the western colonial apparel of a white shirt and pith helmet (1994: 13), Baligi is shown in the following image in an African headscarf and skirt drinking the juice from a melon, the separation and adjacent placement of the images furthering her exotic Othering as her physical and cultural difference from Louis is emphasized. The obscuring of her features with a melon in her individual panel furthermore renders this frame another fractured, incomplete depiction of Baligi. With only one un-fragmented image of her face in the sixteen panels in which she appears, this African woman embodies the unknown, the exotic and the sexual, much like the Black Venus image that equally fascinated and frightened the western imagination of the nineteenth century.

As noted, the figure of Louis's wife appears in the short story in the remaining pages following these final images of Baligi and her Belgian lover together. The two women are never concurrently visible in 'Congo blanc' – a page-turn conspicuously separates their depiction throughout – with the tale's overarching structure physically separating the clearly visually contrasting figures of the black mistress and the white wife. A brief closer comparison between the strips featuring each of the women shows further that although, as noted above, Baligi's brown skin and curves are exhibited by a distinctive and unconventional layout, the panels representing Isabelle's slender white form are moulded into a relatively simple structure.

Within each of these differing formations, several disparities in representation are further notable between the figures of Baligi and Isabelle, the most visually obvious of these clearly that whereas Baligi's predominantly naked body is sexualized from the title page onwards, Isabelle's is always shown fully clothed and, for the most part, wearing a beige blouse exactly matching her skin tone, emphasizing her whiteness. However, although the physical difference between the women underlines the sexual focus of Baligi's depiction over that of Isabelle, it is through the use of dialogue that a more insidious differing of the women, and a consequent sexual exoticization of Baligi, occurs. Both women appear in equal proportions of the narrative proper, each occupying scenes in two pages and one or two additional panels on following pages. However, to Baligi's five spoken words of dialogue, Isabelle utters 116. This disparity of dialogue divides the representation of the women on two levels. Superficially, the reader learns from this more of Isabelle's personality and background, allowing her character a certain level of individuality, whilst Baligi, apart from her name and her five words – 'Tomorrow' and 'You're my man'[6] (1994: 11) – remains a mysterious but sexualized black female figure. On a less character-concentrated level, however, the disparate concentration of dialogue between the women implicitly reinforces the difference of the core focus on each figure beyond the wife/mistress dyad. In panels depicting Louis's wife, such focus is clearly centred around language and verbal expression, whilst Baligi's relative silence ensures that her body is foregrounded. With this relegation of the entirety of her character to her physical form the figure of Baligi becomes a mere plaything, a visual metaphor for the sexuality of the black female, with her relation with Louis an almost animalistic tryst displaying a level of carnality to the reader that further emphasizes Baligi's physical and sexual difference from her lover's wife upon the latter's appearance in the narrative.[7] Isabelle's furious assertion later within the story during a row with her husband over his adultery only serves to underline this point, as she refers to Baligi as 'that negress bitch'[8] (1994: 14) and screams: '[i]t's ridiculous, you just like screwing her, that's all … it's only sexual!'[9] (1994: 15). Through the words of the scorned wife, Warnauts and Raives verbalize the presentation of their Congolese figure as animalistic, far from the accepted aesthetic standards of (white) beauty, overtly sexually charged, and yet greatly desired by the white male; contrasting qualities again recalling the Black Venus narrative and showing the repetition of this centuries-old, female-focused racial stereotype in the pages of the modern *bande dessinée*.

Adding a layer of complexity to the colonial discourse of 'Congo blanc', the character of Louis is not presented by Warnauts and Raives as a racist or exploitative figure. No mention of the length of their extra-marital affair is made in the short story, but Louis's behaviour towards Baligi in their communal scenes expresses a tenderness towards her pictorially suggestive of a lasting attachment and his final appearance in the strip conveys his visible distress over leaving her to return to Belgium with his wife. However, in a final example of Warnauts and Raives's structural manipulation of the story to exoticize and sexualize implicitly the figure of Baligi, within the closing page of 'Congo blanc', the reader is reminded of Louis's racial and class difference from his mistress against the backdrop of her occupied African homeland (1994: 18). This concluding page of the narrative presents two sizeable panels with small, inlaid images depicting Louis in the bathroom of an airplane, in distress over his final decision to leave Baligi and the Congo to return to Belgium with his wife. Supporting these small scenes, above a half-page image of African countryside showing the comparatively tiny plane carrying Louis and his family away from the country, is a large, faceless close-up of Baligi's chest and breasts, with one hand shown holding a wad of banknotes whilst the other, just visible, holds a handwritten note on which, the caption above tells us, Louis has simply written 'I can't … forgive me … Louis'[10] (1994: 18).

This concluding image of Baligi, focused closely on her breasts, the frame cutting her face out of sight but Louis's money seen clearly in her hand, provides both a closing reminder to the reader of the inalienable distance between this white Belgian man and his Congolese lover and a final striking sign of her character's corporeal sexualization and colonial exoticization within the tale. The presence of Louis's pain in the inlaid panels alongside his brief written apology may indicate the money Baligi holds to be an acknowledgement between the two of her lower-class status in the colonized Congo and, thus, destined as a parting gift. However, the symbolic image of money held against Baligi's black naked chest with her face out of frame whilst the white 'colonizer' Louis is pictured fully clothed in the inset panels returning to Europe despite his distress cannot help but exude allusions to prostitution. With this image at the close of 'Congo blanc' the character of Baligi is finally symbolized as a faceless courtesan – a sexualized, depersonalized, racially Othered Black Venus, with the cross necklace worn just visibly between her breasts, a subtle reminder of her body's subjugation to white colonial power.

This introductory story of Warnauts and Raives's *Equatoriales* illustrates several features of the *bande dessinée* that are manipulated to heighten the Othering and exoticized sexualization of the African female. However, it is perhaps important not to ignore the possible influence of the temporal setting of 'Congo blanc' in the colonial era on this examined depiction. To provide a fuller picture of the black secondary woman in Warnauts and Raives's late twentieth-century work, an examination of a text illustrating a more contemporary, 'decolonized' setting is important.

Lettres d'Outremer

Lettres d'Outremer, published in 1996, provides the opportunity for this comparative consideration, differing significantly from the narrative examined above in its placement in modern-day, post-colonial Guadeloupe. It again, however, focuses on the exploits of a white European man – in this case the Parisian Jean – in a foreign but francophone land and his fleeting sexual relationship, seen from his Eurocentric, male perspective, with a woman native to this 'exotic' location, this time named Souana. Temporally set much closer to the present day, *Lettres d'Outremer* textually engages to an extent with the post-colonial debate over the development of France's ex-colonies (Guadeloupe remains a part of the French Republic, but is no longer designated as a 'colony'). However, the sexualization and exoticization of the Guadeloupian female figure Souana again indicates the employment of the Black Venus stereotype in Warnauts and Raives's modern-day BD representation of the woman of colour.

As seen in *Equatoriales*, again in *Lettres d'Outremer* the creators exhibit their ability to manipulate the formal specificity of the *bande dessinée* to accentuate the racially and erotically alterior representation of their female characters. However, in contrast to the text previously analysed, much of this sexualized differentiation lies in the frequent focus on the racial distinction between the Frenchman Jean and Guadeloupian Souana. The interracial couple has become, as Mark McKinney notes, a prevalent trope in the emergence of the post-colonial *bande dessinée*, used iconically to signify several social or political outlooks – as symbols of post-colonial reconciliation or an unattainable ideal for marginalized immigrant groups – but in many cases simply 'as (neo-)colonial erotic encounter between dominant First-World and subaltern Third-World characters' (1997: 170). In *Lettres d'Outremer* the interraciality of Jean and Souana's brief relationship adheres largely to the latter symbolic function with specific artistic and textual techniques used to heighten attention to Souana's exoticism and difference from Jean's ideologically implied 'normality'.

In addition to the basic tonal contrast of their characters' white and black skin, colour on a wider scale is effectively exploited by Warnauts and Raives to heighten Souana's Othered, depersonalized sexual representation, which is most clearly notable in the scenes depicting the couple's first intimate encounter (1996: 44). The sequence begins with a series of four progressively narrower and elongated panels, each focusing more closely on Souana's body than that which precedes it. As Souana is preparing dinner for herself and Jean, he approaches, and as he touches her face, the sexual sequence begins. Significantly, as seen most closely in the final panel of this 'cinematic' close-up, Souana's hands are partly white from the flour she has been using to prepare the food. During this first erotic moment the very blackness of her skin is emphasized by the white flour. The contrast of colour between her dark skin and white fingers as Jean touches her body seem to signify her no longer as 'black' but, rather, as 'not white' – she is the striking opposite of Jean's 'natural' white European appearance. In the following page, finger-shaped traces of flour are seen over the furniture and on the sheets and floor, illustrating the passion of their love-making. The fact that the white marks from Souana's hands are used as a symbol of their sexual union highlights the importance of racial difference in the eroticization of this encounter, heightening the exotically sexual intrigue of this 'non-white' female figure.

Souana's exotic sexual difference is further underlined in the second erotic sequence between the couple in the *bande dessinée*. The morning after their first sexual encounter, the pair again makes love (1996: 57). Apparently bathed in light from the rising Guadeloupian sun, Jean's skin is rendered the same pink shade as the sheets, the walls and the bedside lamp. Only Souana's body remains its natural colour, her brown skin the single contrast to the unified surroundings as her position above Jean exhibits her figure as the sexual focus of the page. Through the alteration of shading between these two erotic scenes, Souana's difference is doubly accentuated. In the former the focus lies on her skin tone as a negation of the norm – her body is emphatically presented as not-white – whilst in the latter the emphasis falls instead on the corollary of this negative chromatic definition. The fact of her blackness emphasized during the second erotic scene highlights this as the focus of her exoticism, the single colour uniting Jean's skin and the room around them, designating his appearance as natural and her skin as symbolically, strikingly Other. This exploitation of colour present in *Lettres d'Outremer* provides a powerful connection between Souana's eroticized characterization and her race. The reader implicitly understands that she is highly sexualized *because* she is different, because she is exotic, because she is black. That this implicit visual assertion is made in Warnauts and Raives's text strongly accentuates the presence and perpetuation of the Black Venus stereotype in this example of the *bande dessinée*, this contention furthered by several other aspects throughout *Lettres d'Outremer*, not least by Souana's position as the only character to speak words of Creole in the strip.

In the first story of *Equatoriales*, as noted above, the black woman's exotic difference is implicitly pictorialized using specific formal features of the *bande dessinée*, with the only textual recognition of her erotic alterity present in the racist insults hurled by Louis's wife. *Lettres d'Outremer*, however, also briefly accompanies the visual exhibition of the black woman's exotic sexuality with a textual consideration of the white man's desire for this eroticized figure, this appearing in the form of a short discussion between Jean and Antoine, a politically outspoken Guadeloupian journalist. Asking candidly of Jean's relationship with Souana: 'Because the fact that she's black doesn't factor into your desire to see her again?'[11] (1996: 37), Antoine is sceptical of Jean's indignant reply and suggests that it might be more honest to admit that it is, in fact, her bodily difference that attracts him.

This brief but overt exchange considering the underlying persistence into the modern day of the white male's colonial desire to possess the black woman sexually reveals a certain level of conscious analysis within the text of the continued fetishization of black female sexuality. However, this explicit contemplation of the underlying components of the Black Venus narrative does not preclude its continuation, albeit in a modernized form in keeping with the work's late twentieth-century Guadeloupian setting, in various forms throughout the rest of the album. Perhaps the most symbolically significant of these comes in several short sentences uttered by Souana as the work begins, in the course of her first conversation with Jean. She notes to her new French acquaintance that she has just returned from Paris, not, as the latter supposes, from having studied there, but from touring France and Belgium as part of an Antillean dance spectacle.

While this fact once spoken is not revisited, its import and placing in the introduction of Souana's character should not be underestimated. Throughout the history of the visual representation of the black woman in the West, and spanning almost all visual media, the question of subject-agency has been paramount with portrait artists, daguerreotypists and modern-day music video directors alike often claiming moral amnesty for their creation of (neo)-colonial, stereotyped images of black women due to their production with the consent and, often, the remuneration of the subject (see Williams and Willis 2002: 35, 36, 48–49). The *bande dessinée*, as one of the only forms of visual expression and narration not to use live subjects, however, finds itself exempt from this debate, with its artists, consequently, fully responsible for their created representations. Warnauts and Raives to an extent tactically side-step their accountability in exhibiting the figure of Souana throughout *Lettres d'Outremer* by specifically presenting her from the outset of the work as a female figure who chooses to be displayed. She is noted as a woman who exhibits her body and her Antillean specificity by choice to European audiences, thus surreptitiously supporting the creators' exposed depiction of her figure, the character of Jean's enjoyment of her body (Jean's supposition that Souana is a student before she corrects him also absolves him from interpretations of exploitation) and, importantly, giving the modern western reader the implicit permission to look at her displayed black form.[12] The Black Venus narrative stems from the conception of the dark-skinned female as a hypersexual being, often nude and certainly comfortable displaying her body, and Warnauts and Raives seem to add Souana to this (pre-)colonial caricatural tradition by stating in the character's first appearance in the 1996 work her willingness to display herself to the European audience.

Although, thus far, several features of Souana's representation illustrate the repetition of the Black Venus type in *Lettres d'Outremer* with no vast structural or thematic variations in depiction to *Equatoriales*'s Baligi relative to the sizable difference in temporal setting, it must be noted that in contrast to the latter text's Congolese female character, Souana is quite as talkative as the work's male characters and, further, is endowed with a certain degree of intellectual autonomy. This most clearly represented in her sporadic comments concerning post-imperial politics: for example, in the course of a short conversation with Jean, whose Republican assimilationist political outlook compels him to state of Guadeloupe, '[t]his country? But it's France'[13] (1996: 59), Souana indicates a post-colonial resistance to her dual French-Guadeloupian identity in her reply. 'This country is Guadeloupe', she responds. 'It's only "your lot" who really believe that we're in France here. You and some self-serving politicians'.[14] However, despite such brief indications of anti-colonial protest that might have served to balance *Lettres d'Outremer*'s dominantly erotic representation of Souana, her intellectual contributions to the post-imperial debate are almost entirely overshadowed by those of the male

Guadeloupian characters in the strip. Jean's journalist colleague Antoine is a resolutely militant critic of metropolitan France's role in Guadeloupe, repeating several times throughout the *bande dessinée* his strongly worded sentiments. Similarly, the figure of the psychiatrist, only fleetingly present in the story, has wise words to say about the history and progression of post-colonial protest on the island (1996: 94). Souana's political opinions in comparison seem to fluctuate in correspondence with her femininity as, for example, her maternal instincts prevail in discussing the heavy-handed French riot police: '[i]t's the climate. It makes them nervous, the poor dears'[15] (1996: 80). Warnauts and Raives do attempt to include the figure of Souana in their work's discussion of post-colonial Guadeloupe, but ultimately her role returns to that of the racialized woman – feminine and subaltern. To an extent, the creators endeavour to give their modern-day Black Venus a voice, but ultimately, this aspect of her representation is over-powered both by the male characters surrounding her, and by her dominant representation as womanly, exotic and sexually driven.

Conclusion

In the introduction to T. Deanan Sharpley-Whiting's *Black Venus: Sexualized Savages, Primal Fears and Primitive Narratives in French* the author notes that in the common imaginations of her chosen media 'black females are rendered "slaves of the idea that others have of them", slaves of their black femaleness' (1999: 10). A continuation of this conception onto the pages of Warnauts and Raives's *bandes dessinées Equatoriales* and *Lettres d'Outremer* is certainly clear following the above examination of respective characters Baligi and Souana. What is further evident from the consideration of the strips by Warnauts and Raives, however, is that the Black Venus type is not only visible within them, but the structural specificity of the *bande dessinée* medium has been used, even more so than previously noted in *La Vie de ma mère*'s depiction of types, to adapt and, in some cases, amplify her presence. As visible from the examples noted, that the medium necessarily places the Black Venus within a sequential visual narrative certainly allows her a level of identity and individuality beyond her eroticized exhibition that is more easily omitted from non-narrative art. However, the manipulation of layout, disparity of dialogue and exploitation of colour used within Warnauts and Raives's drawn strips to emphasize the sexualized exoticism of their secondary black women characters suggest the *bande dessinée* to be a potentially potent medium in the modern-day continuation of female types such as the Black Venus, which are predicated on both desire and fear, and display the inclination for containment and limitation of these particularly 'troubling' women.

9

Secondary Women in the BD New Wave: The Female Figures of *Le Combat ordinaire*

Introduction

The mid-to-late 1990s marked the beginning of a particularly interesting period in the Franco-Belgian *bande dessinée*'s (BD's) development in terms of both form and content, as well as critical acclaim and industry structure. The influence of newly emerged independent publishers eventually filtered back to the larger, established presses, carrying with it their focus on the artists, rather than their regular characters, as the stars of the industry (see p. 31 and p. 93 of this book and Beaty 2007). Manu Larcenet has emerged since this mid-1990s progression as one of the best-known and critically celebrated *bande dessinée* creators.[1] An Angoulême prize winner and author of several best-selling series (*Le Retour à la terre*, *Le Combat ordinaire*, *Blast*), his presence in the contemporary medium has been, and continues to be, sizeable.

Larcenet is also a key figure in the development of the new genre direction of the *bande dessinée*. Moving away from the established features of heroic fantasy or historical realism, a significant strand of strip creation over the last fifteen years has leant towards what Grove describes as a 'New Wave' in *bande dessinée* production, featuring 'an everyday subject matter intended to provoke reflection on the nature of our existence rather than escapism' (2010: 52; see also Chapters 1 and 4 of this book).[2] Strips from this New Wave, in addition to this introspective, quotidian focus, are often presented with humour or light-hearted satire in contrast to the grim every-day direction of urban strips like *La Vie de ma mère*.

The depiction of secondary female characters in the four-part *Le Combat ordinaire* by Larcenet will be discussed below. In this work, in contrast to those examined in the previous three chapters, the artist both presents and questions traditional female stereotypes. How he does this – and how specific features of the *bande dessinée* medium are manipulated in so doing – will be studied, showing that although the *bande dessinée* is a form that, as previously contended, has traditionally favoured stereotypes, its expressive capabilities also allow it a unique opportunity to contest the static nature of such types.

Le Combat ordinaire

Published between 2003 and 2008, *Le Combat ordinaire* was critically acclaimed, with the first tome winning the 2004 'Best Album' award at the Angoulême festival. The series follows photographer Marco (a character who bears a certain resemblance to Larcenet himself; see Simon 2008) through various formative struggles as his father dies and he meets and has a child with his partner, Emilie. Much of the narrative is punctuated by the protagonist's anguish over, and photographs of, the decline of the shipyards in which his father worked, which are eventually demolished in the last episode after a lengthy, but ultimately failed, strike. This, alongside the suicide of Marco's father following a battle with Alzheimer's and his own worries about settling down with Emilie and becoming a father himself, establishes this series as a reflection on the changing nature of masculinity in the twenty-first century – although the text makes no direct allusions to this and frames the loss of the shipyards within a discourse lamenting the demise of the traditional working class.[3] Female characters in *Le Combat ordinaire* are decidedly secondary in representative terms and always appear accompanied by a male figure – there are no instances of female-only interaction in the entirety of the four-album series. However, an examination of their depiction relative to the subtextual discourse on modern masculinity interpretable from the narrative yields noteworthy results, and reveals how traditional female stereotypes are recognized and delimited in this work.

Le Combat ordinaire presents three minor, but featured, female figures – Emilie, Marco's mother Suzanne, and Naïma, the partner of his brother 'Georges' (a nickname; his real moniker is never revealed). All three incarnate in differing ways a similar role throughout the series – that of the carer/healer. Emilie is a vet and meets Marco when he rushes, hysterical and shaking, into her surgery with his badly injured cat. Naïma is a nurse and adopts something of a maternal role towards her partner, Georges. Suzanne, Marco and Georges's mother, appears during the first two albums as the full-time carer of the boys' father, Antoine, who suffers until his suicide from degenerative dementia. Quite unusually in comparison to those *bandes dessinées* already considered in this study of secondary characters, however, despite these related roles, each woman exhibits a certain amount of individuality and, in certain cases, character evolution throughout the series: Larcenet subtly laces the comparative characterization of each with a commentary on the changing place of women in post-industrial France. This is most clearly seen in the figure of the elderly Suzanne, to whom attention shall now be turned.

Suzanne is initially presented in a manner consciously identifying her with the traditional type described by Ferguson as the 'castrating, all-powerful' (here an apt synonym might be 'overbearing') mother (see pp.100-101 of this book). As she greets Marco on the doorstep in her first appearance, wearing a blouse and apron dress, the protagonist's head is gradually covered by a speech bubble growing panel by panel while his mother immediately delivers a harangue regarding his health: '[o]oooh but you look so pale! You must not be eating properly. Ever since you were little you've had problems with food. And how's the constipation? Ooh and look you haven't shaved and your clothes are all wrinkled [...]' (Figure 9).[4] Larcenet's comically visual exaggeration of Suzanne's concerned chiding of her adult son suggests his awareness of the clichéd nature of her introduction (indeed, this initial depiction reminds readers of that of Astérix and Obélix's mothers in *Astérix et Latraviata* (see again pp.100-101 of this book). Her representation in this role continues throughout this first, kitchen-based sequence – her last words to him are '[o]h my God, I'm so worried for you'[5] (2004a: 18) – and through a subsequent phone call in which Marco struggles to find a pause in which to speak (2004a: 50). Her depiction as a traditional housewife and 'involved' mother continues into the opening of the second book as she is shown serving dinner to her husband, Marco and Emilie (here Suzanne is, again, linked to the domestic space of the kitchen), leading the conversation before being visibly stunned by the news that Emilie is actually a partner and, thus, a 'boss' in her veterinary practice (2004b: 5).

However, despite this beginning and although she appears only sporadically throughout *Le Combat ordinaire*, over the course of the series the character of Suzanne is strikingly developed beyond this traditional type. Following the suicide of her husband, Suzanne's depiction changes sartorially (she now wears trousers rather than her apron dress) and her personality changes markedly – a progression clearly seen in both sequences that feature Suzanne in the third volume. Each episode focuses on the aftermath of Antoine's death: in one, Marco helps Suzanne empty Antoine's workshop and in the next, the two sit outside to discuss the reaction of others to Antoine's decision to take his own life. Neither shows Suzanne's previously obsessive worry for Marco – indeed, this feature of her depiction is never seen again – and in both sequences, Larcenet peppers their discussions, no longer restricted to domestic, indoor spaces, with several silent panels. These dialogue-free instances serve two purposes: first, they provide a striking visual contrast to Suzanne's tongue-in-cheek introduction to the narrative, indicating a stark break with her previously typed personality to the reader. Second, they disrupt the narrative rhythm of their respective pages: their verbal emptiness gives no indication of temporal duration and thus evokes the seemingly timeless depth of Suzanne's grief.

Her final appearance of the series, in the fourth book, again shows a progression in her depiction. In this closing episode for the figure, Suzanne is characterized by her independence: she is once again shown outdoors, both defying an 'official' authority figure by painting her house shutters a bright orange in opposition to the tourist board-sanctioned 'village of character' guidelines (2009: 23), and strongly voicing her opinion to Marco on the dangers of holding on to the notion of 'roots' and 'tradition' – 'it stops us from moving forward. "Roots" are for ficuses' (2009: 24).[6] This last development in her depiction not only reinforces her evolution from the typed nature of her narrative beginnings, but also presents Suzanne as a symbol of women's changing place in the modern world. Much of *Le Combat ordinaire* focuses on the demise of the traditional male figure, represented by the dementia and death of former dockworker Antoine and the closing of the shipyards, in addition to the effects of this demise on the younger generation of men. When the reader's gaze is repositioned to focus on the minor representation of women such as Suzanne, however, a concurrent narrative showing the delimitation of the female figure beyond traditional roles and types also becomes visible.

A further, if incidental, example of the evolution of the traditional female role set against the corresponding male figure's disappearance comes a few pages after Suzanne's last appearance as Marco goes to visit his father's grave. As he lies in the grass next to Antoine's tomb an old woman approaches a nearby grave and speaks aloud to the memory of her husband, interred within. The deceased spouse is quickly identified as a man who in life held a traditionally patriarchal view of society, as his widow notes conversationally: 'there's a female candidate in the presidential elections, you know! And she has a real chance, she's not just a token woman, can you believe that?! Of course, you would have hated her [...]'[7] (2009: 30). The elderly woman's tone then quickly changes from wistfully melancholic to accusatory as she remembers her life with her husband:

> Sometimes I think about you ... where did the shy boy in his Sunday best who asked my father's permission for my hand in marriage go for all those years? Life must have knocked the stuffing out of you, run over you like a train [...] for you to turn into the idiotic, hateful and compassionless narcissist who ruined my life.
>
> (2009: 30)[8]

After this abrupt condemnation of her now-deceased husband there follows three silent panels – one in which the widow stands emotionlessly looking at her spouse's tomb, the next showing her walking away and the final image a close-up of Marco smiling to himself. Whereas in sequences featuring Suzanne following Antoine's death, Larcenet sporadically uses silent panels as a marker of the depth of her emotional shift, here they are used as an indication of finality, serving as closing punctuation for the scene. The lack of dialogue both indicates the old woman's continued reflection on her just-pronounced words and underlines the fact that no response is forthcoming – the repressive figure of patriarchy represented by her late husband is now dead. The panel simply depicting the old woman leaving the cemetery again points to the survival of the female figure, and, to an extent, the enhancement of her life, following the demise of the traditional male. Marco's presence in the final panel of the page, smiling in the empty cemetery following the old woman's sharp words, finally indicates the emotional distance of the younger male generation from this fading traditional figure.

Larcenet's depiction of the evolving female role as seen in the case, particularly, of Suzanne is not uniformly visible across all secondary women in the strip – neither Emilie nor Naima, lacking a comparably traumatic life-change, exhibit the same level of character development as Marco's mother. However, again re-directing the gaze to focus on these minor women does reveal another layer of complexity to Larcenet's subtextual commentary on women's roles in contemporary France.

Generational differences between women's roles are acknowledged early in the series. Despite her later character development, Suzanne, as noted, is surprised at the opening of the second volume that Emilie holds a management position in her veterinary practice: it is immediately established that the younger Emilie's role as a woman and as a partner to Marco is significantly different to that of Suzanne's role and position as a mother and housewife. Between Emilie and Naïma, however, two women visibly of the same generation, there also exist social differences within the narrative.

Naïma is the least-featured of the three secondary women (she is not seen at all in the fourth book, for example) but is the first female figure to appear in the series when she is briefly depicted returning home after working a nightshift in her job as a nurse to Marco and Georges's proud assertion that they too were awake all night smoking joints (2004a: 11). Emilie's introduction mid-way through the first volume is also linked to her job but, unlike Naïma, whose introduction occurs in the home, the reader's (and Marco's) first encounter with Emilie happens in a professional setting, her veterinary surgery. The physical location of the first appearances of each woman sets the scene for their characterization, as seen earlier in the case of Suzanne. Naima is quickly established as a surrogate mother figure to her partner (and to Marco, to a lesser extent): whilst throughout the first two episodes, the brothers spend their time together playing video games and smoking various substances, Naïma is sporadically present in the background of these scenes, when not out at work, washing dishes or taking care of Chahida, the daughter she has with Georges, born in the temporal gap between the first and second albums. Emilie, who immediately upon meeting Marco is placed in a role of calm authority in contrast to his fragility and distress (his cat has been injured by a neighbour's dog), often adopts a paternal role when faced with Marco's frequently impulsive and eccentric behaviour, reacting sternly and confrontationally in contrast to Naïma's maternal tolerance of male immaturity.

Both women, in addition to their respective parental roles towards their romantic partners, become mothers during the series (Emilie and Marco's daughter, Maude, is born after Chahida, between the third and final volumes of the strip). However, here also a crucial difference in their depiction appears. Whereas Emilie decides that she would like to have a baby – this desire, and Marco's resistance to it, provides a substantial portion of the sub-narrative within the first three tomes – in her second scene of the first book, Naïma simply appears six-months pregnant, a vessel for the unborn child Georges proudly refers to as his 'chef-d'œuvre' (2004a: 37). Although Naïma is, at times, shown to be outspoken – when angry after learning that Jean-Marie Le Pen has reached the second round of the 2002 French presidential elections, Naïma, of North African descent, notes that '[t]he French are so afraid for their homes that they're forgetting that it was our parents who built them'[9] (2004a: 38) – this fact, in addition to her surrogate mother role noted above, suggests Naïma to be closer than Emilie to the traditional female figure represented by the elderly Suzanne before the suicide of her husband (although Naïma appears as the positive, 'selfless' side of the mother-type division). Social class (hinted at by the difference between their respective professions) again appears as a contributing factor in the differential roles obtaining between the two younger women, as it did briefly between Suzanne and Emilie. Connected to this, Naïma's status as a second-generation Algerian immigrant may play a part in their varying characterization, with Larcenet indicating the progression of women's place in French society to be more moderate amongst those of working class and/or non-European origin.

The above contention in place, however, it must be noted at this juncture that Chahida, the baby daughter of Naïma and Georges, symbolizes quite a different female role than that of her mother. Ann Miller's analysis of the first three tomes of *Le Combat ordinaire* focuses closely on the lingering but largely repressed echoes of the Algerian war that haunt the early episodes (2007: 168–71). Speaking briefly of Chahida, Miller contends that perhaps this baby girl represents in the narrative 'the possibility of a new beginning for Franco-Algerian relations' (2007: 170). Side-stepping the post-colonial symbolism of this infant as concisely conjectured by Miller to return to the minor narrative aspect focused upon in this study – the depiction of women in the text – it can further be contended that Chahida (followed in a variant fashion by Maude, Marco and Emilie's daughter), who appears only sporadically throughout the series, represents a further striking symbol of the survival and thriving of the modern female in the face of traditional male disintegration. The clearest example of this comes in the second album, during a scene in which Marco takes care of Chahida whilst her parents go out for an evening. The standard gender relations between Georges and Naïma are re-enforced as the scene begins by the sight of the former breezing immediately out the door on his brother's arrival while Naïma stays behind to give Marco instructions for the care of their daughter. Once left alone with the baby Marco suffers a panic attack while holding her, pulling a bookcase on top of them as he collapses. Waking up in hospital beside Georges and Naïma, Marco is told that Chahida is safe with a neighbour and that when the pair returned home to find him unconscious on the floor, Chahida was sleeping unperturbed in his arms. This incident, although a decidedly minor aspect of the four-part narrative, nonetheless is important in subtly conveying the causal interconnectedness (rather than mere corollary nature) of the collapse of the traditional male figure and the surviving and flourishing of the female within the text. As already contended, Antoine's dementia becomes through the early episodes of *Le Combat ordinaire* a powerful symbol of one of the narrative's unspoken foci – the disintegration of the traditional male figure against the changing backdrop of modern life. Marco's recurring panic attacks, then, further symbolize the struggle of the younger male figure to live in modern western society without any defined patriarchal role present as in previous generations. His panic attack in this instance, during his first moments alone with Chahida and during his occupation of the traditionally 'feminine' position of the child-minder, seems to indicate a crisis not only of anxiety, but also of identity, as he is faced with this transitionally gendered role. The baby Chahida, by the fact that she remains entirely safe during a potentially dangerous occurrence, in addition to her comfort in the face of this literal male collapse – as indicated when Naïma notes she was found sleeping in Marco's arms – potentially represents a striking symbol of new-born female strength thriving as male identity struggles in the modern world and suggests that, despite its current socio-economic and racial limitations, the evolution of women's societal position continues into the new generation.[10]

It is interesting to note that within *Le Combat ordinaire*, two male deaths occur alongside the birth of the baby girls. Antoine takes his own life at the close of the second album, whilst Marco's elderly neighbour Mesribes – a further symbol of the traditional French male with an added layer of post-colonial complexity due to his questionable behaviour during the Algerian war – dies suddenly in the final tome. The two girls, Chahida and Maude, make their respective appearances within the narrative earlier in each of the albums within which Antoine and Mesribes are noted to have died. It seems to an extent that it is the arrival of these young girls, and their place as symbols of the new generation of French women, which is the final contributing factor to the demise of the equally symbolic elderly male figures.

Conclusion

When one's gaze is repositioned to concentrate on a decidedly secondary aspect of *Le Combat ordinaire* – the representation and development of the female characters – an undercurrent of this narrative depicting the progression of women in modern France from minor to major becomes visible. Rather than the shocking and sudden arrival of female dominance that is mockingly depicted in *La Rose et le glaive*, *Le Combat ordinaire* paints a slowly evolving and nuanced picture of changing female roles set against the progressive decline of traditional male authority.

Again in contrast to *Astérix* but also to *La Vie de ma mère* and the studied works of Warnauts and Raives – all narratives that rely heavily on traditional female 'types' in their characterization of secondary women – Larcenet in *Le Combat ordinaire* consciously questions the limits of female typing and, thus, the necessity of 'containing' the problematic female figure. The strip does recognize female-oriented character shorthands and makes use of them (particularly via the figure of Naïma), but also reflects on their real-world legitimacy (as contended in the comparison of Naïma and Emilie). Through the figure of the elderly Suzanne, Larcenet is most clearly able to consciously confront traditional female typing and shows how both narrative and visual elements may be combined to develop a female character clearly beyond the limits of her initial recognizable, but restrictive, outline. As noted, *Le Combat ordinaire* is one example of the 'New Wave' *bande dessinée*, a turn-of-the-millennium genre that favours introspection over action and the narrativization of daily life over adventure sagas. It is also one example of how the traditional typing and limiting of women figures may be challenged from within the medium even when such characters occupy minor roles.

SECTION 3

WOMEN CHARACTERS BY WOMEN CREATORS

10

The Women that Women Draw: An Introductory History of Female Characters Drawn by Women Artists in the Francophone *Bande Dessinée*

The history of male-developed, notable female characters in the modern *bande dessinée* (BD), as set out in the first chapter, begins in 1905 with the birth of Bécassine.[1] The chronology of female figures fully created by women artists and writers within the medium has no such identifiable starting point, however. The beginnings of this counterpart history are ambiguous for several reasons. Searching where one would expect to find examples of female creators in the early medium – within the pages of *illustrés* aimed at girls – many strips are unsigned. Those strips bearing signatures usually display names that are male or are unidentifiable as either male or female. Where female names are distinguished, often little or no information that would shed more light on the identity and œuvre of the artist is available. What does seem clear, however, is that very few women were active in the production of *bandes dessinées* for *illustrés* in the early years of the twentieth century. To take publication *Fillette* as an example, a table listing the principal BD series of the *illustré* between 1909 and 1942 in an article written for *Le Collectionneur de bandes dessinées* (2001) shows no strips that are attributed to clearly female names (Denni 2001: 26). It is possible that women drew under male pen names in order to increase their chances of publication in this very male-dominated profession. Yvonne Luce, for example, drew for *La Semaine de Suzette*, *Lisette* and *Ames Vaillantes* throughout the 1930s and 1940s under the pen-name Yves Gohanne (Frémion 2005: 47) presumably for this reason. However, the likelihood remains that women were largely uninvolved in BD production at this time. It is possible that the almost total male domination of caricature – David Kunzle has noted this art form to be a more gender-biased artistic domain even than painting (1986: 133) – remained as the *bande dessinée* developed as its off-shoot and thus discouraged women from attempting this male-associated art. Female contribution is apparent in *illustrés*, but is overwhelmingly limited to textual narratives or illustrations for stories. The early issues of *Fillette*, for example (starting from its first publication on 21 October 1909), regularly printed plays attributed to Clotilde Leclerc and a feature entitled 'La Mode de Fillette' with instructions on dressing dolls signed by 'Tante Tartalane'. Short stories also appeared signed by female names such as Clotilde Leclerc, Marie de Bosguérard and Camille Vert.

Certain exceptions to the absence of women artists in early *bandes dessinées* exist. Illustrator Collette May Pattinger, for example, occasionally drew strips for *Lisette* in the early 1920s – her first strip, a one-page narrative featuring an anthropomorphized female weasel entitled *Dame Belette, un Beau Matin*, appeared in October of 1921. However, it is not until after the Second World War that female production of *bandes dessinées* is more apparent. The Catholic girls' journal *Bernadette* featured several female contributors. Often these women continued the text or illustration pattern noted above; however, certain strip signatures attested to all-female creative teams. Regular strip *Geneviève, Bergère de Paris*, which commenced in February 1954 and recounted the young life of Geneviève, patron saint of Paris, was drawn by Manon Iessel and written by Geneviève de Corbie, whilst *La Petite Fille aux lions*, a *bande dessinée* story following the life of young orphan girl Michol in the second century AD, first appeared in October of the same year and was produced by Manon Iessel and Henriette Robitaille. A regular contributor to *Bernadette*, Henriette Robitaille teamed up with Janine Lay in 1957 to produce *Priscille et Olivier* (later renamed *Les Jumelles*) for the *illustré*, which subsequently moved to publications *Nade* and *Lisette* until its conclusion in 1974 (Lambiek 2009). Janine Lay, in turn, collaborated with Rose Dardennes in the 1960s to produce two strips: *Mirella* and *Nik*.

Although more women artists were visible in the medium from 1945 onwards, it was not until the late 1960s that a real change in the prominence of female creators in the *bande dessinée* was felt, as the radical maturation of the medium throughout the decade began to manifest in female-created strips featuring women. In 1969, Claire Bretécher produced the first notable francophone female-created strip for an older audience with the series *Cellulite*. This strip, pre-published in *Pilote*, featured the humorous exploits of the eponymous character – a princess in the Middle Ages – in her daily life and never-ending quest to find a husband. Despite the fairytale premise, Cellulite (as her comic name suggests) was far from resembling the classic princess figure of popular fables as she was variously represented as loud, moody, scatter-brained and man-crazy. Bretécher used her chosen setting to humorous effect, mixing via the figure of Cellulite both archaic customs and anachronistic behaviours concerning women. In the tale 'Symphonie en Flute Majeur' for example, Cellulite's reaction upon learning that several suitors are on their way to ask for her hand in marriage (tempted by the promise of an impressive dowry) is 'Yay! I must get my cucumber face mask on!'² (1972: 27). When considered against the social context of the strip's publication from the late 1960s onwards, the medieval/modern mixture present in Cellulite's personality and actions suggests a nod to the contemporary position of women following the sociopolitical movements of the 1960s that added new feminist ideas to traditional views of the female role in society.

Cellulite certainly presents a female character who breaks with the stereotypical women figures present up to this point in the wider developing adult-oriented *bande dessinée* (one thinks particularly of the 'Losfeld ladies': Barbarella, Pravda, Epoxy etc.); however, the strip does contain elements reminiscent of previously published strips. The influence of *Astérix* is particularly evident in the use of anachronisms for comic effect and the artist's brief, captioned narrations. The presence of René Goscinny (with whom Bretécher had collaborated to create 1963 strip *Le Facteur Rhésus*) is directly visible in the 1972 album collection *Les Etats d'âme de Cellulite*, in fact, as he provides a short prologue introducing the origins of the parodic fairytale and Claire Bretécher as its artist: 'the beautiful fairy was named Claire Bretécher and in a few strokes of her magic pencil she transformed what could have been mild and insipid into something sophisticated, appetising and incredibly hare-brained' (quoted in Bretécher: 3).³

It is interesting that this first example of a female-written, adult-oriented *bande dessinée* featuring a female character should be published with a narrative introduction not by Bretécher, its original artist, but an established male creator of the époque, not least because several years later in 1978, the first album to be published by Chantal Montellier, *1996*, would be printed with a preface by Jean-Claude Forest. The allographic preface, as Gérard Genette describes in *Seuils,* principally functions as a recommendation for the principal text: the preface contributor – usually a writer (or, in the case of the *bande dessinée*, an artist) whose reputation is more firmly established than the creator of the prefaced work, or one who is capable of adding value to it – applauds the merit of the creator and their œuvre in an attempt to encourage the reading of the work(1987, p. 246). Allographic prefaces are not overly common, Genette asserts, and it may be added here that they remain even less so in the *bande dessinée* than in literature. Both Bretécher and Montellier would go on to become common contributors to the *bande dessinée* industry over the years that followed their introductions – between 1978 and 1986, for example, there is only one identifiable year without a publication from either Bretécher or Montellier – and are undoubtedly amongst the most acclaimed female artists in the history of the medium. That the inclusion of the relatively unusual feature of an allographic preface, mediating the publication of these early works of female artists by more reputable male artists, was deemed necessary (or, at least, desirable) is indicative of the large and perhaps divergent step the introduction of these elsewhere in the contemporary medium. Depictions of these characters varied greatly between strips, however, with little evidence of female-created 'types' appearing across issues. *Ah! Nana* lasted only nine issues before publication ceased due to censorship but, during this time, it exposed international artists such as Americans Trina Robbins and Shary Flenniken to francophone audiences for the first time, thus briefly extending the visible range of female characters and artistic styles of strips featuring women figures. *Ah! Nana* also introduced several new and relatively unheard-of European female artists to the industry. Chantal Montellier, who from publishing her first strip series within the pages of *Ah! Nana* (although her first *bande dessinée* publications appeared in *Charlie mensuel* in 1974) would go on to publish three *bande dessinée* albums before the end of the 1970s.

Across the 1980s, Chantal Montellier continued her prolific *bande dessinée* production, with eleven albums published between 1980 and 1987. Displaying a *nouveau réaliste* style strikingly different to the artistry of any of her female contemporaries, Montellier consistently confronted social issues in her work. Although her œuvre at this time did not necessarily favour the depiction of female characters – her series *Andy Gang* is particularly male-populated – some strips proved prescient of the artist's later female focus. *Odile et les crocodiles* (1984; see Chapter 12), for example, follows rape victim Odile's quest for murderous revenge against a bleak urban background. In 1985, Montellier joined forces with fellow female artists Nicole Claveloux, Florence Cestac and Jeanne Puchol in penning a letter, published in *Le Monde*, which condemned certain aspects of female depiction in the contemporary *bande dessinée*. Entitled 'Navrant',[5] the letter took aim at 'this so-called new form of expression crippled by the oldest and scummiest macho fantasies'[6] in which, amongst other things, 'fetishism, sexism and infantilism'[7] were noted as rampant (Montellier et al. 2012). It is interesting to note that Montellier's cosignatories Cestac and Puchol, whose first *bande dessinée* album publications appeared at the end of the 1970s and the early 1980s respectively, and who would both go on to produce an impressive list of albums, certainly did not perpetuate the style of female depiction they criticized but largely echoed at this early point in their careers Montellier's lack of particular focus on female characters in their works.[8] This would later change for both artists.

Returning to the production of female characters by women artists, it is notable that francophone *bandes dessinées* created by and featuring women were not completely limited to European artists at this time. Congo-born Chantal de Spiegeleer created the first of the five-part *Madila* series in 1988. Set in an imaginary town named Madila Bay, de Spiegeleer's series was unusual in that it featured several black women as principal figures. Combining dramatic inter-character relationships alongside the Hollywood-reminiscent superficiality of Madila Bay to create a soap-opera-esque narrative, the stand-out aspect of de Spiegeleer's series is its bold, angular style inspired by 1980s *haute couture*, rendering this strip a particularly visually striking example of female-led *bande dessinée*.

As clear from the works noted thus far, the female characters featured in *bandes dessinées* created by women were varied in their early manifestations, with relatively few commonalities of genre, characterization or artistic style visible among them. This continued to be the case as the 1980s gave way to the last decade of the millennium and Chantal Montellier's character Julie Bristol appeared in *Fluide Glacial*. With the figure of Bristol, Montellier followed a characterization path already well-established in women drawn by male creators: that of the female investigator or mystery-solver (a trope employed in *Line, Prudence Petit-Pas* and, of course, *Les Aventures extraordinaires d'Adèle Blanc-Sec*). Unlike the *bandes dessinées* that preceded it, however, in the Julie Bristol series Montellier used the catalyst mystery and her heroine's attempt to solve it as just one layer of a complexly interwoven narrative, often evoking or replaying the lives of forgotten female artists.

The year 1995 saw the publication of the first album to be drawn collectively by four female artists and one of the first to show the complex nature of the modern woman, as Florence Cestac, Dodo, Edith and Nathalie Roques joined forces to produce *Quatre Punaises au club*. This work mixed several different styles–diary writing, illustrations and *bande dessinée* – in addition to the artistic talents of each of the four creators to tell the story of a group of women on holiday at a resort. Two general points of view are presented: one, that of a young female holiday-maker, is entirely conveyed via the text of her journal writings; whilst the other, that of the four women denoting (or at least inspired by) the artists, is represented through drawings, sporadic strips and the occasional *illustré*-inspired 'games page'. Using this unconventional mix of styles and media, *Quatre Punaises au club* portrays with humour different sides of the modern woman in opposition with one another, as the positive naivety, sensitivity and sentimentalism of the journal writer is contrasted with the pessimistic and mocking artistic reactions of the four 'artists'. This comedic work is indicative of an introspective character trend examining the different facets of modern womanhood that would become particularly apparent in the early years of the new millennium and across several genres, as will be discussed below. Cestac, a female *bande dessinée* pioneer in several senses as an early woman artist and an industry figure (founding in 1974 alongside Etienne Robial the publishing house Futuropolis) would almost immediately continue this trend in one of her next albums, *Le Démon de midi ou 'Changement d'herbage réjouit les veaux'* (1996) in which the character of Noémie, a mother-of-one, discovers that her husband is cheating on her with his secretary. Noémie would appear in 1998's *La Vie en rose ou l'Obsessionnelle poursuite du bonheur*, a funny reflection on various facets of growing up female, including menstruating in the 'pre-Tampax' era, and in two other volumes of the *Démon de midi* tryptich, *Le Démon d'aprèx-midi ...* (2005) and *Le Démon du soir ou la menopause héroique* (2013), which provide funny takes on growing older as a woman and, as the title of the latter indicates, the menopause, rendering Noémie a relatively rare example of a middle-aged female bande dessinée character. This focus on female-oriented concerns has continued beyond the character of Noémie in Cestac's works with, for example, *Des Salopes et des anges* (2011; written by Tonino Benacquista and drawn by Cestac) reflecting on the introduction of abortion in 1970s France. Cestac's distinctive rounded visual style and witty narratives have earned her particular critical success: she is, in 2018, the only woman to have won the coveted *Grand Prix* at the Angoulême festival.[9]

In the same year as Cestac's first *Démon du midi* narrative, a French-language *bande dessinée* by a Canadian female artist, Julie Doucet, was published by L'Association. Doucet had previously worked and published in the American comics industry, the influence of which was clear in 1996's *Ciboire de Criss*, rendering it stylistically and thematically different from anything as yet published by her French female counterparts. In her work, Doucet made herself the main character of a collection of eclectic strips. Combining both the personal and the surreal, Doucet autobiographically approached female bodily issues rarely represented in French-language *bandes dessinées*, with a bluntness directly inspired by US underground commix. Two years later, Doucet continued her autobiographical work with the publication of *Changements d'adresses*, a one-shot detailing three key stages in her life as a young woman and an artist. Although works featuring self-referential features by female artists (such as Cestac) appear previously in the *bande dessinée*, these strips by Doucet are the earliest examples identified during this study of a single-author, French-language, female-created autobiography: a genre that, as shall be discussed more fully below, would soon become the most clearly visible trend in female-created strips – and thus in female-created women characters – in the *bande dessinée*. By comparison, the history of American women's creation of life narrative comics, from which Doucet drew influence, significantly predated its francophone corollary, with autobiographical strips by artists such as Aline Kominsky-Crumb appearing during the underground commix movement in the 1970s.[10]

Alongside this development of the autobiographical trend towards the end of the millennium, a diverse range in characterization in works by female artists seen earlier in the 1980s and 1990s continued towards the end of the decade. The comic reflection on women's lives seen in Cestac and Doucet's work was further visible in, for example, Jeanne Puchol and Anne Baraou's two-part *Judette Camion* series, the albums published in 1998 and constituting a collection of short black-and-white *bande dessinée* narratives reflecting comically on such issues as the pain of cohabiting with a man and being a woman who does not wish to become a mother. Other works by female artists are more difficult to categorize. *Ascension*, by Belgian artist Séraphine (published in 1999), told the part-realist, part-fairytale coming-of-age story of the eponymous character, a young woman stuck in a life she hates, who dreams of flying away from her home on the beloved family sow. Although *Ascension* shares little in common with any female-focused *bande dessinée* previously noted, the album is interesting to note in this history as it shares a paratextual aspect with the earliest examples of female-created *bandes dessinées*: it features a preface by a prominent male *bande dessinée* artist, in this instance François Schuiten. Despite *Ascension*'s 1999 publication, Schuiten makes reference to the rarity of female artists in the industry and notes that when he and Séraphine met at art school to study the medium, the thought of women working as *bande dessinée* artists 'seemed fairly unimaginable' (Schuiten quoted in Séraphine 1999: 2).[11] Like the allographic prefaces of Bretécher and Montellier's work discussed above and published some twenty years previously, this male-scripted addition contributes to a delineation – and hence a certain 'minoritization' – of *bandes dessinées* created by women as belonging to an exceptional sub-category. Despite the increase in numbers of female artists in the Franco-Belgian medium from the start of the new millennium, the industry tendency to circumscribe female-created strips was identified as a particular concern of the *Charte des créatrices de bande dessinée contre le sexisme* in 2016, when they stated in their manifesto that 'women's bande dessinée is not a genre' and that 'publishing "women's" collections [of *bande dessinée*] is misogynous' (Collectif des créatrices de bande dessinée contre le sexisme 2016).[12]

Towards the end of the 1990s, certain strips emerged from women creators that took the (still) very unusual step of representing lesbian characters. The self-published, black-and-white *Les Marsouines* (1997) by Arbrelune and Jour de pluie depicted a community of exclusively gay women, and represented their relationships and often their discussions concerning their sexuality. A very different tone was struck by the colourful *Lucie* series, which began in 1999 from the collaborative efforts of Catel and Veronique Grisseaux. Following the rise of *bandes dessinées* depicting the 'everyday' seen elsewhere in the medium towards the end of the 1990s onwards, the four *Lucie* albums were another early examples of a semi-comedic series focusing on the exploits of a modern woman in her day-to-day life, and happened to sporadically feature homosexual female secondary characters.[13] The exceptional nature of these strips underlines and echoes the lack of lesbian characterization in the wider *bande dessinée* medium of the late twentieth and very early twenty-first centuries, something that would begin to change towards the end of the 2000s with the publication and rapid translation into French of Alison Bechdel's *Fun Home* in 2006, the appearance of Lisa Mandel's *Princesse aime princesse* (2008), the series *La P'tite Blan* (from 2009) by Blan and Galou, and, particularly, the publication of Julie Maroh's acclaimed *Le Bleu est une couleur chaude* in 2010. Minne suggests that the development of representations of homosexual characters (both male and female) in the Franco-Belgian *bande dessinée* has, in a sense, been inhibited by the association of such depictions with publications from other graphic novel markets, notably Japan (he notes particularly the presence of homosexuality in manga genres *shonen-ai* (boys' love), *yaoi* (erotic) and *shojo-ai* and *yuri* (both of the latter showing relationships between young women) (2010: 175). Interestingly, Groensteen (2014) also cites the growing popularity of manga in the Franco-Belgian market through the 1990s and, in particular, the 2000s as one of two clear reasons for the rise in the number of women artists beginning their *bande dessinée* careers at this time, indicating the particular importance of the popularity of *shojo* (for girls) manga, which was almost exclusively drawn by women artists and appears to have inspired young francophone female artists to develop their interest in the *bande dessinée* beyond readership and into creation.

The second notable reason for the influx of women artists to the *bande dessinée* industry following the turn of the millennium indicated by Groensteen is the success of Marjane Satrapi's *Persepolis*. Published in four instalments between 2000 and 2003, this autobiographical work chronicled the childhood of Iranian Satrapi during the Islamic Revolution and her difficult adolescence split between Austria and Tehran, in a strip combining comedy, tragedy and a feminist critique of the consequences of the aforementioned Revolution. The extent of the success of this *bande dessinée* (and its later cinematographic adaptation of the same name [2007]), both in the francophone market and worldwide, increased the visibility of female-created *bandes dessinées* and, in Groensteen's words, 'seems to have "allowed" other young women from across the world to express themselves via the drawn strip'.[14] Within the Franco-Belgian medium, the vogue for autobiographical creations, begun most clearly in the 1990s by artists such as Fabrice Neaud and David B., then developed by Julie Doucet to include reflections on specifically female experience towards the end of this decade and, finally, rendered internationally visible by Satrapi in the early 2000s, attracted several new female artists. Johanna's *Née quelque part* (2004), Dominique Goblet's *Faire semblant c'est mentir* (2007) and Zeina Abirached's *Le Jeu des hirondelles: Mourir, partir, revenir* (2007) are three strips that, via a detailed and artistically varied recounting of the artist's personal life experiences, contribute complex, un-sexualized and intimate (self-)portraits of womanhood to the medium. Aurélia Aurita's autobiographical *Fraise et chocolat* (2006) specifically confronted the question of women's sexualization in the *bande dessinée*, presenting a humorous and uneroticized account of a sexual relationship with another artist. This work will be analysed fully in Chapter 13.

By virtue of its self-representative nature (Aurita is French of Chinese-Cambodian origin), *Fraise et chocolat* is a rare example of a *bande dessinée* representing a female figure of Asian descent, the female-created medium as much as its male counterpart remaining during the 2000s, in spite of the arrival of some artists from outside of France and Belgium, heavily weighted towards characters of white European origin. One strip that defied this lasting trend was the *Aya de Yopougon* series by Marguerite Abouet and Clement Oubrerie. Script-writer Abouet, who has repeatedly noted Satrapi to be a key influence, combined a fictional story within a physical setting based on her own experience to create the world of principal character Aya, a young Ivoirian woman living in the city of Abidjan during the 1970s. This strip, which, via the contrast of studious Aya with her less professionally driven female acquaintances, illustrated a variety of facets of young womanhood, has become the most recognized *bande dessinée* featuring characters of African origin of the contemporary medium (its later adaptation into a film [2013] cementing this position); as indicated, however, it remains largely exceptional in this regard.

At the very end of the period studied in this book (1905–2008), as the autobiographical *bande dessinée* developed presenting an opportunity for the diversification of female characterization beyond the stereotyped norms so often associated with the medium, a corresponding sub-genre drawn by women artists also developed, which, to some, threatened to confirm traditionally held views about women's lives and interests. The development of *bande dessinée girly* ('chick-BD') in fact appeared from a confluence of factors: the growing interest in, and success of, graphic life-narratives by women, but also the vogue for 'chick-lit' novels from the mid-1990s onwards and the growing importance of the Internet blog for, particularly, the unpublished *bande dessinée* creator. Strips associated with this genre often related anecdotes from the daily lives of the artists that portrayed a heavily stereotyped comedic notion of the modern woman's existence, centred around shopping, diet or dating woes. Popular artists whose work emerged in this context and following this pattern were Penelope Bagieu, Margaux Motin and Diglee, whose first non-virtual *bande dessinée* publications were album collections of humorous strips featuring themselves as central characters (*Ma Vie est tout à fait fascinante* [2008], *J'aurais adoré être ethnologue* [2009] and *Autobiographie d'une fille gaga* [2010] respectively) adapted from regular blog posts. Since its appearance, this genre and its outputs have been criticized – artist Tanxxx famously and virulently critiqued its representation of women and the *bande dessinée* industry's eagerness to publish it in a 2011 blog post – as has the name attached to it: the charter of the *Créatrices de bande dessinée contre le sexisme* movement states that 'the appellation "girly" only reinforces sexist clichés'.[15] As the emergence of this genre lies largely outside the temporal scope of this study, these issues will not be fully studied here. What is interesting about the advent of 'girly' *bande dessinée*, however, are the questions this genre raises about the kind of female imagery regularly published within the modern industry and the responsibilities that women artists may be perceived to have in combating the dominant stereotypes of female figures that persist in the medium.

Over the history of women's creative involvement in the medium from the early 1900s as laid out here, female figures drawn by women appear largely to defy categorization and certainly no 'female aesthetic' is visible. Throughout the twentieth century, women artists have shown themselves, on the whole, to be more likely to represent female figures – this is particularly true of the late 1990s and through the 2000s – however, there are certain periods (the early careers in the 1980s of certain women artists who would go on to become the most female-focused *bande dessinée* creators, for example) during which this is less noticeable. Compared to their male counterparts, women artists also show themselves to be significantly less likely to create sexualized female characters, although, again, some artists, such as Annie Goetzinger, do produce traditionally eroticized depictions. Otherwise, the representation of women characters of colour is as scarce in female-created *bandes dessinées* as it is in the wider medium and lesbian figures are a distinct minority amongst female characters created by women – although the frequency of depiction of homosexual figures appears to be increasing, pointing to a mitigated, gradual diversification of women characters in the medium. The last ten years studied in this history has shown both a marked increase in the number of female artists publishing *bandes dessinées* and the emergence of certain trends within their depictions, notably in the domain of autobiography and comic depictions of modern womanhood (two trends that often overlap).

With such variation across much of the history of representations of women drawn by women, then, it is imperative to analyse closely specific examples of female characters by women artists in order to ascertain more fully if, and how, such figures may differ from the characters previously assessed in this book and to consider how women artists may conform to, or, indeed, use the *bande dessinée* medium to challenge, the notion of the 'problematic female'. The following chapters undertake this task.

11

The Rise and Fall of *Ah! Nana*: France's First and Only All-Female *illustré*

Introduction

As the foregoing historical account attests, the process of female integration into *bande dessinée* (BD) creation in the twentieth century was slow, with women linked to this domain much more likely to inhabit the role of writer or illustrator, and particularly for children's audiences. In the late 1970s, however, as Bretécher and Goetzinger made their mark as pioneering female creators in the medium, a new publication appeared with the potential to expedite the slow integration of women artists into the BD, providing an unprecedented vehicle both for semi-established and previously unpublished women artists to present their work. The journal *Ah! Nana* did not fulfil this potential, however, and after falling foul of strict censorship laws and the restrictive economic sanctions that accompanied them, folded after only nine issues.

Ah! Nana was certainly short-lived, producing its first issue in October 1976 and its last in September 1978. However, as the only journal in French history created entirely by women featuring regular *bandes dessinées* (although male artists were also occasionally invited to contribute) it constitutes an interesting experiment in the development of the adult francophone *bande dessinée*. In spite of this, it has, like so many other female-led artistic endeavours, been largely ignored in chronologies and encyclopaedias of the medium. Patrick Gaumer's 2004 *Larousse de la BD* does not mention *Ah! Nana* at all, whilst the 2003 *BD Guide* devotes one short paragraph of its 1525 pages to the journal, simply noting its creation by women, the name of its editor Janic Dionnet, and the fact that it was eventually censored.[1]

Although also often absent from standard non-encyclopaedic texts studying the *bande dessinée*, *Ah! Nana* has occasionally been a focus of scholarship: two articles published in 2006, for example, by Blanche Delaborde and Virgine Talet respectively, consider the publication, concentrating on its creation, publication history and censorship.² Each article constitutes a valuable source of information on the *illustré*, but close analysis of the *bandes dessinées* present in the periodical is not part of their scope.

In order to consider how women were represented in early examples of female-crafted adult *bande dessinée* this chapter will consider the *bande dessinée* content of this pioneering but under-recognized journal. Following a brief introduction and contextualization of *Ah! Nana* drawing on the work of Delaborde and Talet, this chapter will add a new focus to the existing study of the feminist *illustré*, analysing selected strips from the entirety of *Ah! Nana*'s nine-issue print-run and closely focusing on the representation of women therein.³

Ah! Nana 1976–78

The first issue of *Ah! Nana* was published in October 1976 and featured 66 pages of *bandes dessinées*, culturally focused articles and reviews, and occasional short stories. Its first editorial, presumably written by editor-in-chief Janic Guillerez but humorously signed 'Edith Orial', described the conception of this new publication in the following way: '[a] group of female artists, colourists and journalists was complaining to each other about having to include male fantasies, presented as the key to successful publishing, in our work. We decided to act, sketching out the idea of a journal [...] Entirely unconvinced, the publisher Les Humanoïdes offered their printer. Thanks, I suppose' (Orial 1976).⁴

The first two issues of *Ah! Nana* contained articles and strips on widely varying subject matter with the sole commonality being their creation by women writers and artists. From the third issue onwards, however, themes were introduced to each publication attributing a common thread to at least part of its content. Beginning with the provocative title of 'Nazisme aujourd'hui'⁵ in issue three, these themes moved on to discuss 'La Mode démodée' ⁶ and 'Hommes'⁷ in the following publications before developing more sexualized content in the last four issues with 'Le Sexe et les petites filles', 'La France cruelle', 'Homosexualité, Transsexualité' and 'L'Inceste'.⁸

Despite these themes featuring boldly on the front cover of each issue, informing its illustration and taking pride of place in the following editorial, in each publication only about ten of its standard 66 pages were devoted to textual evocations of the chosen subject. Other regular features made up the remainder of the journalistic portion of *Ah! Nana*, such as the 'Gazette', an artistic round-up featuring reviews of cinema, theatre and literature, often with a focus on female-produced work; a regular opinion piece by female film director Sotha; and, in the latter issues, 'Feminiscope', a page featuring facts and news items concerning the current state of the feminist movement.

The *bandes dessinées* present in *Ah! Nana*, as will be discussed more fully below, did not follow even this imprecise thematic structuring adhered to by the textual content. In certain issues, some strips conformed to the theme announced on the cover, although most did not. Furthermore, whilst some artists at times used the journal to publish *bandes dessinées* with a feminist focus, the current of the women's movement of the time was much less apparent amongst the artistic content as a whole than it was in the textual features.

It is interesting to note that just as the *bande dessinée* content did not mirror the journalistic material in the publication, *Ah! Nana*'s articles and cultural 'Gazette' seldom included references to, or reviews of, the *bande dessinée* medium. As a pioneering journal in the francophone tradition for the dissemination of female-created *bandes dessinées*, and a journal that dedicated a significant page-ratio to examples of the medium, *Ah! Nana* might have proved a natural vehicle for theoretical discussions of female-created sequential art, but textual elaborations on the nature of the medium and its relation to women were largely avoided (Delaborde 2005: 73). The 'Gazette' featured only two reviews of *bande dessinée* albums throughout its nine-issue run, with short columns on Annie Goetzinger's *Légende et réalité de Casque d'Or* and Bretécher's *Les Frustrés* (*vol. 2*) both in the second issue. A very short column in all but the eighth issue written by Pierre Couperie (the only regular male contributor, present from the journal's beginning) also briefly elucidated biographical details about a chosen female artist under the title 'Histoire de la BD féminine'. Elsewhere in *Ah! Nana*'s textual content the *bande dessinée* was considered only once more, in an opinion piece as part of the eighth issue's theme of 'La France cruelle', entitled 'Les Dessinateurs de bandes dessinées sadomasochistes: Une bande d'impuissants?'[9]: an article strongly criticizing the representation of women in male-created strips featuring sado-masochist themes. In an interview concerning *Ah! Nana*, Janic Guillerez noted in 2005 that it was her decision as editor-in-chief to separate the journalistic and artistic aspects of the publication in order to make *Ah! Nana*, unlike its contemporary publications such as *Métal Hurlant*, a 'magazine' rather than a *bande dessinée* periodical (Delaborde 2005: 17).

Despite Guillerez's intentions to differentiate *Ah! Nana* from the other journals around it, it was nonetheless undeniably linked to the *bande dessinée* industry of its day and particularly to *Métal Hurlant*. Published by Les Humanoïdes Associés, a company instigated by the creators of *Métal Hurlant*, several of *Ah! Nana*'s editorial team were professionally or personally linked to the sci-fi journal.[10] The creation of *Ah! Nana* was announced in the editorial of *Métal Hurlant*'s September 1976 issue, alongside the announcement of a sanction that would also eventually befall the all-female journal, but for quite a different reason. Indeed, *Métal Hurlant* had been issued a ban forbidding its sale to minors due to its degrading representation of women: the *Commission de contrôle et de surveillance* specifically condemned 'the explicit and immediately obvious agenda of dehumanising content, only directed at women, who are depicted as objects'[11] (quoted in Delaborde 2006: 68). The consequences of a 'censored for minors' label were economically serious for a journal as such publications were subsequently banned from advertising anywhere that was likely to be seen by children and were removed from the shelves of airport, train and metro kiosks, resulting in an immediate loss of approximately thirty per cent of any revenue (Delaborde 2005: 44).

Although the editors of *Métal Hurlant* eventually succeeded in overturning the ban they had received, when, in August 1978, *Ah! Nana* fell foul of the same fate it proved a fatal blow for the fledgling feminist journal. No clear reason was given by the Commission for the imposed censorship, but a note to the reader printed on the inside cover of the ninth and final issue of *Ah! Nana* clearly suggested that a sexist attitude to female expression was the cause. This editorial began with a large illustration, drawn by Chantal Montellier, of a young woman wearing a 'Rosie the Riveter' tee-shirt, standing beside the group of men from Montellier's *Andy Gang* strip, which appeared in each instalment of *Ah! Nana*.[12] As the woman, frowning directly at the reader, begins 'Ah! Nana – the only *bande dessinée* journal made by women!', the group of men reply, smiling directly at her: 'Forbidden by men!!!'.[13] The text below (signed by Carine Lenfant) explains the bitter tone of the sketch, noting the seriousness of such a severe economic sanction for the journal: '*Ah! Nana* will die ... Censorship wins once again. Surrounded by nudie magazines, we fall'[14] (Lenfant 1978). Of the reason behind the censorship, the text goes on to cite the provocative nature of the journal's chosen content – particularly the specific themes for each issue: '[w]e don't often see women being so direct and outspoken. The often vengeful and iconoclastic tone of our drawings and texts was what earned us this punishment'[15] (Lenfant 1978). Whatever the official reason for the censorship, no attempt to assuage the censors was made by the editorial team of *Ah! Nana*, who went on to consecrate the rest of this issue to the theme of 'incest', with a cover image of three girls dressed in short, bow-adorned dresses, each holding a sash over the top of their bare legs that together read 'Happy Father's Day'.[16] This cover, shocking in its representation of three young women apparently presenting themselves as sexual gifts to their fathers (any ambiguity removed by the bold-print presence of the issue title, 'l'Inceste', over the middle character's body), was *Ah! Nana*'s last.

Ah! Nana *and bandes dessinées*

Whilst a limited amount of consistency was discernible from the textual elements of *Ah! Nana* in terms of adhering to the theme of each issue and illustrating general feminist concerns, as indicated above, the *bande dessinée* content of the journal was much more varied and without even a general focus.

Presenting itself from the first editorial as a very 'cosmopolitan' publication, which would feature female artists from the United States to Italy and, of course, France, the ethos of *Ah! Nana* seemed to be the inclusion of as many women artists as possible, as it concluded the inaugural message to its readership with a call to artistic arms: '[d]on't be surprised to find so many female artists together in the same place. We have officially counted fifty in France but we're sure there must be more of you out there. Ladies, we're waiting for you' (Orial 1976).[17]

Throughout the nine issues of the journal, *Ah! Nana* certainly featured strips by scores of artists, with an integrated mix of (relatively) established names such as Trina Robbins, Shary Flenniken, Florence Cestac and Nicole Claveloux and less well-known or previously unpublished female artists such as Chantal Montellier, Aline Isserman or Cecilia Capuana.[18] While most of the former are still recognizable names from the *bande dessinée* industry, several names of the latter category that appeared only once or twice have since fallen into obscurity and little (if any) information is available concerning their contributions to the journal or their later work.

As to be expected in a publication hosting such a diverse international company of artists, the styles of the *bandes dessinées* present in *Ah! Nana* varied widely. One generalized difference was evident between the work by American artists and that of their European counterparts. Trina Robbins, Shary Flenniken, Sharon Rudhal and Mary Kay Brown were the four artists that made up the US contribution to the journal. All had links with the American underground commix movement, which influenced both their rounded, cartoony styles and the distinct mixture apparent in their strips of classic comic gags and, particularly in the case of Robbins (the most regularly appearing of the four US contributors), nudity and explicitly sexual scenes. It should be noted that the work that appeared in *Ah! Nana* from all four artists was originally intended for an American audience, as each submitted translated material to the journal that had already been published in the United States (Delaborde 2005: 29).

Bandes dessinées provided by European artists were very different to those drawn by their American colleagues. Most were created specifically for *Ah! Nana* and despite adhering to no fixed style or theme, contained common traits that set them squarely within the context of the contemporary francophone adult *bande dessinée* vogue, led in the late 1970s by *Métal Hurlant*. In contrast to the US-imported strips, these *bandes dessinées* were much less likely to have a linear narrative and often combined realistically-drawn characters and surroundings with fantastical, surrealist or science-fiction themes.

The *bandes dessinées* of *Ah! Nana* as a whole certainly featured female characters most prominently; however, considering the strips collectively, no significantly-recurring trends of female representation are apparent in these early creations by women artists. This lack of cohesion constitutes in itself a break with tradition in the *bande dessinée* medium which, as previously noted, often restricted women to typed and/or hyper-sexualized roles. However, the depiction of women characters in the journal overall was not noticeably 'positive' in response to this enduring depiction of *bande dessinée* women elsewhere, despite certain strips – but by no means a majority – featuring feminist themes (some examples are analysed below). An example of the range of non-traditional but negative depictions of women characters is identifiable from the collection of strips featuring mother figures throughout the nine issues. Although the depictions of mothers varied beyond the overbearing/angelic dyad identified by Ferguson, and, in this way, may be considered an innovative contribution to female depiction in the *bande dessinée*, over the course of the journal's life span these maternal characters were variously depicted as sadistic (see Nicole Claveloux's strips in *Ah! Nana* (nos. 1 & 3)), uncaring (see Marie Ange Le Rochais's strip in *Ah! Nana* (no. 9)) and even cannibalistic (see Cecilia Capuana's strip in *Ah! Nana* (no. 8)).

Additionally, despite the notable variety in female characters and the genres through which they were depicted, little diversity is evident in the racial and sexual identities of the women portrayed. Although *Ah! Nana* consecrated an issue to the theme of homo- and transsexuality, the publication as a whole prefigured the landscape of the future female-created medium by featuring no lesbian presence in any strip throughout the entirety of its print-run. Women characters of colour were also almost non-existent, with only Trina Robbins depicting black characters, most noticeably in the recurring figure of African-American high-class prostitute/drug dealer/war-time double-agent Lulu (*Ah! Nana* nos. 3 & 5).

As evident from the above findings, *Ah! Nana*'s artistic goal was clearly to provide a platform for women *bande dessinée* creators to publish their work and not necessarily, despite the indications of the first editorial and its expressed frustrations with male-oriented content, to present positive female characters or feminist-inspired narratives to combat the dominant depiction of women figures prevalent in the medium at the time. A small percentage of strips did use the journal to disseminate such characters or themes, however, and as such were unique in the history of the medium up until this point. The following section will closely examine a selection of these strips, considering the representation of women in the first feminist *bandes dessinées* of the adult medium.

Ah! Nana, Bandes Dessinées and the First Feminist Focus on Women

Although the advent of second-wave feminism in France and the creation of the Women's Liberation Movement (MLF) had resulted in a series of important victories for women's rights in the years preceding the publication of *Ah! Nana*,[19] most of the strips interpretable as feminist throughout the publication's nine issues depicted women as victims of violence, misogynistic traditions or societal expectations. As will become evident, however, the role of 'the victim' was interpreted in widely varying ways to disseminate each strip's message.

La Conasse et Le Prince Charmant *by Nicole Claveloux* (Ah! Nana [*no.* 2])

This five-page strip was one of the first in *Ah! Nana* to present a commentary on women in contemporary society, and did so by mixing one of Claveloux's signature bulbous-styled, fantastical settings with an exaggeratedly-clichéd female character in order to present a sarcastic reflection on women's traditional romantic expectations to the female readership of the journal.

Beginning with two strips of huge, elongated panels and featuring a tiny cherub figure as narrator, this strip commences by visually charting the growth of the principal figure – known only as 'La Conasse' (silly cow) – as she grows from baby to middle-aged woman (1977: 27). Above her illustration as an infant, the cherub-narrator opens the narrative by telling the reader that La Conasse had known, ever since she was very young, that she would meet her prince charming, before announcing over each subsequent image of her growth that she was waiting for him 'patiently', 'tenaciously', 'still' and 'continually' (1977: 28).[20] As La Conasse decides to go out to look for this overdue prince charming, a third page of smaller, overlapping panels is presented, the change in layout from the consistent, structured panels of the introduction to this page of superimposed, non-linear panels emphasizing the panic and desperation also clear in the words and thoughts of La Conasse, ranging from '[b]ut this prince charming has got to be somewhere, surely!'[21] to 'I can't see anything coming'[22] and finishing by '[s]till nothing! I'm starting to get discouraged now'[23] (Figure 10).

Overleaf, for the final two strips of the tale, the narrative jumps forward in time and the reader sees the La Conasse alone at home, lighting the candles for her 95th birthday. Large, heavily shaded panels show the curmudgeonly old woman, all good humour apparent from earlier scenes dissipated, thinking to herself as an old man appears at the door: '[s]omeone's always bothering me! ... Well I'm definitely not sharing my cake!'[24] (1977: 30). Learning in the final page that this elderly man is her prince charming finally arrived, the shock proves too much for La Conasse, who collapses and dies on the spot, the strip concluding with the image of the nonagenarian 'prince' looking in surprise and confusion at her lifeless form.

A short strip with fantastical elements – such as the cherub-narrator or the counterpart little devil figure who appears by La Conasse's side as she starts to lose hope, whispering discouraging thoughts to her – Claveloux's contribution to the second issue of *Ah! Nana* nonetheless presents a contemporary feminist message to the journal's readers. As an ironic take on the standard fairytale narrative which suggests that women wait in the hope of being found by their ideal man after which they will live happily ever after, the clichéd central character is presented as a willing victim of this passive and restrictive paradigm in her initially blind, exaggerated faith in it. Named 'La Conasse', she is unequivocally and humorously represented from the title onwards as particularly stupid and, despite her principal role, the fool of the narrative. The ironic circumstances surrounding her death point to the conclusion that an uncritical adherence to the traditional notion that the goal of a woman's life is to meet and marry her ideal man is a waste of female potential and happiness.

Untitled Strip *by Cecilia (Back Cover*, Ah! Nana [*no. 6*])

The critical feminist view of contemporary woman as willing victim, or to varying degrees complicit in her own disenfranchisement, appears in other strips throughout *Ah! Nana*'s nine issues in varying ways. A short six-panel strip by Italian artist Cecilia Capuana, signed simply 'Cecilia', which closed the sixth issue of the journal on its back page certainly depicts this feminist trope (Figure 11). Unlike Claveloux in the above strip who used irony, clichéd exaggeration and a manipulated layout to transmit her message with humour, however, Cecilia's brief strip disseminates its meaning via the use of contrasting colours and a shocking visual conclusion.

Presented as a set of instructions on how to apply make-up, this strip begins with a long, horizontal panel featuring a dressing table full of pink and purple beauty products against a jet-black background (colour is exceptionally present in this strip as it occupies the back cover of the publication; all content within *Ah! Nana* issues was printed in black and white). A woman's face is visible in the dressing-table mirror, her reflection showing a maniacally gleeful expression as she contemplates the pots and vials before her, her hands raised to seize them. Following this introductory image, the remaining two strips of the page are divided into panels, each showing the woman at different stages in her make-up application with instructions in the caption below explaining them. Following four fairly innocuous images of mouthwash, foundation, eye shadow and lipstick appliance, each focusing on close-up fragments of the features, the strip finishes with a full view of the woman's face. As the caption states '[s]tep 5: Lightly highlight cheeks with razor blade. Blend ...'[25] (Capuana 1977b), the woman is shown smiling as she draws a razor blade across her face, causing blood to pour from her cheeks. A visually shocking comment on the lengths to which women accept to go to conform to artificial notions of beauty and the masochism involved in maintaining these 'standards', the final panel of this short *bande dessinée* presents its female character as a willing victim of this anti-feminist societal practice, smiling as she cuts into her face supposedly to improve her appearance. The colour clash throughout of the black background and gutter space with the pastels of the make-up add to the woman's incongruous glee in this last image and manic expression in the first panel to lend a dark, dystopian atmosphere to the strip. A work critical of female complicity in those societal trends that ultimately contribute to women's repression, not unlike the Claveloux strip discussed above, its artist Cecilia also eschews humour to heighten the shocking self-harm of the woman's actions by contrasting the 'normality' of this figure's initial make-up application, emphasized as 'routine' via the accompanying generic textual instructions and very familiar to the contemporary female readership, with the smiling, self-imposed violence of the final image.

Une Histoire exemplaire *by Mona* (Ah! Nana [*no. 4*])

Whilst both strips discussed thus far representing the feminist *bande dessinée* content of *Ah! Nana* negatively present their principal female characters, using their depicted stupidity or self-harm to criticize women's own involvement in continuing female societal disenfranchisement, not all *bandes dessinées* representing women as victims were so uncompromisingly critical.

Artist Mona's contribution to the fourth issue of *Ah! Nana* is a four-page strip, rare for the journal in its thematic conformation to the chosen theme for the issue: fashion.[26] Featuring a mix of human and fantastical beings to create a world not unlike that of *Alice in Wonderland*, this short strip, presented as a play in two short 'acts' followed by an epilogue, recounts the tale of a girl who, after falling and hurting herself whilst wearing dangerously high heels, is raped by a passing man while watched by an excited rabbit and two small creatures representing a priest and a nun.

The story begins with the girl naked and masturbating in bed on a stage framed by billowy curtains, watched by the rabbit, the priest and the nun (1977b: 89). The latter figures, respectively representative of three figures of misogynistic society – the sexist male (embodied by the rabbit), the religion that restricts women (the priest) and the traditional woman who fears the empowerment of the modern female (represented by the nun) – are varyingly horrified as they look on, with the rabbit announcing the girl to be a 'tart',[27] the priest claiming she is possessed, and the nun fainting from shock.

Deciding she must get out of bed to start her day, the woman then dresses, putting on a blouse, tight pencil skirt and knee-length high-heeled boots: an outfit that is praised by her trio of onlookers, particularly by the nun figure, who announces to the reader her relief that she's dressed decently like a proper lady (1977b: 90). Her clothes prove too restrictive, however, and the woman falls hard as she tries to rush in her tight belt and high heels. Overleaf as 'Act II' begins, the creatures look on as the injured woman, spotting a passer-by, calls out to the man for help. The latter agrees to come over, but immediately starts to take off his trousers as he approaches her, much to the woman's surprise and the rabbit's indignant exclamation that this strange action is the fault of the woman: '[t]he tart, look what she's making him do'.[28] In the final panel of this strip, also the final panel of the narrative proper, the man rapes the woman as she cries for help. Whilst the priest looks away in horror, announcing that the woman is 'un démon', the rabbit looks on eagerly, exclaiming 'she's coming, she's coming',[29] and the nun once again collapses from shock (1977b, 91).

Overleaf, the curtains on the stage have been drawn and a female clown-figure appears before them to explain the moral of this *bande dessinée*-play: '[a]nd there you have it, friends, the sad cautionary tale of Angelique [...] perched on high heels, strapped in to skirts, paralysed by our belts, bras and corsets, fashion ties us up and hands us to our attackers'[30] (1977b: 92). Pushing the three fantastical creatures off the stage as from their position in the wings the priest cries '[o]h! It's the MLF! Don't look, Sister Immaculate, the pope has forbidden it!',[31] the clown-figure calls to a group of naked women who have suddenly appeared on the stage, each criticizing herself for not conforming to beauty or fashion ideals, '[l]ove yourselves, girls. Everyone else, out'.[32] The final panel of this strip shows the clown alone and leaping across the empty stage, concluding her message with a gag: '[a]nd remember, to be able to run and jump is to come for a good time!'[33] (1977b: 92).

Whilst the strips discussed above present their female characters as complicit in their own victimization and, thus, accountable for the suffering they incur, this *bande dessinée* depicts its female principal figure not as responsible for her attack (although she is considered as such by misogynist others) but unable to remove herself from the position of 'victim' because of her compliance with female-focused societal expectations – in this case linked to fashion. The clown-figure's frank explanation of the narrative's moral for the audience/reader and the priest's designation of the former as 'le MLF' make this strip perhaps the most outspokenly feminist artistic contribution to *Ah! Nana*'s nine issues. Its message to women not to hinder or even endanger themselves in restrictive clothing is directly stated, and an implicit criticism of those who consider that a woman's sartorial choice may render her in some way 'responsible' for being raped is also present (most notably via the priest's reaction to the attack and the rapist's description of his victim as a 'tease'). In addition, the appearance of the insecure, naked women on stage in the penultimate image, the central figure amongst whom is shown peering closely at a copy of *Elle* magazine, implies a critique of the 'feminine media' in the creation of such insecurities, whilst the figures of the priest and the nun implicate Catholicism's role in the restriction both of women's political empowerment and (re-)connection to their bodies.[34] Clearly, the layering of textual, visual and stereotyped symbolism is used to continual effect to transmit the artist's message throughout this four-page strip.

It is interesting to note that although *Ah! Nana* by no means predominantly presented feminist *bandes dessinées*, the depiction of rape present in Mona's work noted above was not the only invocation of this crime, with several references appearing throughout the journal's print-run. Whilst the rape in *Une Histoire exemplaire* was depicted to indicate an extreme and violent consequence of women's conformation to restrictive societal demands, other strips, such as Clodine et Fèvre's *Fantasme et Réalité* (*Ah! Nana* [no. 8]), made the shocking violence of this predominantly female-directed crime, and the effect on women as helpless victims of it, their focus.

Although the feminist *bande dessinée* content of *Ah! Nana* reflected that of the wider artistic presence in the journal in its variation of themes and styles, from the three strips discussed above, it is clear that the figure of the woman as victim of gender-biased traditions and practices was used as a repeated trope via which to disseminate a feminist message. Although some strips in *Ah! Nana* presented their female victims purely as innocent sufferers of either figurative or literal violence against women, such as Clodine and Fèvre's *bande dessinée* noted above, the three short strips chosen for closer analysis in this study indicate an exploration of the idea of women as victims in more ambiguous and hence more complex ways. A critical dimension was often incorporated into the characters' representations – particularly in the case of Cecilia and Claveloux's work – which implied the complicity of women in certain situations in their own victimization.

It is important to note, however, that not all feminist-focused *bandes dessinées* in *Ah! Nana*'s nine issues presented women as victims. In addition to one or two that satirized the societal fear of the 'feminist' as a Maestria-like brash and vicious hater of men – such as Florence Cestac's unnamed one-page strip in *Ah! Nana* (no.4), which showed a towering and broad-shouldered woman, naked except for a pair of high-heeled boots, terrorizing a cartoon penis with a whip and forcing it to jump through a hoop – a small minority focused on women as strong and positive figures who challenge the misogynistic bias of society. One such strip, drawn by Cecilia Capuana, is discussed below.

Visite inattendue *by Cecilia Capuana* Ah! Nana (*no. 3*)

This strip, relatively long for *Ah! Nana* at ten pages, is drawn in Capuana's standard style of large detail-laden, semi-realist panels, with layers of visual symbolism used to disseminate her feminist message. It begins with several images of four elderly people – two women in dresses and two men in three-piece suits – having tea (1977a: 18). A long, narrow panel of a chest of drawers laden with old photographs and a ticking clock, featuring speech-bubbles bearing expressions such as 'in my day' and 'as time passes',[35] emphasizes the age of these figures and the time they have spent sitting quietly in their comfortably opulent surroundings. A doorbell suddenly rings and several panels follow depicting the shocked and wary figures, clutching guns and knives, making their way down long corridors and staircases towards the door (1977a: 20). At first believing no one is there, the four are suddenly aghast at the appearance of a young woman, shown reflected in a grandly framed mirror. This first representation of Capuana's heroine is couched in metaphor as her reflection, fragmented by the mirror's division into several panels, is depicted next to two white lilies that have been placed in front of the glass but are not reflected within it – this incongruity separating the image of the girl from the virginal and virtuous symbolism of the chosen flowers. Overleaf, an elongated vertical panel shows a full-length view of the young woman, naked and holding a bag from which the head of a snake is seen extending itself. As the four elderly figures stand horrified before her in the following panels, this Eve-inspired woman states 'I finally found you after all this time hiding behind your traditions. But I'm not so easy to exorcise!'[36] (1977a: 22), before the elderly figures riposte furiously on the opposite page (1977a: 23), the final panel of which depicts them as slight and decrepit, with one figure visible through the parted legs of the young woman, a clear allusion to the power of 'modern' female sexuality. Overleaf, large panels show the four figures looking increasingly inhuman and deranged, crying 'Order', 'God' and 'Family',[37] (Figure 12), before the young woman pulls open a large curtain, and, screaming in the light, the faces of the four elderly characters shrivel and decompose (Figure 13). The narrative closes with a strip showing the young woman, surrounded by neighbours, explaining how she came to the door and simply found the elderly residents dead and decaying (1977a: 27). In this final image, the girl is fully dressed and visibly shocked, with only the small figure of a snake at her feet connecting her presence and identity to the foregoing narrative.

A story clearly rich with symbolism, layered across both the *bande dessinée*'s textual and visual content, this feminist narrative shows the demonized figure of Eve taking a stand against the outdated opponents of women's liberation who hide behind buzz-words claiming to defend order, religion or the traditional family. Capuana's style, presenting large panels and frequent facial close-ups in striking contrasts of dark and light shading, contributes to the contrasting of 'traditional' and 'contemporary' established by the narrative. The female figure, depicted as non-virginal in her visual opposition to the metaphor-laden lilies, and naked throughout most of the narrative, is presented as the figure of the modern woman, reclaiming her body from the shame thrust upon it by tradition or religion. Careful not to isolate the reader by characterizing her central female figure entirely as a metaphor, Capuana's fully clothed depiction of the girl at the tale's close as she chats with the neighbours presents her finally as a normal young woman and thus identifiable to the reader. With no hint of victimization in the Eve-figure's characterization, this strip contrasts to those *bandes dessinées* noted above, whilst certainly retaining a very feminist theme showing the victory of female strength over withering misogynistic tradition.[38]

Conclusion

Considered as a whole, the *bande dessinée* content of *Ah! Nana* indicates no clearly significant trends of female representations in its early examples of female-created sequential art, other than the very general white European and heterosexual identifiers as noted above. What is discernible from the examination of the feminist complement of strips in the journal – which, as noted, by no means constitutes a thematic majority of *bandes dessinées* present but is, nonetheless, an identifiable sub-section – is that these first uses of the medium as a disseminator of feminist themes, consciously focusing on societal expectations and depictions of women, utilized a range of styles and structural manipulations to convey their messages. Certainly not restricted to unfailingly positive and strong representations in order to contrast with the dominant depiction of women in the male-created medium as might be expected – although as clear from Capuana's *Visite inattendue*, these *bandes dessinées* did exist within the pages of the journal – female figures in these strips were often presented negatively, with satirical humour and shocking visuals used to indicate their own culpability in the discrimination against, and restriction of, women in contemporary society. Confronting the norms and processes of female representation in these strips, then, involved a challenge to women readers as much as to male-defined traditions. Although considerations of the reception of these pioneering strips remain largely speculative due to lack of evidence in this regard, given the lack of information on the future careers of several of the *Ah! Nana* women artists following the journal's close, it is reasonable to conclude that such feminist-focused strips were not wildly popular with the *bande dessinée* reading public.

One artist whose presence in the *bande dessinée* progressed considerably in the years after *Ah! Nana*'s demise, however, and whose œuvre has garnered a certain level of critical attention over the past three decades, is Chantal Montellier. It is to this artist and her *nouveau réaliste* work that the focus of this study turns in the next chapter.

12

Murdering the Male Gaze: Chantal Montellier's *Odile et les crocodiles*

Since her débuts in *Charlie mensuel* and *Ah! Nana,* Chantal Montellier has been one of the most active female *bande dessinée* (BD) creators within the Franco-Belgian industry. Unlike her contemporaries Bretécher or, later, Satrapi, her works have largely remained untranslated, keeping her from international success[1]; however, with over thirty albums published in French since 1978 in addition to countless strips appearing in periodicals, her contribution to the francophone market has been impressive.

Bande dessinée scholarship has taken some notice of Montellier since the turn of the millennium. Ann Miller's 2001 article 'Chantal Montellier's *Faux Sanglant*: Sex, Death, Lies and Video Tape' introduced many scholars to the artist via its concentrated study of the second Julie Bristol narrative. The social focus of Montellier's œuvre was also discussed in a 2004 article by Nua-Hoa Nguyen and Philippe Sohet, with the latter further examining the artist's style in monograph *Images du récit* (2007).

As noted in the previous section, one of the first strips by Montellier to reach the general public was *Ah! Nana*'s *Andy Gang*, which, despite the journal's feminist agenda, displayed no clearly female-focused politics or even any notable women characters. Over the course of her career, however, Montellier's work has become increasingly politicized, and frequently feminist in nature, and has certainly represented female figures.

During the late 1970s and throughout the 1980s, Montellier produced albums such as *Blues* (1979) and *L'Esclavage c'est la liberté* (1984) that illustrated the artist's stylistic *nouveau réalisme* and tendency to evoke themes of social violence and exclusion in her works (Nguyen and Sohet 2003: 115). Her three-album series featuring documentary maker and amateur detective Julie Bristol (*La Fosse aux serpents* [1990], *Faux sanglant* [1992], *L' Île aux demons* [1994]) is probably her best-known creation. Bristol, a filmmaker whose documentaries often result in her coming to the defence of abused women who in turn have become violent, is intelligent and unemotional and in some ways resembles a more feminist-focused incarnation of Tardi's character Adèle Blanc-Sec. Indeed, Montellier in some scenes of the Julie Bristol narratives directly links these two female figures either by drawing Bristol or other characters in Tardi's style in chosen single panels or, on occasion, ironically recreating the image of Blanc-Sec in the bath from *Adèle et la bête* with Bristol in her place (see, for example, Montellier 1994: 17).

Sorcières, mes sœurs, published in 2006, is Montellier's most openly politically feminist album to date. Taking the misogynistically charged symbol of the witch as its theme, it compiles seven short narratives featuring female characters accused of witchcraft with each story focusing on the fear invoked by talented or seductive women. In addition to this politicized trope, *Sorcières mes sœurs* is also evidence of Montellier's outspokenness concerning the position of women artists in the *bande dessinée*—also exemplified in her founding of the 'Association Artémisia', a group dedicated to the recognition of female-created *bandes dessinées*. The collected work opens with a two-page authorial preface by the artist in which she discusses the symbol of the witch and its relevance in the modern world before proceeding to lament the difficulties faced by women artists in the contemporary *bande dessinée* industry, thus likening the female artist to the feared and oppressed symbol of the witch.[2] The circumstances surrounding the demise of *Ah! Nana* are particularly noted in this introduction, as Montellier states, '[t]he women's BD publication *Ah! Nana* fell victim to an entirely male-determined censorship [...] Patriarchal society has excellent reflexes, it's a shame that they are particularly used to shatter female talent' (Montellier 2006: 7).[3] She closes her text with a brief discussion of the struggles faced by specific female artists such as Jeanne Puchol and Catel Muller and concludes with a warning to women creators: '[t]he Inquisition's stakes are still burning, even if those who fan them look like they're on our side'.[4]

Montellier has become an increasingly vociferous figure in the *bande dessinée* industry as her career has progressed, culminating in this fierce metaphorical preface to *Sorcières mes sœurs*. Long before 2006, however, the content of Montellier's sequential narratives was notable for its interweaving of political, often feminist, and certainly female-focused metaphors. In *Images du récit*, Sohet discusses the recurrence of particular motifs or figures across Montellier's texts, citing a 'dynamic between repetition and narration'[5] present in her collective œuvre (2007: 280). Several of these repeated motifs make reference to women as artists or as objects of art, and as victims and perpetrators of violence, with these varying tropes sometimes overlapping, such as in the repeated figure of Artemisia Gentileschi. Montellier resurrects and recalls the memory of Gentileschi, an accomplished seventeenth-century Baroque painter raped by her art tutor and forced to endure torture during the trial for the crime, in *La Fosse aux Serpents, Faux Sanglant* and *Sorcières mes sœurs*.[6] References to this figure also appear very briefly in the 2008 re-edition of *Odile et les crocodiles* but, interestingly, are not found in the original

1984 strip. As an artist and a rape victim, Gentileschi is a powerful symbol used by Montellier to evoke both the creative and the abused woman. Her metaphorical presence also links to another symbolically laden female figure that Montellier equally uses as a repeated motif: the Biblical Judith whose act of beheading Holofernes (recounted in the deuterocanonical Book of Judith) provided the focus for Artemisia Gentileschi's most famous painting, *Judith Slaying Holofernes* (*c.*1611). With such a dense and often elliptical tissue of motifs permeating her work, Montellier, perhaps more than any other female *bande dessinée* artist, creates something of a continuing narrative across her collection of disparately-themed texts. Although not all repeated visual symbols are specifically related to women, the recurrence and powerful use of such motifs as Gentileschi and Judith alongside the contemporary, fictional female characters appearing in her texts (such as Julie Bristol) indicate Montellier's desire to situate her female characters within a wider narrative concerning women, art and violence.

It is already clear via this short introduction to Montellier's work that this *bande dessinée* artist depicts particularly complex and un-typed female characters throughout her texts. In what follows, a key work from Montellier's oeuvre featuring a female lead figure will be considered closely in order to present a case study of the intricacies of her representation of women within the *bande dessinée* and the challenge it represents to the dominant modes of female depiction predicated on neutralizing the 'woman problem'.

Odile et les crocodiles *1984–2008*

Montellier's *Odile et les crocodiles* is an early incarnation of what would become one of the artist's repeated themes – that of the woman as victim of violence who then turns to violence herself. Via a first-person narrative, the 61-page text tells the story of the eponymous Odile, a theatre actress, who is raped by three men in an underground car park after a performance. Her rapists are tried but acquitted and, in anger over the attack and the injustice of the court case, Odile turns to murdering those who show sexual attraction towards her.

The text was first published by Les Humanoïdes Associés in 1984 and was followed over twenty years later by a second edition, published by the Groensteen-founded Actes Sud–l'An 2. The 2008 edition constitutes more than a simple re-printing of the book: in addition to some stylistic changes mostly related to the inversion of colours used for various scenes, the diegesis contains a small number of discrete additions that add to the characterization of Odile (for this reason, the 2008 edition is specifically studied in what follows). Paratextually, one principal alteration is visible between the 1984 and the later version. Both contain a two-page preface reflecting on the narrative, but whilst in the earlier edition this introduction is written by fellow artist Anne-Marie Schropff, the latter contains a preface written by Montellier herself. Bearing the Rimbaud-inspired title 'Je est une autre', this introduction is a response by Montellier to the opinion apparently formed following the 1984 publication of *Odile et les crocodiles* that the text was symbolically confessional for the artist and that the principal character represented, to an extent, Montellier. Alongside her assertion of 'I am not Odile B.' (2008: 5),[7] however, the artist does use this short preface to note that the violence suffered by Odile in her creation comes from a fear of sexual aggression that is real to both herself and many women. Montellier again shows herself to be an increasingly politicized artist, situating the fictitious fate of the female character of her *bande dessinée* via this added preface firmly within the realm of contemporary reality.

Odile et les crocodiles (*2008*)

This text begins with a feature present in several albums by Montellier: an introductory splash-page outside the narrative proper that foregrounds the story's principal elements. Unlike the corresponding page for *Faux Sanglant*, however, which constitutes a crowded full-page mix of images that will feature in the ensuing narrative, this visual overture features one large panel in the middle of the page with blank space above and below. The long, horizontal panel shows Odile in its centre walking alone in a darkened stone-walled space while into the frame, but largely outside it occupying the white non-diegetic space, protrudes a crocodile with its jaws open, ready to strike.

The scene here presumably prefigures the moment leading up to the catalytic event of the narrative – the rape – showing Odile making her way towards her vehicle in the poorly lit car park while the spectre of sexual aggression looms, symbolized by the figure of the crocodile (the play on words with *croc-odile* no doubt adding to this choice of motif). It also provides an introduction to the figure of Odile, however. The full-length view of the character as she walks provides a visual overview of her androgynous appearance, from her cropped hair and slender, boyish frame to her baggy clothes: it is largely the addition of certain accoutrements of femininity, such as a handbag (although, here, largely concealed) and small heels on her shoes, that visually denote her in this first instance as female. Her lone position in the centre of a larger panel whose perspective extends it seemingly infinitely backwards into darkness also highlights Odile's isolation, which will become a focus of her characterization until the end of the narrative. A socially excluded individual who is denied justice following a horrific act of violence,

Odile's fight against the 'saurian nature' of male-led society is undertaken, with the exception of her encounters with those she murders (or considers murdering), entirely alone. The position of the menacing crocodile, awaiting its prey outside the frame, recalls Montellier's words in the preface, indicating the real danger of sexual violence outside of fiction. The same image of the crocodile is used as a narrative marker throughout Odile's story, with entire pages completely blank except for the reptile's threatening presence following each of Odile's ritualized murders.

This opening panel introduces one final aspect pertinent to the story that follows. Set against the bright whiteness of the blank page space above and below, the panel itself is coloured only in this same shade of white, a contrasting dark black and, for Odile's coat, a wall fixture and, most importantly, the crocodile, an icy shade of turquoise green. These colours remain the predominant chromatic trend for the rest of the album, with only shades of grey added to this combination within the narrative proper. The overwhelming presence of the turquoise green shade that frames each page and occupies the gutter space contributes a desolate and glacial atmosphere to Odile's physical world and adds to the nihilist claims that the 'ice age is coming' (see, for example, p. 32; this phrase is written in English in the text) repeated in the form of graffiti on walls and statues throughout the depicted desolate cityscape.[8] The graffiti represented in Odile's urban environment are not limited to this single slogan, with politicized, often anarchist, scribblings found on stone structures in almost every outdoor scene, sometimes contrasted with literary quotations that are also shown daubed on walls. This, in addition to the striking colour scheme and the proliferation of newspaper scraps and crumpled pages of unidentified texts that sweep the streets, provides a derelict and decaying urban backdrop to Odile's murderous journey, entirely in keeping with Montellier's *nouveau réaliste* style.[9] The mixture of English-language slogans and French-language dialogue and narration heightens the atmosphere of a post-globalized, decaying world.

The main narrative begins with a page depicting Odile onstage, performing in a play. In three consecutive panels the focus moves progressively closer towards the figure of Odile, whose words encased in a speech bubble become gradually readable, revealing her monologue to be the words of a woman trying to accept being regularly beaten by her husband 'as the fate of all women' (2008: 8).[10] The following page shows Odile in her dressing room after the performance, in turmoil over having to pronounce such words on stage. These first two pages immediately precede the sequence leading up to the rape: the reader has little time to learn about Odile before the crime, but her reflection upon and refusal to accept archaically patriarchal power relations, even in a fictional scene, is significant in its narrative placement here. The first image of Odile after the rape, following several panels that feature her words in speech bubbles but focus solely on exterior scenes of the crumbling, derelict building from within which she is speaking (2008: 15, 16), reinforces the absence of physical and mental vulnerability in her portrayal. In this image she is shown without clothes and recumbent on a bed facing a naked man while both smoke cigarettes, each visual element of their representation coded to imply a sexual union has just taken place. In choosing to depict a sexualized first view of Odile following the rape, Montellier presents a clear message concerning her protagonist: the sexual nature of the attack against her does not negate Odile's sexuality as a woman. Each aspect of her presentation to readers in the early pages of this album, then, is crafted to depict a resilient, aware and un-typed female character.

In the construction of its narrative around the sexual attack against the eponymous character, *Odile et les crocodiles* may be situated within a literary and visual tradition that Alexandra Heller-Nicholas refers to as 'rape-revenge', in which the act of rape becomes the diegetic catalyst for the raped woman, or an agent acting on her behalf, to enact violent vengeance (Heller-Nicholas 2011: 3). In this *bande dessinée* text, the rape takes place early in the tale and, significantly, is not directly shown. Before the attack, Montellier consecrates four pages to the sequence of Odile walking from the theatre, situated in a shopping centre, to her car in the underground lot. As she descends the floors of the mall, the continuous automated tannoy announcements indicate both the services available to customers and, equally, the degradation of Odile's surrounding society into an increasingly soulless, commodity-driven culture. It is noted that '[i]n addition to its 1200 shops, the centre boasts [...] numerous cinema screens, a theatre [...] and in-house call-girls' (2008: 12),[11] before customers are reminded that '[e]very Sunday morning, a robed priest leads a religious service with pre-recorded choir songs. An automatic wafer distributor is situated in the 'religious articles' department (2008: 13).[12] The last message before the intercom completes its series of announcements by thanking its customers for their patronage is a reminder that the police station and the morgue are situated in the basement (2008: 13).[13] With sex and religion established as commodities, this equation of justice with death comes immediately before the final evidence of the depravity of the society: the rape of Odile.

As noted, unlike the *Ah! Nana* strips that feature sexual violence directly, the rape is not shown. The final scene of the four-page sequence leading to the crime shows Odile setting eyes on her attackers: three men, with one wearing a clown's nose and another the mask of a pig's head.[14] This image occupies the bottom right panel of the page. Overleaf, in the first instance of what will become a repeated motif throughout the album, the page is blank with only the open-jawed crocodile seen in the introductory page present in its centre. Constituting a formal device unique to the *bande dessinée*, the strategic page turn between the final image before the attack and this symbolic representation of the crime entirely arrests the flow of the narrative. The short-circuiting of the diegetic tempo is used by Montellier to convey the trauma and violence of the implied attack, with this formal exploitation heightened by the effacement of the marks of the medium: the reptile is the only figure on the page, which is entirely devoid of panel structure.

The rape of Odile is certainly a causal event for the character's subsequent series of murders but also proves to be the starting-point for a change in narrative structure that will carry the diegesis to its conclusion. Immediately following the symbolic representation of the attack are two pages in which Odile's narration begins as she reflects on her descent into criminality to her male companion. As previously indicated, all but the last panel of these two pages show a derelict set of buildings with the character's words indicated via speech bubbles. The reader understands by Odile's disembodied narration that the story has jumped forward in time as the character briefly mentions her struggle with her attackers (2008: 15), before discussing the trial of her rapists, which she describes as the worst part of her experience. In four speech bubbles issuing from a crumbling construction that seems to symbolize Odile's mental state, her mind separated from her body by the horror of her attack and the ensuing trial, the character explains that her rapists were ostensibly acquitted due to a lack of evidence, but that the trial judge clearly focused during the proceedings on the difference in social status between the accused men – all from 'good families' – and Odile, as an impoverished young woman with a history of mental health problems: '[m]y rapists were "sons of good families", luxury rapists – for a poor girl like me, almost a godsend! [...] I was no longer a violated woman but a lowly tease!...' (2008: 16).[15] Emphasizing that this legal injustice is based on class as well as gender inequality, Odile also notes that several weeks prior to her trial, the same judge had immediately sent the rapists of a young woman possessing a higher social status to jail for a minimum period of ten to fifteen years. Via this added piece of information, a continuation of theme between Montellier's earlier works featuring narratives of social injustice and exclusion and this variation of the 'rape-revenge' script is elucidated.

Above Odile's head as she is finally revealed to the reader, lying naked with her male partner, is a dark green poster with the letter 'O' in a star at its centre. This is a motif particular to the 2008 re-edition of *Odile et les crocodiles*, and is repeated several times throughout the album, which links the principal character to the enslaved and degraded eponymous figure from Pauline Réage's *Histoire d'O*. However, whereas 'O' – said to be, on Réage's admission, an abbreviation of the name Odile (Ciuraru 2011), is throughout this novel presented as a willing slave to the sexual demands of others – Montellier reverses the representation of the female object of desire in this *bande dessinée* by proceeding to show repeatedly Odile murdering those who would wish to sexually objectify her.[16]

The repeated 'O' symbol is the most prevalent reference to depictions of women in wider literary and artistic culture made by Montellier in *Odile et les crocodiles* but is neither the first nor the last. Following her monologue onstage earlier in the text, Odile is shown standing in front of a poster publicizing the play in which she is performing. This proves to be *La Peau dure* by Raymond Guérin, a story that follows three women, all victims of male abuse, in the late 1940s. The combination of this reference, the immediately subsequent rape of Odile and then her link to 'O' in her first depiction after the attack, create around the main character of this text a *mise-en-abyme* effect in which the physical and sexual abuse of women is replayed between artistic media. This is furthered in the sequence following Odile's first visual connection to 'O' in which the character, attempting to overcome her trauma, consults a psychoanalyst who will become her first murder victim.

Odile's visit to the psychoanalyst spans four pages and is the first sequence viewed by the reader as the principal character retrospectively narrates. Much like the trial judge before him, the psychoanalyst belittles Odile's ordeal, describing it as a 'sexual mishap'[17] (2008: 19) and suggesting that her disturbed mental state most likely stems from a sense of sexual frustration from not climaxing during the crime, in addition to an absence of mental discipline due to her parents' behaviour during her childhood years (2008: 18). He advises Odile that she must start having sexual relations again as soon as possible (2008: 19) in order to recover from her ordeal before approaching her suggestively, stroking her face and complimenting her appearance (2008: 20). Odile's response is sudden as, following this advance, she seizes a letter-opener from the man's desk and plunges it into his neck, leaving him dead on the floor amongst his books.

This sequence featuring the psychoanalyst is intrinsic to the narrative as it illustrates the first in Odile's long series of murders, which will see her kill other symbols of a male-dominated society – a misogynist, a priest, a soldier, a burlesque club owner – with her first victim's letter-opener. It is also central to Montellier's continual placing of Odile within a wider narrative of artistic representations of the abuse of women as the layering of symbolic imagery over these four pages is highly dense. As the psychoanalyst tells a shocked Odile that her inattentive upbringing has meant a life devoted to the selfish pursuit of personal pleasure, the image of the man sitting behind his desk – significantly but unwittingly holding the fateful phallic letter-opener as he talks – is dwarfed by a large sketch of Magritte's *Le Viol* above his head (Figure 14). Montellier's reproduction of this famous image during the psychoanalyst's speech confirms his treatment of Odile as a further symbolic rape of the character, the man abusing his (professional) power to attack his already weakened victim mentally. The appearance of this image also, like the references to *La Peau dure* and *Histoire d'O* before it, links Odile's experience to that of other women. However, whereas the connection to the women of the play and novel worked to situate Odile within a textual discourse amongst other fictional characters, the appearance of *Le Viol*, with its clear symbolizing of the silencing and reducing of 'woman' to her sexual role, widens Odile's experience to that of all women.

The following panel depicting Odile's appointment with the psychoanalyst continues this dense artistic layering (Figure 14). As the latter pursues his damning diagnosis of the character, proclaiming '[y]our life is solely guided by the pursuit of pleasure! You want everyone to like you! [...] Clearly an indication of a hysterical condition ...'[18] (2008: 19), the office setting is not seen, and instead the panel shows Odile, naked and holding a candle, in a long narrow room being watched by two men in bowler hats facing away from the reader, in the forefront of the panel. This image again evokes the work of René Magritte, particularly via the motif of the bowler hat, but does not seem to correspond to a specific work by the surrealist artist. Rather, the figure of Odile appears in this panel as the psychoanalyst speaks, naked and under the scrutinizing gaze of modern art in general, a watched object kept at a distance and entirely silent.

Considering this album in the context of the *bande dessinée*, a further, but connected, meaning may be drawn from this panel. The figures of the two men in bowler hats, only seen in this panel from behind as they look at Odile, cannot help but remind the reader of two very famous, similarly dressed *bande dessinée* characters: Hergé's Dupond and Dupont. The combination of this and the series of references to *Histoire d'O* – which, in addition to being an (in)famous literary text charting the willing degradation of a woman, also became a well-known and quite explicit *bande dessinée* by Guido Crepax – suggests Montellier's use of Odile, woven amongst her intricate web of literary and artistic references, as a character symbolizing the objectification and over-sexualization of the female figure in the *bande dessinée* as a whole.[19] It is worth noting in defence of this supposition that the open letter lamenting the general representation of women in the *bande dessinée* and signed, alongside other female artists, by Montellier (see p. 145 of this book), appeared in *Le Monde* within several months of the publication of the 1984 edition of *Odile et les crocodiles*.

In addition to direct references to the *bande dessinée*, as now is clear, Montellier uses *Odile et les crocodiles* as a vehicle to explore and respond to the proliferation of the sexualized female form across differing pictorial media. Each of Odile's first three murder victims is introduced against a visual backdrop of naked or partially clothed women variously featured in 'artistic' photographs, such as those shown adorning the walls of the psychoanalyst's office (2008: 17), pornographic photos (seen at the home of her second victim [2008: 25]) or in sculpture, as visible in the cemetery in which Odile will murder a priest (2008: 33). The recurrence of erotic images of women surrounding each of these victims suggests that other than the men themselves, each of whom spouts misogynistic lines either directly about Odile or concerning women in general, the true target of Odile's wrath as she wields her letter-opener is the sexual objectification of the male gaze.[20] This is made most clear in the scenes surrounding the second murder she commits. Followed along the street at night by a man intent on drawing her into a conversation, Odile accepts his invitation to have a drink at his home. Immediately upon entering, as the man remarks about his flat that 'this place needs a woman! [...] rather than making women do the housework, I always have something better to suggest' (2008: 25),[21] Odile is shown in two panels – one particularly large, making up fifty per cent of the page – looking worriedly at numerous X-rated photographic images showing nearly naked women in underwear in provocative poses. Overleaf, as the man pours drinks and puts on music, Odile imagines herself as one of the posing women, dressed in a bondage outfit, trying to flee an anthropomorphized crocodile that appears in a visual state of sexual excitement (2008: 26). Two pages later, after she has stabbed the man in the jugular, two consecutive panels link his murder to his visual objectification of women. In the first panel, and for the second time in the album (the first appearing after Odile has stabbed the psychoanalyst), the figure of Judith with the head of Holofernes at her feet appears, with, in this instance, the X-rated photographs (with one of Odile now added) on the wall behind her (2008: 28). A long-held artistic symbol of (violent) female triumph over male tyranny, Montellier's depiction of the biblical Judith after each of Odile's murders, acts, to a certain extent, as a visual justification of her crimes – the reader understands that like Judith, Odile's crimes somehow serve the greater good. In this first panel following the violent image of the still-unnamed man with the letter-opener protruding from his neck, as Judith stands with Holofernes' head at her feet, it is the pornographically presented women in the images behind her – 'protected' by her – that are suggested by Montellier to be the true victims of violence. In the second panel, the displayed women have stepped out of their paper confines and stand, three-dimensional, around the man who is dying on the floor. Odile/Judith's murderous act has rendered them real: they are no longer lifeless objects to be watched by others. This panel might be considered the artist's visual declaration that the female gaze can only become active following the death of the traditional male gaze; this declaration is supported by Montellier's admission in a 1994 interview that part of her reason for creating *bandes dessinées* is 'to conquer, in a symbolic way of course, the right to look instead of being looked at, instead of being judged'[22] (quoted in Miller 2001: 217).

Of Odile's later murders shown in the text, two out of three particularly suggest a link with the symbolic murder of the male gaze. The first shows Odile stabbing a soldier following a panel in which he orders her to undress, shines a spotlight on her (still-clothed) form and states 'I like fat women better but ... you've got to make do with what you've got, eh?'[23] (2008: 40). In the second, her victim is a symbol of the gaze itself: a cabaret director who chooses and styles women to perform onstage. Several panels before his murder, as he describes his profession in the following way: '[a] woman can be manufactured from A to Z [...] She becomes the canvas and me the painter'[24] (2008: 43), Odile imagines a woman in bondage gear under a spotlight. Behind this performer in the shade appears once again the image of Odile naked and holding a candle. Referring back to the earlier panel that consciously recalled the sexualization of the female in modern art and, more specifically, the *bande dessinée*, thus bringing this critique to the fore again, Odile's appearance in this panel also serves simply to equate the image of the burlesque dancer as the object of a sexualized gaze with her own experiences of erotic objectification. Several panels later, she again takes her violent revenge.

The murder of the cabaret director proves to be the last killing committed by Odile within the text. It is interesting to note that immediately after this murder, the motif of Judith does not appear as it has following each of the earlier crimes. On the opposite page, however, Odile is shown lying on her bed in three consecutive panels reflecting on what she has done. In an addition not present in the original 1984 text, the word 'Artemisia' appears in a poster above her head, retaining the link to the female icon who claims her revenge (2008: 45). Also present on this wall behind the figure of Odile are the translated name of the George Orwell text *Keep the Aspidistra Flying* and the motif of the 'O' set within a green star. The former reinforces the social dimension underlying the main narrative, made clear earlier in the text during Odile's description of the rape trial,[25] whilst the latter once again draws parallels and contrasts between Odile and her abbreviated literary namesake.

Above this trio of symbols, Odile's narration explains what finally stops her series of murders. Finding a stack of paper on the floor in the abandoned building where she stays following the killing of the cabaret owner, she begins to write the story of her crimes, describing through narrated captions the cathartic effect of this act: 'every word, every phrase that I wrote freed me a little from my fear. I began to hope again [...] I thought to myself that maybe, if I did this, I wouldn't want to kill any more ...'[26] (2008: 45). However, although Odile is not seen committing any further murders in the text, her literary therapy is short-lived. After meeting a fellow writer in a café, the man's pressing critiques of her text and continual suggestions for its 'improvement' removes Odile's personal connection to it as her text comes to reflect not her voice but his. As she explains this retrospectively to her still-anonymous male companion (2008: 53), the open-jawed crocodile appears again, hissing words that appear in large green speech-bubbles. Montellier's repetition of the reptile motif here seems to indicate that Odile has once again been the victim of a crime. The artist this time uses the visual symbol to underline the threat posed to female creativity by predatory male intellectual intervention, briefly expanding her critique of female representation in visual arts to encompass the restriction of women's self-expression in the arts more widely.

Throughout the majority of *Odile et les crocodiles*, the eponymous figure remains the only female character present in the narrative and, with the exception of her unnamed companion (only sporadically shown while she tells her story), each male character is presented as dangerous, lecherous and misogynistic. However, whilst up to a certain point in the narrative this text might seem guilty of vilifying its male characters, and thus men in general, one significant sequence towards the conclusion of the story redresses this gender imbalance.

Following her experience with the writer, Odile, in need of money, tries to find employment. After unsuccessfully attempting various jobs (as a waitress, cleaner, assembly-line worker) she finally secures an interview at a feminist publishing house (2008: 56–58). Her interviewer – a stocky woman wearing a shirt and tie with dark glasses – behaves towards Odile in much the same manner as the ill-fated male characters of the story. Like them, she talks incessantly, neither listening to Odile nor allowing her to speak, before proposing a sexual encounter. Here, however, the interviewer's discourse is entirely couched in militant feminist clichés. She spouts buzzwords and pseudo-politicized slogans ('your body is words')[27] to such an extent that after several panels they merely appear in speech bubbles behind her head whilst she launches into a long monologue concerning the feminist nature of her publishing house and the importance of female expression to, ironically, a silent Odile. The nude female form is also visible in a sense here, in the form of bald and naked female shop mannequins who appear in increasing close-up views as the editor continues to talk, each figure adorned with feminist slogans scrawled across their bodies. As the sequence progresses, and the woman becomes sexually suggestive towards Odile – '[o]ne must be either bestial or very masochistic to agree to make love to a man ... To a woman, on the other hand ...'[28] (2008: 58) – the editor's body is replaced by the symbolic open-mouthed crocodile, who seems to speak her words in her place. Via each of these three elements – the silencing of Odile by her incessant talking, the prominent place of the naked female form (literally objectified and reduced to a bodily canvas for another's point of view) and, finally, the motif of the crocodile – Montellier presents the editor as a danger to Odile to the same extent as any of the male characters who have come before. The restriction of women by women, in this sequence symbolized by the exaggerated depiction of the narcissistic, dictatorial editor despite her ironic claims to an inclusive feminist perspective, is critiqued here in the same way as the various representations of phallocentric society – the church, the military, the gaze – that have preceded in the narrative.

Odile's experience with the editor is the last episode in the retrospective telling of her story. In the last two views of Odile, as she blows out the candle in the room of the abandoned building in which she has recounted her tale to her male partner (now revealed to be a policeman), she is shown entirely naked, kneeling in one image and curled into the foetal position in the next. This final depiction of the exposed female is significant on several levels. Although appearing on the final page of the narrative, it constitutes the first representation of Odile (or any female figure) partially or fully undressed whilst acting directly within the diegesis and thus not appearing either as background decoration (in a photograph or as a statue) or as an imagined or hallucinated image. The presence of her unclothed form here confirms that Montellier's critique of the often-exposed representation of women in art that runs consistently through *Odile et les crocodiles* stems not from a desire for censorship of the naked female body but from a concern with the objectified eroticism that entirely defines these representations. In these final views of Odile, free from surrounding images of over-sexualized female nudity and the dangerous, erotic gaze of the 'crocodiles', Odile is able to appear, simply, naked, and free to govern her own body. Her final scene, showing her curled up in the foetal position, further suggests a rebirth for the character as her story is now told. This 'birth' adds a sense of innocence and purity to her nakedness in a marked contrast to images of exposed female figures appearing previously in the narrative.

Odile: A Conclusion

In *Odile et les crocodiles*, Montellier presents a highly unconventional *bande dessinée* character: she is physically androgynous, laconic and extremely violent.[29] However, despite Odile's position as the narrator and principal, eponymous character of the story, her history and personality remain relatively unexplored. Instead, Odile is used by Montellier as a figure via which to explore and critique the representation of women in textual and modern art and, in particular, in the *bande dessinée*. By representing Odile alongside a series of intertextual and, on occasion, extra-diegetic references to other depictions of women, Montellier places her isolated, solitary character within an identifiable culture of female representation. Odile's violent acts against those bearing a sexualized gaze suggest precisely this to be her, and Montellier's, target, the artist taking revenge for the artistic rape of the female image with her pen as Odile wields her letter-opener against the crocodiles.

Produced by one of the most actively feminist of women *bande dessinée* creators, *Odile et les crocodiles* consciously pits itself against standard representations of the 'problematic' woman in traditional, male-created *bandes dessinées*. This 1984 album, updated and re-issued in 2008, also presents a different view of female characters than many of the contemporary female-drawn publications of the years surrounding its re-edition, however, many of which, issuing from the growing, frequently light-hearted, 'girly' vogue, often sport an entirely dissimilar view of the modern female.[30] In the following, final chapter, however, one example from the trend for female-created 'autobioBD' will be examined, which, like *Odile et les crocodiles*, but using significantly different artistic tactics, aims to challenge and redefine the image of the female body in the *bande dessinée*.

13

Everyday Extremes: Aurélia Aurita's *Fraise et chocolat*

In 2009, artist Aurélia Aurita published an autobiographical *bande dessinée* (BD), *Buzz-moi*, reflecting on the popularity of, and media interest in, her earlier work *Fraise et chocolat* (2006; followed in 2007 by *Fraise et chocolat 2*). 'This book', she stated, 'created a "BUZZ"'[1] (2009: 6). The reasons behind this buzz concern the interaction of the content of *Fraise et chocolat* and the identity of its author: it is a graphically sexual *bande dessinée* narration, by a young, hitherto-unknown French female artist, of the intimate relationship between a well-known BD creator – Frédéric Boilet – and a character, Chenda, who appears to be a representation of the book's author.

Certain elements of the book's content and creation link it to previous works of literature and *bande dessinée*, thus situating the work, to an extent, within various existing traditions. The openly sexual nature of the narrative and its expression by a French woman has led to comparisons to the explicit, feminist literature of French authors such as Virginie Despentes and Catherine Millet – indeed, in *Buzz-moi* Aurita notes that she is frequently asked, when interviewed about *Fraise et chocolat*, for her opinion on these writers (2009: 88). Reyns-Chikuma and Gheno suggest, in fact, that the title of *Buzz-moi* is a tongue-in-cheek reference to Despentes's famous *Baise-moi* (2013: 117). The *bande dessinée* presentation of this sexual explicitness and the apparently autobiographical nature of *Fraise et chocolat* has also led to comparisons with the work of Fabrice Neaud in his *Journal* series (1996–2002) – Aurita has, indeed, indicated Neaud as an influence (Reyns-Chikuma and Gheno 2013: 110) – and, indeed, with that of Boilet, an artist who frequently interweaves autobiographical elements and explicit representations of (often Asian) women in his work.[2] The interaction of explicitness and life narrative combined with the artist's gender have also suggested an indirect link to certain North American women comics artists, particularly Aline Kominsky-Crumb (see Ladurie 2016) and Julie Doucet (the latter comparison particularly arising from the unabashed depiction of certain realities of women's bodily experience (menstruation, for example) present in both women's work. However, despite the validity of these individual links, it is in the combination of all the noted aspects of *Fraise et chocolat* that this work has established itself as unique. Compounding the still relatively uncommon fact of the artist's gender in 2006 – again, this work bears an allographic preface written by a more prominent male artist (Joann Sfar), in which he underlines the artist's exceptional position as a woman – although graphic explorations of women's experiences of sex were present in female-written autobiographical comics from their earliest inception in the United States (see Chute 2010), the same was not visible in their later Franco-Belgian equivalents. The incidence of francophone female artists drawing nude characters and sexually explicit content more generally, outside of the autobiographical genre, has also remained low throughout the history of the medium (see Ladurie 2016: 2; Filippini: 2006). Aurita's work, therefore, stands by the noted criteria as exceptional in the francophone medium.

Beyond the challenge to publishing norms posed by the basic outline of *Fraise et chocolat*, however, several more complex aspects of the narrative also confront and defy dominant representations within the medium (and indeed elsewhere in other media) of women and of women's sexual behaviour. Aurita de-idealizes via various visual and textual means the depiction of the naked female form and of the sexual act throughout *Fraise et chocolat* and, further, challenges through the figure of Chenda certain popular expectations concerning female sexuality. This final chapter studies these aspects of Aurita's work, with an aim to showing further how the *bande dessinée* may be used to consciously undermine the image of women so often presented within the medium and examining how the autobiographical expression of the female body may be used, to an extent, to 'reclaim' the image of woman from these dominant modes of depiction.

Aurita's Autobiographical Approximation

Explaining Philippe Lejeune's definition of autobiography as presented in his famous text *Le Pacte autobiographique* – '[a] retrospective account in prose which a real person gives of his/her own existence, with the accent on his/her individual life, and in particular the history of his/her personality' (Lejeune quoted in Miller 2007: 215) – Ann Miller notes Lejeune's understanding that autobiography usually requires 'a [shared] nominal identity between author, narrator and protagonist, either through the use of names attested in text and paratext or through metatextual commentary' (2007: 215). Throughout *Fraise et chocolat* Aurita does not explicitly comply with this referential pact assumed necessary by Lejeune nor does she expressly attest to the veracity of the experiences she recounts in other ways. Rather, the artist hints at the autobiographical nature of her work, allowing identifiable references to progressively appear towards the end of the text (and then throughout *Fraise et chocolat 2*). The *bande dessinée* is based loosely on a journal format, presenting a mix of date-stamped diary pages containing several lines of prose accompanied by sketches with short chapters that follow a more classic *bande dessinée* structure. Although the prose of the former and the captions of the latter are both written in the first-person narration of the principal female figure, a French sequential artist of Asian origin like Aurélia Aurita, suggesting the voice of the character to be that of the work's creator, no name is attributed to this figure until close to the end of the book, when she is designated simply as Chenda. This contrasts to the identification of Chenda's partner, whose first name is used from the third page of the narrative and whose full name, Frédéric Boilet, is noted later. Via this contrast, Aurita appears to play with the notion of autobiographical identification: the precise naming of Boilet, a successful *bande dessinée* artist whose moniker is likely to be familiar to at least a part of the readership of *Fraise et chocolat*, lends the narrative an air of autobiographical authenticity; the naming of Chenda is less clearly confessional as, although this is the given name of the artist (Aurélia Aurita is a pseudonym), the lack of accompanying explanation – and the creator's relatively unknown status as an artist in 2006 – renders the link between character and creator less definitive. As indicated above, however, Aurita does progressively reveal that she and Chenda are one and the same. Shortly after noting her name, very close to the end of the narrative, a diary page containing particularly explicit details of Chenda and Frédéric's sex life is accompanied by a small sketch of the latter, irritated, asking his bashful partner if she is sure that she wants to reveal these intimate secrets (2006: 126). This brief self-referential detail suggests Chenda to be the artist of the work being read (this then goes on to be confirmed in the second volume of the *bande dessinée* when Frédéric and Chenda discuss the future publication of *Fraise et chocolat*). Despite this apparent confession, Aurita then plays with the notion of autobiographical truth on the final page of the book when, following an epilogue that shows her reflecting on past lovers while ironing, she concludes the narrative thus: '[t]he story that you have just read is fictional because, of course, I have never in all my life ironed a single one of Frédéric's shirts. Aurélia Aurita, Tokyo, 12th February 2006'[3] (2006: 142). The convergence of the personal pronoun, the reference to Frédéric and the inclusion of Tokyo (where *Fraise et chocolat* largely takes place) as place of writing all indicate that Aurélia Aurita and Chenda are one and the same. The tongue-in-cheek statement, however, questions the lived nature of the experiences presented in the preceding narrative.

The autobiographical uncertainty of *Fraise et chocolat* – Ladurie also points to the 'caricatural' nature of Aurita's drawing style (discussed below) that renders her pictorial avatar visually 'dissimilar' to the artist's physical appearance

(2016: 9) – impacts the narrative in two principal ways. By drawing what (progressively) appears to be her own body and graphically expressing her own sexual experiences, Aurita's work participates in the 'reclaiming' of the female body, deemed necessary by Cixous in 'The Laugh of the Medusa', from dominant (male-created) expressions. As Cixous proclaims, '[w]oman must write her self: must write about women and bring women to writing' (Cixous et al. 1976: 875); 'By writing herself woman will return to the body which has been more than confiscated from her, which has been turned into the uncanny stranger on display' (1976: 880). By writing her apparent 'self', Aurita presents an authentic female body and experience at odds with the imagined and idealized femininity presented elsewhere in the medium, thus reclaiming the female form from the frequently distorted norm. By retaining a certain level of ambiguity as to her shared identity with Chenda throughout most of *Fraise et chocolat*, however, Aurita is also able to present a less individualized depiction of the sexual woman: as the identity of the main character is not entirely 'fixed', the figure depicted is able to retain a certain level of (female) universality – she is, for much of the book, *a* woman artist rather than *the* woman artist credited on the book's cover, this avoiding the sometimes-alienating specificity of autobiographical expression.

Sex and the (Un)Ideal Woman

Although the autobiographical nature of *Fraise et chocolat* in relation to the female body depicted on the page is often ambiguous, the challenges Aurita issues in this work to dominant representations of sex and, particularly, to the female experience of sex via her depiction of this body are visible from the beginning of the text and continue throughout.

Certainly an explicit *bande dessinée* containing multiple sex scenes that illustrate a variety of acts (vaginal and anal intercourse, fellatio, cunnilingus, use of sex toys etc.), *Fraise et chocolat* avoids categorization as an 'erotic' *bande dessinée* by its focus in many of these scenes on either mundane aspects of everyday life – early in the narrative in a scene showing Frédéric performing oral sex on Chenda on a balcony, for example, Chenda's dialogue 'normalizes' this situation by drawing attention to the fact that she is cold (2006: 7) – or on the occasional, less pleasant side-effects of sexual intercourse, particularly those linked to the realities of the female body. The title, *Fraise et chocolat*, seemingly romantic in its alliterative connection of Frédéric and Chenda to two gastronomic aphrodisiacs, in fact, refers to two memorable sexual mishaps represented in the book – one involving the unexpected start of Chenda's period and the other an accidental excretion during anal sex.

This narrative, often comedic, reinsertion of everyday reality into the sexual act, so often represented in visual or textual works as a seamlessly choreographed, exalted moment, set distinctly apart from the mundanities of 'real life', is accompanied by two notable elements of Aurita's artistic style. One is her use of visual details, specific in their formatting to the *bande dessinée* medium, to draw attention to quotidian elements: during one of the first sex scenes of the book, for example, Aurita sketches an arrow pointing to a close-up panel of Frédéric holding on to her foot, distracting the eye from the intimate images which otherwise dominate the page (2006: 16); she also on several occasions adds onomatopoeia to sexual scenes to emulate the sometimes-amusing noises associated with sex (2006: 71, 85). The other aspect of Aurita's style that greatly contributes to this de-eroticization of sex is the simplicity of her drawings of the (particularly female) human body. Sketches of Chenda and Frédéric dominate *Fraise et chocolat*, with other characters entirely limited to background panel detail in scenes occurring in public (this is not true of *Fraise et chocolat 2*, in which several other characters are named and participate in the narrative). Aurita's style fluctuates somewhat in her rendering of Frédéric, particularly on the aforementioned diary pages – Reyns-Chikuma and Gheno cite one such example from *Fraise et chocolat* (I) presenting a much more detailed drawing of Frédéric (see Aurita, 2006: 95), which 'shows that the artist knows how to draw more academically' than the unconstrained style she employs throughout most of the book, which they suggest to be 'between sketch and caricature'[4] (2013: 115). Her visual presentation of Chenda, however, remains very simple throughout. Chenda, in a manner somewhat similar to Charles Schulz's comics figures, is drawn with a large, very round, head and her facial features are indicated by single lines or circles. On occasions, bodily outlines that should be invisible remain part of the drawings presented – the curve of a shoulder behind Chenda's chin, for example (2006: 81) – this providing the sketches with an intentional air of rapid creation and carelessness that contributes to the loosely followed 'journal' premise of the book. During scenes of nudity and sex, Chenda's body is depicted with very little detail: two semicircles represent breasts while a single curved line and an 'x' denote genitals. This overall lack of detail attributed to Chenda contributes to the certain level of (female) 'universality' in the figure's depiction also maintained, as noted above, by the autobiographical ambiguity of the book, allowing Aurita to depict *a* woman's experience of sex, rather than a visually (and, for much of the book, nominally) very specific woman's experience. It also contributes to the 'challenge' implied by *Fraise et chocolat* to dominant representations of women and sex in the *bande dessinée* medium in two interconnected ways. First, the extremely simple representation of the nude female form before, after and during sex presented by Aurita contrasts strongly with the most well-known representations of women, female nudity and sex seen elsewhere in the medium. In *Barbarella*, for example,

Jean-Claude Forest repeatedly highlights visual markers of the main character's sexual difference (her long hair, large lips, prominent bust; see analysis of Barbarella in Chapter 3 of this book). The artists most famously known for depicting naked female figures and erotic scenes – Milo Manara and Guido Crepax (although both Italian artists, their works have been widely translated and were published in France) – are, in turn, celebrated for the detailed draughtsmanship of the intricately drawn, beautiful depictions of sexualized female figures such as Claudia Cristiani (*Le Déclic*, Manara), Valentina or Emmanuelle (*Valentina*, *Emmanuelle*, Crepax). François Bourgeon and Enki Bilal, neither known as creators of BD erotica like Manara and Crepax, nonetheless sexualize women in their work by drawing attention to their beautified, voluptuous forms (Bourgeon; see p. 27 of this volume) or by using colour to draw attention to certain bodily features such as nipples and pubic hair (Bilal; see p. 28). Finally, Frédéric Boilet's own work is notably marked by beautifully rendered displays of women's bodies, often fragmented to focus on elements of their sexual difference (and to occult the visible presence of their male companions during sex scenes). Aurita's very understated and undetailed sketches of the naked female form sit in stark contrast to these now-normalized interpretations of women's bodies. The lack of definition in her drawings removes the expected emphasis on sexual corporeal features and aesthetically pleasing silhouettes and, thus, de-idealizes the visual conception of the nude female form.

This simplicity and de-idealization also contributes, as indicated above, to Aurita's reconceptualization of sex as a quotidian, bodily act removed from imagined and often unrealistic eroticism. Chute notes of Aline Kominsky-Crumb's bulbous, somewhat grotesque style of depicting bodies that it presents 'a deliberate challenge to the idea that any image of a naked woman is supposed to be arousing' (2010: 38). Aurita's aesthetic is very different to that of Kominsky-Crumb, yet it produces a similar effect with regards to woman and the sexual act. The lack of detail in the imagery and of any corresponding invitation to the reader to focus particularly on Chenda's body beyond that required by the specific narrative context of the page discourages the 'freezing' effect that female bodily presence may have on narrative progression, as explained by Laura Mulvey: 'her visual presence tends to work against the development of a story line, to freeze the flow of action in moments of erotic contemplation' (2009: 19–20).[5] Chenda's body, reclaimed by its simplicity from the continual eroticization associated with the female form in the *bande dessinée*, becomes one element on the drawn page amongst several, allowing the reader to direct their attention to other details of the scenes presented, such as the comedic, every-day banalities or mishaps noted above. The fluidity of Aurita's adherence to the traditional structuring mechanisms of the *bande dessinée* – *Fraise et chocolat* swings between pages divided into panels and strips and those without on which different sketches are placed freely, unframed, on the white space of the page – also sometimes contributes to this diffusion of the reader's attention away from the expected eroticism of the female form during representations of sex. As Ladurie notes of a specific sexual sequence presented in the latter manner (see Aurita, 2006: 15), the lack of BD 'architecture' on the page allows the look of the reader to wander between the images without being directed in a specific manner by traditional sequential structuring. Unlike the work of the well-known *bande dessinée* authors noted above, in which the look of the reader is frequently guided across the page to better focus on the female figure's exaggerated sexual features, in *Fraise et chocolat*, Aurita denies this specific positioning of the gaze, thus allowing for a plurality of visual foci. To borrow Chute's phrasing, the combination of visual and narrative features making up Aurita's aesthetic present a challenge to the idea that any image of women and sex must be eroticized. This fluid use of *bande dessinée* architecture and, in particular, the artist's reclaiming of the female body from the standard sexualized 'ideal' are key components of this challenge.

Fraise et chocolat *and Myths of Female Sexuality*

Whilst the visual depiction of Chenda, as noted, is crucial to Aurita's re-imagining of women and sex in the *bande dessinée*, several elements of her narrative characterization within *Fraise et chocolat* are also notable as part of this reconceptualization as they confront and attempt to correct popular societal myths concerning female sexuality.

Chenda is depicted as possessing a sizable sexual appetite: she frequently initiates sex with Frédéric and is indicated to take as much (or more) pleasure in it as he does. She is also sexually curious and adventurous – one key incidence of humour in the book comes when, suddenly taken by the idea of seeing what her body looks like with a sex toy anally inserted, Chenda wiggles 'like a caterpillar' along the floor towards the mirror (see Figure 15). These elements of Chenda's personality contrast with the dominant myth that women are less prone to experiencing sexual desire and pleasure than men and, thus, passively accept rather than initiate sexual advances.[6] Sara Cooper states in her work on female sexual myths that this notion, whilst predating the advent of psychoanalysis, has been amplified by the popularization of Freud's theories that present 'a model of female sexuality based on the concept of absence, on lack [...] [The woman] lacks a penis which, according to Freud, is conceptualized in infantile fantasy as the major organ of sexual pleasure, the active genital' (1995: 158). This understanding of women as the passive recipients of male desire corresponds to their frequent depiction in traditional visual narratives as passive vessels for the sexualized masculine gaze, coded, as Mulvey's puts it, to exude 'to-be-looked-at-ness' and consequently excluded from active participation in the narrative (2009: 19–20). Aurita's refuting of this sexual lack via the behaviour of her avatar Chenda both contests the enduring popular understanding of women's relationship to sex and, combined with her rendering of Chenda's body, presents an alternative to many of the dominant depictions of women in the *bande dessinée*.

In Cooper's work, she identifies the notion of the 'sexually lacking' female as emanating from one side of the archetypal, ahistorical understanding of womanhood as split between two extremes: 'the virgin, pure, untouched, and untouchable and the whore, the depraved, uncontainedly sexual figure' (1995: 157). In this understanding of womanhood, a place is allowed for the libidinous female but she is necessarily rendered as morally and emotionally defective – no middle ground is ceded to the possibility of a sexually desirous and virtuous woman. This long-standing dyadic myth remains visible in contemporary visual and textual narratives containing women figures – indeed it is identified and discussed in the analysis of Chauzy and Jonquet's *La Vie de ma mère* in Chapter 7 of this book. In *Fraise et chocolat*, however, Aurita consciously confronts and dismantles this division from the book's beginning. One means she employs of doing so again implicates her visual style. The simplicity of her sketches, exaggerated on occasions to the point of rendering her drawings akin to stick-figures (see Figure 16) renders her drawings of Chenda somewhat childlike (see also Ladurie 2016: 8); this stylistic feature, in addition to the humour and apparent earnestness of her sexual exploration throughout the book, is presented alongside her consistently high levels of sexual desire, problematizing the distinction between innocence and depravity implied by the virgin/whore dyad. Chenda is also introspective about and caring towards Frédéric throughout the book, nuancing *Fraise et chocolat*'s sexual focus; she, in fact, makes a clear statement regarding these interconnected elements of her nature in a conversation following the first sex scene of the book: responding to Frédéric's question about what she hopes to experience in her romantic life, she responds 'I'd like to be with someone ... but have lots of lovers!!! I would give my body to them ... but my fantasy is to save my soul for one person, and one person only' (2006, p. 27).[7] By presenting the figure of Chenda in this untyped manner – a figure whose depiction as an authentically 'real' woman is, again, corroborated by the autobiographical insinuations in the text – Aurita introduces a character who defies the classification of women figures still seen, as shown across Section 2 of this book, in the *bande dessinée* medium and, indeed, in the wider public imaginary.

As is now clear, *Fraise et chocolat* confronts and attempts to correct several dominant visual codes and societal myths still strongly attached to the depiction of women in narratives. Aurita's representation of Chenda as emotionally intelligent and also strongly sexually-driven presents an alternative to the long-standing division of women between extreme types seen across visual and textual art forms. Her artistic rendering of Chenda, in addition to her manipulation of the structuring mechanisms of the *bande dessinée*, however, directly challenges the exaggerated focus on the expected eroticism of the womanly body so often seen in the *bande dessinée* medium. This de-idealization of the female form using features specific to graphic narratives shows the possibility of challenging the 'woman problem' identified in this book's introduction: by removing the exaggerated focus on female sexual difference and presenting women's bodies as a normal, un-exalted feature of human imagery, the notion of woman as a visual symbol of (masculine) 'fantasy and dread' (Pollock 2003: 178) is undermined. Whether this, and comparable, technique(s) will be adopted by other artists, male and female, in order to consistently challenge the still-dominant depiction of women in the *bande dessinée* will be a question for future study.

Conclusion: Problem Solved?

Men say that there are two unrepresentable things: death and the feminine sex.

—Hélène Cixous (Cixous et al. 1976: 885)

In Joann Sfar's preface to Aurélia Aurita's 2006 *Fraise et chocolat* (see Chapter 13), after noting Aurita's exceptional place as a woman artist – '[a]h, and for once it's a girl talking'[1] – he continues with an allusion to his own difficulties in drawing female figures: '[h]mm, I really wish I were able to have my female characters express themselves as well as she does. Yes, but she *is* a girl so, really, it's easy for her'[2] (quoted in Aurita 2006: 4). This confession expresses two things of interest here – first, it reinforces the fact that the perceived difficulties of drawing 'real' women (see p.1 of this book) in the *bande dessinée* (BD), noted by artists throughout the twentieth century, have continued into the twenty-first century despite the remarkable evolution of the medium since the days of Hergé and Goscinny. Second, it suggests that the drawing of 'real women' in a medium that has so long restricted them to underdeveloped, typed and often sexualized characterizations is dependent on the growing presence of women artists in the medium. The latter assumption is complex and shall be considered below in relation to the findings presented in the final chapters of this book. Sfar's former expression of his own difficulty in drawing women figures, however, links to what has been an unavoidable conclusion repeatedly drawn during research conducted for the earlier chapters of this volume: that the continued, inexorable existence of the 'woman problem' in the *bande dessinée* – that is, of the understanding that creating and viewing images of women is inherently problematic to the (presumed) male, heterosexual artist and reader of the *bande dessinée* due to women's positioning both in the phallocentric societal paradigm and due to the specific history of the medium – is visible within the depiction of women characters across eras and genres, and that multiple visual and narrative techniques, some specific to the sequential art medium, have been employed to contain and defuse the apparent challenge that femaleness presents.

In response to observations that the *bande dessinée* may historically be considered a particularly restrictive medium for the representation of women (see, for example, Peeters's words on p. 6) several things are now apparent. One is that the artistic features of the form itself may contribute to this. The analysis of Barbarella in Section 1, for example, showed that the very active, controlling gaze of the reader made possible by the artist's positioning of their female character in the static visual narrative process inherent to sequential art may be a contributing factor to the extensive presence of sexualized female figures visible across examples of the form. The study of *La Vie de ma mère* in particular in Section 2 then posited that the traditional importance of characters and character-recognition to graphic narratology as the art-form has developed from caricature (cf. Morgan 2009), in addition to the necessary 'compression' of the characterization of minor figures to fit into the traditional (often 48-page) narrative format, may encourage the use of typing in the medium. It is further established that this especially negatively impacts the depiction of women who are more often than not secondary figures and, thus, are more consistently 'compressed' into types to fit into the *bande dessinée* narrative and who are, across all art forms, much more frequently associated with biologically restricted and frequently 'negative' typing.

Sections One and Two also make clear the extent to which historical influence, both internal and external to the *bande dessinée* medium, has been a key factor in perpetuating the notion of the 'woman problem' in the *bande dessinée*. This external influence is visible from the earliest example of a character examined, Bécassine, whose asexuality and literal alienation seem to have stemmed from the pre-existing fear that any representation of woman to any audience may carry with it implications of sexualization, and from the analysis of Warnauts and Raives's 1990s strips which shows that the figures of Baligi and Souana borrow heavily from the historic 'Black Venus' stereotype seen across other visual and textual media. The importance of influence is also evident from within the history of the *bande dessinée* itself. Tardi has, in particular, noted that the invention of the figure of Adèle Blanc-Sec was complicated by the lack of female precursors in the medium and the analysis of this series undertaken in Chapter 4 suggests one reason for her androgyny to be that she was essentially based on male figures (imagined as a 'female Brindavoine') due to this lack. The repetition of what we might call the 'invisibilization' of women – by over- or a-sexualizing (as seen with Barbarella and Bécassine respectively), Othering (Adèle Blanc-Sec) or containing within a reassuringly delineated stereotype (the *Gauloises*, the women of Chauzy and Jonquet, Baligi and Souana) is then seen throughout the history of the bande dessinée where women *are* present, with every example in the first six analytical chapters of Sections One and Two showing evidence of this. In a paper presented at the 'Forum des femmes' in Suresnes in 2014 in which he discusses the influence of Satrapi's *Persepolis* on the introduction of women to the *bande dessinée* medium, Groensteen briefly discusses a similar understanding of influence – what he dubs the 'permission' phenomenon present in the art-form – suggesting that BD artists tend to restrict their creativity to what they have already previously seen in strips, 'until the day that [they] discover that someone has already done it and then [they], in turn, feel "permitted" to do it' (Groensteen 2015).[3] Although the importance of influence on creation would eventually also benefit female characterization in the medium as a new generation of women artists would be inspired to draw their own lives after seeing it done by others (particularly Satrapi, as Groensteen notes), prior to this, its effects seem to have weighed heavily on the depiction of woman figures in the predominantly male-drawn medium, (re-)producing reductive processes of 'invisibilization' of femaleness that would become for many decades the norm.

The history of women's depiction (or lack thereof) in the medium appears also to have influenced women's depiction of women characters prior to the paradigm-shifting late 1990s and early 2000s. The androgyny of certain of Bretécher and Claveloux's strips and the overall lack of feminist direction in the strips of *Ah! Nana* compared to the *illustré*'s textual content, followed by the lack of particular focus on female characters in the early works of Montellier, Cestac and Puchol suggest that one early reaction of women incoming to the adult *bande dessinée* for the first time was, largely, to avoid the 'problem' of women so artistically present elsewhere in the medium (often, it must be remembered, by the clear absence of women figures) by also avoiding, to an extent, the representation of women's difference. Some other examples noted in the compiled history of women artists' creations of female figures (Chapter 10) indeed further remind us of the fact that when women artists *do* focus on female figures, they are also not immune from the influence of the medium's history and thus from recreating depictions of female characters that largely correspond to those dictated by the concerns of the phallocentric paradigm, thus perpetuating the notion of the 'woman problem'. This fact, in addition to the analysis of *Le Combat ordinaire* by Larcenet (Chapter 9), a male artist, which shows the potential for disrupting the dominant female imagery shaped by said paradigm, contrasts with Sfar's implication noted at the start of this Conclusion that first-hand experience of womanhood is key to the creation of non-typed, developed female figures (Sfar is not alone in holding this general belief; it corresponds, for example, to Cixous's opinion that 'woman must write woman. And man, man' [Cixous et al. 1976: 877]). All three of the analytical chapters of Section 3 studying women figures by female artists *do* reveal characters that defy standard depictions of womanhood in the *bande dessinée* and that show the potential of the medium's formal specificity to challenge the 'normalization' of women as Othered, eroticized or typed. However, despite this focus, the analysis presented in Chapter 9 and the historical findings of Chapter 10 do not support the notion that the female status of the artists studied is necessarily fundamental to their ability to create characters that contest the notion of the 'woman problem'. Rather, it is the conscious, critical engagement within each strip with the clichés and restrictions of dominant representations of women both in the *bande dessinée* medium and in past and present societal imaginations that allows the characters presented to deviate from the established norms of the depicted woman. Each of the final four analytical chapters shows a clear awareness of the issues surrounding representations of women; this conscious approach is visible by various means such as the identifying and dismantling of a restrictive female stereotype (Larcenet), the depiction of women figures as complicit in their own patriarchal subordination and the direct appeal to readers to challenge this (*Ah! Nana*), the explicit visual reflection on the pervasiveness of phallocentrically determined images of women (Montellier) and the simplification of the visual rendering of the nude female form in direct contrast to dominant, eroticized images of BD women (Aurita). As such, each of these strips undermines the notion of the 'woman problem' by engaging directly with the assumptions that accompany it – that woman is 'lacking' and represents, first and foremost, a sexual difference that must be by some means disavowed or contained, and that the history of female representations present earlier in the medium must necessarily influence subsequent depictions in a cyclical reproduction of stylistic neutralizations of womanhood. In the Introduction, it was noted that an important constituent of the 'woman problem' is the consistent placing of the viewer of female imagery – the 'gazer' – as a (heterosexual) male. The publication of certain *bandes dessinées*, particularly since the advent of the new millennium such as those linked to the 'girly' BD trend briefly touched upon, suggests that repositioning the traditionally masculine *bande dessinée* viewer as female is not sufficient to break down certain patriarchal beliefs and stereotypes regarding women in the depiction of female figures (although, as seen in the examples from *Ah! Nana*, the expectation that the reader is female does allow the artist the opportunity to speak directly and explicitly *to* women in their work). Rather, as seen in the final four analytical chapters, it is the adoption of an overt engagement with the assumptions regarding, and history of, female imagery directed to all readers that allows the very notion of the 'woman problem' to be challenged.

This conscious re-evaluation of female imagery, whilst still a decidedly minor element of a medium that largely continues to present traditionally typed and sexualized women figures, does appear, despite the above disavowal of Sfar's view, to be increasing in tandem with the influx of more women artists to the form. It appears true that whilst 'womanness' is not a fundamental criterion of challenging female representations as argued, the particular life experiences of women artists and their continued underrepresentation in the *bande dessinée* industry may, indeed, impact on the likelihood of their critical reflection on issues of women's depiction in their strips (this is particularly true of the autobiographical genre, for obvious reasons). How the continued creation of such 'challenging' women figures will, in turn, influence the future of women's representation across the *bande dessinée* medium remains to be seen; however, evidence of the beginnings of such change is already clear.

This book has examined at length a previously very understudied aspect of the *bande dessinée*: its representation of women across the developing medium as a whole, beyond the study of a single character or genre, and unrestricted by category of publisher or age of audience. In doing this, it has taken a consciously expansive 'Images of Women' approach (see p. 8) – that is, it has selected key examples of strips featuring women in the medium and has analysed the representations of these female figures both within their own narratives and in relation to other depictions of women across the *bande dessinée* as a whole. One obvious concern regarding 'Images of Women' criticism is the need to select specific examples out of many, this raising the question of why certain examples are omitted and to what extent these omitted examples may affect the conclusions drawn. As noted by Carroll (1990) in relation to cinema, however, 'Images of Women' criticism constitutes a valuable empirical step in the examination of female figures in artistic media, and *no* conclusions may be drawn without first studying relevant examples. The intention of this book, thus, is to contribute, via a relatively large and wide selection of analyses, to what must surely be an ongoing process in the study of women in the *bande dessinée*. For a future multiplication of 'Images of Women' studies to allow a nuancing of the conclusions drawn here would be a most useful (and very welcome) development in *bande dessinée* research.

Figures

FIGURE 1: Forest, *Barbarella* (Edition Intégrale: Premier tome) (1994), p. 3 © 2019 Humanoids, Inc. Los Angeles.

FIGURE 2: Forest, *Barbarella* (Edition Intégrale: Premier tome) (1994), p. 14 © 2019 Humanoids, Inc. Los Angeles.

FIGURE 3: Forest, *Barbarella* (Edition Intégrale: Premier tome) (1994), p. 6 © 2019 Humanoids, Inc. Los Angeles.

FIGURE 4: Forest, *Barbarella* (Edition Intégrale: Premier tome) (1994), p. 53 © 2019 Humanoids, Inc. Los Angeles.

FIGURE 5: Extrait de l'ouvrage *Adèle et la bête*, Tardi (2007), p. 27 © Casterman. Avec l'aimable autorisation des auteurs et des Editions Casterman.

FIGURE 6: Extrait de l'ouvrage *Adèle et la bête*, Tardi (2007), p. 21 © Casterman. Avec l'aimable autorisation des auteurs et des Editions Casterman.

FIGURE 7: Extrait de l'ouvrage *Adèle et la bête*, Tardi (2007), p. 22 © Casterman. Avec l'aimable autorisation des auteurs et des Editions Casterman.

FIGURE 8: Extrait de l'ouvrage *La Vie de ma mère: Face B*, Chauzy et Jonquet (2003), p.11 © Casterman. Avec l'aimable autorisation des auteurs et des Editions Casterman.

FIGURE 9: Larcenet, *Le Combat ordinaire* (2004), p.13 © DARGAUD 2003 – www.dargaud.com. All rights reserved.

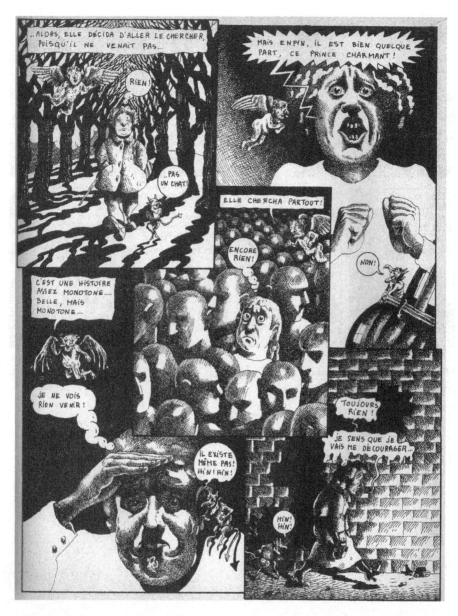

FIGURE 10: Claveloux, 'La Conasse et le Prince Charmant' in *Ah! Nana* (no.2) (1977), p. 29 © Nicole Claveloux (many thanks to the artist for allowing the reproduction of this image).

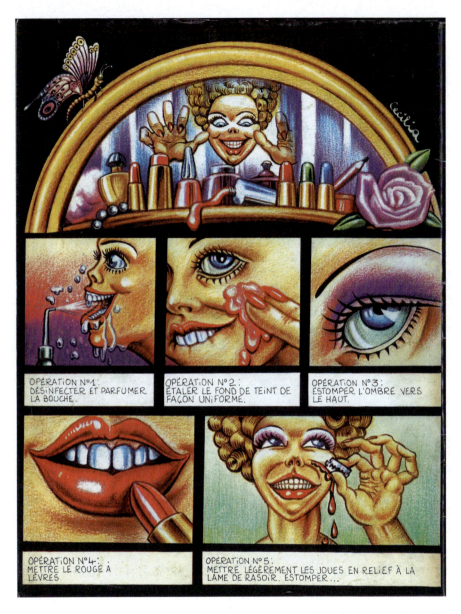

FIGURE 11: Capuana, Untitled Strip in *Ah! Nana* (no. 6) (1977), back cover. © Cecilia Capuana (many thanks to the artist for allowing the reproduction of this image).

FIGURE 12: Capuana, 'Visite inattendue' in *Ah! Nana* (no.3) (1977), p.24. © Cecilia Capuana (many thanks to the artist for allowing the reproduction of this image).

FIGURE 13: Capuana, 'Visite inattendue' in *Ah! Nana* (no.3) (1977), p.25. © Cecilia Capuana (many thanks to the artist for allowing the reproduction of this image).

FIGURE 14: Montellier, *Odile et les crocodiles* (2008), p. 19 © Actes Sud 2008.

FIGURE 15: Aurita, *Fraise et chocolat* (2006), p. 72 © Les Impressions Nouvelles – 2006.

FIGURE 16: Aurita, *Fraise et chocolat* (2006), p. 75 © Les Impressions Nouvelles - 2006.

Notes

Introduction – Women Problems

1. 'Le problème de la femme est, au monde, tout ce qu'il y a de merveilleux et de trouble'. All translations from French in this book are my own, except where otherwise indicated.
2. Throughout this book, the acronym BD is used occasionally for textual variation, although the full term *bande dessinée* is favoured. Whilst the interesting argument of some in the industry who suggest that the full term and its acronym be separated and redefined to indicate a difference in quality or target readership age is acknowledged (see Menu 2005) no such differentiation is implied by the use of the BD acronym here.
3. Response to a question asked by the author of this book during an event at the Goethe-Institut Glasgow on 25 November 2009.
4. 'Je n'ai jamais réussi à dessiner une femme qui soit réelle'.
5. 'Et d'ailleurs…les femmes sont rarement des éléments comiques'.
6. The notion of the 'Symbolic' was first theorized by psychoanalyst Jacques Lacan and is one of three intertwined Orders of human existence, alongside the 'Imaginary Order' and the 'Real'. See Eyers (2012).
7. 'Comment le crayon malhabile, butor, pourra-t-il jamais traduire en la langue la plus vulgaire les délicatesses, la finesse exquise?'. In gathering citations from Nadar, Hergé and Moebius on the subject of drawing women into a footnote of his work on Rodolphe Töpffer, as referenced here, Peeters recognises, albeit briefly, a symptom of what this book describes as 'the woman problem': the apparent difficulty male artists have noted in drawing women.
8. Laurence Grove's *Comics in French* gives examples of negative pre-1960s criticism of the 'general stupidity' of the medium (2010: 232–33).
9. An examination of issues of both *L'Epatant* (begun 1908) and *Fillette* (begun 1909) over their respective first year shows that both publications devoted approximately the same amount of space to *bandes dessinées* (which generally appeared [of varying length] on around 10 out of the 16 pages of each *illustré*) and that both tended to favour depictions of male characters. Strips contained within *L'Epatant* largely focused on male figures with women in very secondary roles (almost always as wives to more prominent men characters); *Fillette* generally restricted any female focus to featured, recurring strips, particularly *L'Espiègle Lili* (see pp. 22–24), with male characters appearing to feature more prominently amongst the bulk of the remaining one-shot strips that filled each issue.

Despite an increase in female presence (both in terms of characters and artists) in the late twentieth century and into the twenty-first, the notion that the *bande dessinée* is 'for boys' seems to have persisted until the present day. The *Collectif des créatrices de bande dessinée contre le sexisme* has explained that one of the several sparks leading to their creation was the attitude of the *Centre belge de la bande dessinée* in 2015 that *bandes dessinées* 'for girls' were 'niche' and only really a 'marketing strategy' ('un plan marketing') (Collectif des créatrices de bande dessinée contre le sexisme 2016).

10. Thierry Groensteen estimated that, as late as 2002, only 6.5% of artists were female (quoted in Lemaire 2009). This is more fully discussed in Chapter 10.
11. In an article on women and comedy in French cinema, Brigitte Rollet notes that, traditionally, the power to create humour is divided between genders much as the sexualized look is: 'women in comedies are the objects and not the subjects of the joke (just as they are more often than not the objects and not the subjects of the gaze' (1999: 129). Subordinating women in both cases upholds the phallocentric status quo.
12. 'Dans la plupart des albums, les visages et les corps féminins demeurent privés d'existence individuelle, tant ils obéissent aux mêmes schémas, aux mêmes clichés de la séduction inexpressive'.
13. The specification of the valorization of the 'masculine' (rather than the 'male') here is important, as both men and women can adopt or exhibit masculine (or feminine) subject-positions and assumed behaviours (although these are traditionally much more associated with biologically male people).
14. Montellier, for example, founded the 'Association Artémisia', a group dedicated to the recognition of female-created BDs.

Chapter 1 – Bécassine to Barbarella ... But What Came in Between? An Introductory History of Female Primary Characters in the Francophone Bande Dessinée

1. 'un journal de qualité destiné aux jeunes filles de bonne famille'.
2. See Chapter 2 for a detailed study of Bécassine.
3. Issues from the year 1922, for example, show Bécassine appearing in at least a double-page strip in every instalment.
4. The marketing tactic of giving the first issue of a new *illustré* away for free with a more established publication seems to have been common at this time, with both *La Semaine de Suzette* and *Fillette* participating in this practice to launch their introductory instalments.
5. 'Faites des heureux en remettant ce journal à une petite fille ou à un petit garçon'.
6. 'la marraine d'un nouveau journal'.
7. It should be noted that the encyclopaedic *BD Guide 2005*, a useful source in the compilation of this historical account, contains an entry on *Nane* that would appear for the first time in 1923, in the pages of *La Semaine de Suzette*. *Nane* will not be discussed here, however, as despite its combination of text and images (with the focus clearly on the former) it uses neither panels nor strips and its images are not intrinsic to narrative comprehension. Therefore, this work cannot truly be considered a *bande dessinée*.
8. *Winnie Winkle* would eventually cross the Atlantic to be published in *Excelsior Dimanche* from 1923. However, the francophone version differed significantly from Martin Branner's

original strip, taking Winnie's little brother as its principal figure and renaming the strip *Bicot* after him. Its original protagonist Winnie (renamed Suzy in the French-language version) appeared only sporadically in *Bicot*.

9. 'paresseuse et gourmande'.
10. See McKinney (2011: 25–41) for a full discussion of colonialism, imperialism and racism in Saint-Ogan's strips.
11. It is certainly true that images of the black female have been habitually sexualized in the *bande dessinée*, however. See Chapter 8 of this book.
12. 'un curieux style géométrique, proche du futurisme'.
13. 'une héroïne antirésistante et antisémite'.
14. 'le banditisme, le mensonge, le vol, la paresse, la lâcheté, la haine, la débauche…'.
15. Grove notes that American import strips were one of the principal targets of the 1949 law, both due to fear of their 'foreign mores' influencing French children and to a desire to protect the sales of French artists (2010: 134). With the law in place, he states, 'it would now be easy to repel the undress of Tarzan ("la débauche"), the double life of Superman and Clarke Kent ("le mensonge") or the daily non-activity of Goofy ("la paresse")' (2010: 134).
16. 'Les éditeurs, en général très bien pensants, refusaient les filles un peu décolletées, les personnages qui commençaient à faire du gringue aux filles. Alors, on s'est habitué à ne pas mettre de femmes dans nos histoires, du moins très peu, mais c'est une chose que la censure nous a imposée'.
17. 'des BD d'agences sans grande originalité, mais des titres comme *L'Humanité* et surtout *France-Soir* […] [avaient] une vraie politique de création'.
18. *Arabelle* was published daily in the newspaper taking the form of one strip divided into panels with all text underneath the images until 1954, when Ache modernized this format by incorporating the use of speech bubbles into his work (Gaumer 2010: 27).
19. Gaumer and Moliterni, for example, state the following in the entry on 'Barbarella' in their 1994 *Dictionnaire mondiale de la bande dessinée*: 'Barbarella is a symbol: she is the first heroine of what we now call adult *bande dessinée*' (Gaumer and Moliterni 1994: 43). 'Barbarella est un symbole: elle est la première héroïne de ce qui est convenu d'appeler aujourd'hui la bande dessinée adulte'. See Chapter 3 for a detailed case study of *Barbarella*.
20. Groensteen suggests that Losfeld played a particularly important role in *bande dessinée* production in the 1960s. Previously known for being a publisher of surrealist texts, Losfeld's tenure as a BD publisher (beginning with *Barbarella*) was short-lived, but the freedom he allowed artists during the 1960s – particularly by ignoring the standard 48-page format for albums and accepting to publish *bandes dessinées* not previously serialized in periodicals – was, Groensteen notes, revolutionary (2000: 174).
21. Grove defines this style, typically associated with *Spirou*, as displaying 'larger-than-life caricatures that nonetheless retain a feeling of realism' (2010: 140).
22. This trend will be more fully discussed in the historical section concerned with women secondary characters (see Chapter 5).
23. For a detailed discussion of the figure of Adèle Blanc-Sec, see Chapter 4.

24. 'comme il en existe peu dans la *bande dessinée*'.
25. Renaud and Dufaux created a 'spin-off' series, *La Route Jessica*, focusing on other characters from the narrative following this final volume of the main story.
26. See Beaty (2007) for a full discussion of the changing *bande dessinée* industry in the 1990s.
27. The first tome of *Aya de Yopougon* won the 'Best First Album' prize (Prix du meilleur premier album) at the Angoulême Festival in 2006.
28. This is also a feature of Juillard's earlier work *Le Cahier bleu* (1994).
29. It is interesting to note that male illustrator Galou, creator alongside (female) scriptwriter Blan of *La P'tite Blan* (first published in 2009, thus slightly outside the temporal scope of this book), has described his position as a male homosexual artist drawing a female homosexual character (the eponymous Blan) as entirely exceptional, describing himself in a 2009 interview as 'the only gay man on the planet to draw the adventures of a lesbian' ('le seul homo de cette planète à dessiner les aventures d'une lesbienne') (Delabre 2009).

Chapter 2 – Bécassine: The First Lady of Bande Dessinée?

1. Christophe's *La Famille Fenouillard* (created in 1889) is an earlier notable *bande dessinée* series presenting recurring characters, but divides its focus between the four Fenouillard family members.
2. Maurice Languereau was not unconnected to the *Bécassine* series or *La Semaine de Suzette* prior to 1913. A nephew to the director of Editions Gautier – and future boss of the publishing house – he had assisted his uncle with the creation of *La Semaine de Suzette* in 1905 (Davreux 2006: 14).
3. Two additional albums outside of the main series, produced for educational rather than entertainment purposes, *L'Alphabet de Bécassine* and *Les Chansons de Bécassine*, were also published in 1921 and 1927 respectively.
4. A further *Bécassine* publication – an alphabet book – drawn by Trubert and written by Vaubant named *L'Alphabet Bécassine* (not to be confused with Caumery and Pinchon's 1921 *L'Alphabet de Bécassine*, which, also an alphabet book, contained different content) appeared in 1961.
5. 'Ce dernier qui séjournait souvent en Bretagne situa l'histoire dans cette région de France tandis que Jacqueline Rivière relata une bévue commise par sa jeune bonne. Cette petite histoire fut donc mise en images et prit le nom de *L'Erreur de Bécassine*'.
6. Paul Gauguin's paintings of Brittany landscapes are particularly prominent examples. Several of Gauguin's Breton scenes, dating from the 1880s to 1890s, feature women in traditional dress sporting white *coiffe*s.
7. A coiffe is a headdress or bonnet, often associated with women's traditional Breton dress. Original text of above translation: 'En février 1900, le journal satirique *Le Rire* met en scène une 'bonne à tout faire', Yvonne Labrutec (on n'est pas très éloigné sémantiquement d'Annaïck Labornez, dite Bécassine, née cinq ans plus tard). En octobre 1903, *L'Assiette au*

beurre s'en prend en couverture à l'obscurantisme clérical des Bretonnes: à l'arrière-plan, une des Bretonnes en *coiffe* et tablier ressemble fort à ce que deviendra le personnage de Bécassine'.

8. This attention continues in the present day – a live-action, feature-length Bécassine film was released in June 2018, directed by Bruno Podalydès.
9. 'les conquêtes sociales et culturelles de la femme au XXe siècle'.
10. 'le thème de la sexualité qui doit être tenu secret à l'égard des fillettes'.
11. Another factor that may have contributed to the severity of Bécassine's physical defeminization is her publication in *La Semaine de Suzette*, which was directed towards young readers of the Catholic faith – the latter encouraging modest behaviour and dress to women of Bécassine's time (and long before) (Bechtel 2003: 2014). This would not seem to account for all factors of Bécassine's muted appearance, however (her lack of lips or eyelashes, for example).
12. '[elle est] amour comme tous les amours réunis'.
13. This observation once again indicates the possible influence of *La Semaine de Suzette*'s Catholic focus on Bécassine's characterization.
14. Although the creators' intentions are not of paramount importance to this analysis, it remains worth noting, as Lipani-Vaissade does in an article briefly discussing Bécassine, that in any case, the Breton maid was not purposely depicted as a symbol of female liberation by Pinchon and Caumery (2009: 153). In fact, as Zancarini-Fournel, in turn, notes, unlike much of the other content created for La Semaine de Suzette, the *Bécassine* series was not intended to instruct or morally influence the readership of the *illustré* – it was solely intended to entertain (2005: 182).
15. The serialization of *Bécassine pendant la guerre* in *La Semaine de Suzette* occurred after the publication of the album, its first instalment not appearing in the periodical until February of 1916.
16. *Bécassine en apprentissage* was serialized in 1914 in *La Semaine de Suzette* but not published in album form until 1919.
17. The album following these three works, *Bécassine chez les Turcs*, also sets its narrative against the backdrop of the war, but was not published until 1919.
18. A 'marraine de guerre' – a 'war godmother' – was a woman who volunteered to write to a deployed soldier during war-time. This practice began in France in 1915.
19. 'Possible qu'il y aura la guerre, mais comme c'est avec des gens qui n'existent pas, ça ne présente guère de risques …'.
20. Bécassine says 'sur le front'. This is a play on words using 'le front', which in French means both 'the front line' and 'the forehead'.
21. Marie Quillouch is presented in many ways as Bécassine's polar opposite. Her features are sharp and protruding in comparison to Bécassine's lack of facial detail and she is frequently depicted as bad-tempered and manipulative. In *Bécassine pendant la Grande Guerre*, Marie and the strip's usually docile heroine become involved in a physical altercation during which Bécassine throws a bucket of water over her cousin and the latter angrily pulls off Bécassine's *coiffe* to expose her hair.

22. This same visual tactic has been used over centuries to 'animalize' the representation of certain drawn figures, notably those not of white/European origins.
23. '[L]'étude des caractères d'après les bosses du crâne'.
24. 'Parfait! ... voici la bonté, le dévouement, la simplicité d'esprit ... Quel document pour l'ouvrage que je prépare!'
25. It is possible to posit a link between Bécassine's continued depiction as 'underdeveloped' and the concern held in some circles in nineteenth- and early twentieth-century France with 'degeneration' amongst the French people, which led to the development of certain eugenicist policies. This hypothesis is speculative in nature; however, the depiction of phrenology as a way to 'prove' Bécassine's difference in this strip (phrenology has been particularly linked with practices of scientific racism and attempts to show different levels of evolutionary development between human subjects) somewhat supports the suggestion that Bécassine may have been a humorous example of such theories of degeneration. For a full discussion of the notion of degeneration, see Brauer and Callen (2008).
26. '[D]emande donc à voir la nommée Bécassine. C'est ce que nous avons ici de plus curieux/ Eh bien! Qu'on me montre cette curiosité'.
27. 'C'qu'elle est drôle!'
28. 'Méfiez-vous, Madame! Le trop potage va vous manger le bras!'. When Bécassine says 'trop potage' in this scene, she is trying, and failing, to say 'anthropophage' (cannibal).
29. This manipulation of Bécassine's naiveté and stupidity in order to alienate her from other figures differentiates her characterization from other notable 'fools' in the *bande dessinée*. The low intellect of certain 'stupid' characters appearing in the medium both before the creation and after the demise of Bécassine often appears as inclusive – that is, it is shared by other characters and thus used to establish a link between these figures. The idiocy of le sapeur Camember – the eponymous figure of the early strip by Christophe, first published in 1892 – for example, is shared (at least on occasion) by his commanding officer le sergent Bitur. Similarly, the dim-wittedness of Obélix (perennial sidekick in the *Astérix* series), is matched by that of the bard Assurancetourix, and sometimes even the village chief Abraracourcix. In contrast, Bécassine's stupidity serves, as noted, to separate her from fellow characters and isolate her as an 'alien' presence.

Chapter 3 – Barbarella: Study of a Sex-Symbol

1. See Grove (2005: 138) for a series of citations on this subject.
2. Jean-Claude Forest was also involved in the making of the film. He consulted on the script and designed all the sets.
3. '[U]n fond iconique de référence pour tout ce qui concerne l'érotisme et les *sixties*'. The cultural influence of Barbarella appears to have continued into the twenty-first century. In 2004, a musical entitled *Barbarella*, based on Vadim's film and written and produced by British composer David A. Stewart, premiered in Austria. Also, in 2012, Gaumont

International TV announced that they would be producing a new television series continuing the character's adventures.
4. 'Je n'en suis pas morte mais on en a fait un film…'.
5. Although this was the reason given by the *Commission de contrôle et de surveillance*, it is suggested in *Astérix, Barbarella et Cie* that the censorship of *Barbarella* was less motivated by the content of this strip and more by the desire of the Committee, shocked by this new adult direction of the *bande dessinée*, to discourage the further development of sexualized sequential art within the French market (Groensteen 2000: 174).
6. 'This is barbaric censorship'. Note the play on words in the original French with 'barbare est là'/Barbarella.
7. 'Malheureusement, de cette bande dessinée […] on n'a retenu trop souvent que le coté sexuel: une histoire de fesses. Cela vaut à Forest la réputation réductrice de pornographe, ou pour le moins de spécialiste des BD érotiques'.
8. Forest here joins René Giffey as an example of an artist who drew both children's *bandes dessinées* and erotic adult strips simultaneously or in quick succession in their careers.
9. Many of Forest's sketches and cover illustrations show his inclination towards the science-fiction genre. His work for magazine *Fiction* is a good example of this.
10. This differs from the film *Barbarella* in which the mission of the eponymous character, to find Earth scientist Duran Duran, is outlined from the start.
11. '[U]ne fille libre, sauvage, indépendante. Ce n'est pas une suffragette pour autant, ni un gendarme'.
12. In *Les Colères du Mange-minutes*, during a conversation with a defective sex-bot that Barbarella proceeds to repair, she informs her robot companion that she studied social sciences at Nanterre University (Forest 1994: 46). Although this surprising piece of information defends the intelligence of Barbarella, the rarity of personal details provided concerning the character throughout the series in addition to the creation of this second narrative between 1966 and 1969 (although it was serialized from 1967), suggests her admission to be a reference in support of the May '68 protesters rather than a detail that was always destined to be included. That a major catalytic force for the May '68 protests was the implied prohibition of sexual relations between students at Nanterre (due to the strict gender segregation of university accommodation) strengthens the suggestion that the sexually-uninhibited Barbarella's unusual personal divulgence is a reference to these real-world events.
13. Although male characters may be grounded by incidental aspects of a particular narrative, Lathers suggests that grounding as a general practice is not seen in the depiction of male figures whose exploits into space are largely presented as heroic, rather than in some way unnatural or problematic.
14. Although this *bande dessinée* is often labeled 'erotic', it is by no means explicit. Barbarella is shown naked in the arms of different men over the course of the narrative indicating that they have had sex; however, the act itself is never shown.

15. Scenes from the brothel sequence that show various unnamed female figures in a variety of poses and attached to (or suspended from) various apparatus recall certain images from Guido Crepax's 1976 *Bianca*. The mutual influence of French and Italian adult sequential art from the 1960s onwards and the serialization of *Les Colères du Mange-minutes* in Italian journal *Linus* (home publication to Crepax's most famous creation *Valentina*) suggest that the Italian artist may have been directly influenced by Forest's work in this narrative.
16. The etymological origin of this planet's name – from the Greek 'gyne' meaning 'woman' – suggests fertility and reproduction to be a fully female-focused affair.
17. Barbarella is, unusually, somewhat eroticized *while* pregnant, however. She is briefly shown on Gyn-Gyn with a rounded stomach and in each panel in which her pregnancy is visible she is depicted nude and often in a provocative pose, her fetishized eroticism overshadowing the fact of her enlarged stomach as the most visible part of her depiction.
18. Lefèvre-Vakana notes in his biography of Forest that the artist's wider œuvre echoed this stylistic progression away from the image and saw him increasingly give priority to textual expression until two years before his death when he abandoned visual art entirely to write novels full time (2004: 17).
19. Elements that involve the imaginative participation of the reader may be ones that the *bande dessinée* is simply unable to provide – such as the sound of a character's voice – or they may be one that the artist has chosen to withhold. In Scott McCloud's *Understanding Comics*, he discusses a technique used by sequential artists in which the detail with which a character is drawn is varied to invite – or discourage – the identification of the reader with the character. Generally speaking, the less detailed the visual depiction of the character, the more the reader participates in the completion of their representation, often seeing themselves in this *tabula rasa*, and thus becomes actively invested in the narrative (1994: 36).
20. 'Pourquoi m'ont-ils jetée sur ces pierres tranchantes...?'
21. The use of the male pronoun in reference to the reader of *Barbarella* is intentional here – as discussed in the Introduction to this book, it presumes the masculinized viewing position adopted by a reader of either sex. Forest clearly positions the incoming gaze not only as masculine but also as heterosexual: despite occasional moments of homoeroticism between Barbarella and female figures such as the Medusa or the Queen of Sogo in their brief interactions, these women are subsequently punished (via death and dethroning respectively) while Barbarella resumes her flirtation with men, this discouraging the real establishment of a homosexual gaze.
22. In this panel, two male figures are present in the background looking upon Barbarella (one administering the 'protective' vapour), in accordance with Forest's structuring technique for panels displaying the female character. A third figure does occupy the foreground with Barbarella; however, this diminutive, child-like alien neither resembles a man nor occupies the role of an adult male character in the narrative, and thus is not a threat to the established hierarchy of the gaze.

23. 'sa curiosité de connaître la tendresse d'un Orhomr'. The placing of a clothed or covered man behind a recumbent, naked and displayed female is seen in Renaissance art, notably in certain paintings of Venus and Mars. Examples of this are Titian's *Venus, Mars and Amor* and Giordano's *Venus and Mars*.
24. The cinematic version of *Barbarella* is less provocative throughout in terms of nudity than its *bande dessinée* inspiration. A clear example of this from the film is that the repeated trope used to indicate that Barbarella has been intimate with a male companion is audible rather than visual – Barbarella sings or hums contentedly.
25. 'tout…et très soigneusement'.
26. 'Viktor vous avez du style!'. Barbarella's interesting use of the formal 'vous' in reference to her robotic partner perhaps indicates the esteem in which she holds sexual prowess.
27. Blindness is often identified as a signifier of castration in the psychoanalytic paradigm. See Rand and Torok (1994: 198).
28. In *The Sign of the Cross: From Golgotha to Genocide*, Daniel Rancour-Laferriere describes crucifixion as, amongst other symbolic significations, a tortuous method of feminizing the sufferer as their body is penetrated by phallic tools (Rancour-Laferriere 2011: 82).
29. '[L]a fille que j'ai toujours rêvé de rencontrer…'.
30. In fact, Mulvey notes that one example of Allen Jones's sculpture that she analyses in 'Fears, Fantasies and the Male Unconscious' or 'You Don't Know What Is Happening, Do You, Mr Jones', entitled *Hat-Stand*, is based on a publicity still used to promote the film *Barbarella* (2009: 9), which shows Jane Fonda's incarnation of the character bound in leather and awaiting torture.
31. There is some evidence in the *Barbarella* series that suggests Forest to be aware of Freudian theory, although such knowledge on the part of the creator is not necessary for a post-Freudian psychoanalytic reading of his work. In the second album, a young girl rescued by Barbarella is taught Galactic Esperanto by being attached to 'le système Freud et Comabluzier' that instills the knowledge of language by stimulating the libido (1994: 12). In the fourth album, Barbarella undergoes psychoanalysis in a bid to understand the source of her presumed hallucinations. More anecdotally, the second-hand copy of *Le Semble-Lune* used in the preparation of this chapter bears a hand-written inscription apparently from Forest dedicating 'this hugely Freudian story' ('cette histoire furieusement freudienne') to its original owners.

Chapter 4 – Solving the Mystery of Adèle Blanc-Sec

1. *Tardi: Entretiens avec Numa Sadoul.* Sadoul's previous interviewees have included BD heavyweights Hergé, Moebius and Uderzo.
2. Tardi's style has influenced that of other BD artists, including Chantal Montellier. A further brief consideration of echoes of Tardi's work in Montellier's œuvre is noted on p.167.

3. In addition to appearing in album format, *Les Aventures extraordinaires d'Adèle Blanc-Sec* have also been serialized in various publications, notably *(A Suivre)*. For a full account of Adèle's appearances in periodicals, see Gaumer (2010: 7).
4. 'Il est certain que le personnage n'a pas du tout la mentalité d'une femme de son époque. Adèle est plutôt un personnage féminin d'aujourd'hui'. *Le Livre d'Adèle* is accredited to both Jacques Tardi and Nicolas Finet, and was published in 2010 to coincide with the release of Besson's cinematographic adaptation of Adèle's adventures. However, it seems clear from the extensive quotation of Tardi throughout the book, and from Finet's thanks to the artist for his 'contribution' at its conclusion, that Finet is the author of the prose with Tardi the subject of interview and artist of several images, mostly of Adèle, apparently drawn specifically for the book. It does, as noted, constitute the most in-depth study of the series and its eponymous character. However, it is not strictly academic in nature (and resolutely uncritical, no doubt in deference to Tardi's involvement), and, whilst an undoubtedly useful source, may fall under the category of 'fandom'.
5. This comes mid-way through *Tous des monstres!* when Adèle replies to a man who is loudly lamenting the conditions suffered by men during the First World War: '[y]ou're throwing important truths at us, but you're forgetting women'. ('Vous nous assenez des vérités considérables, mais vous oubliez les femmes...' [Tardi 1976: 33]).
6. 'C'est la deuxième fois qu'on essaye de me tuer cette nuit...Je me demande si je dois rester debout ou me recoucher.'
7. In this respect the setting of Adèle's adventures is comparable to that of Malet's *Nestor Burma* series (one thinks particularly of the 1956 novel *Brouillard au pont de Tolbiac*).
8. This perhaps explains why Adèle and Edith are so visually similar. The latter wears glasses over a longer, sharper nose; however, this is the only real difference in their physical depiction.
9. The possibility of Adèle's place as the narrator draws a parallel between her mysterious adventures and the *Sherlock Holmes* detective series, in which a character, Dr Watson, is the narrating voice.
10. 'Notre jeune et belle héroïne désarma les deux brigands, puis d'un coup sec arracha les masques hideux qui cachaient leurs visages'.
11. 'Tout est paisible dans l'appartement de notre jeune et belle héroïne'.
12. The *Adèle Blanc-Sec* series begins in 1911. In 1909, following an amendment to a previous decree, it was made regional law that women in Paris were only permitted to wear trousers when riding, or holding the handlebars of, a bicycle. According to *The Telegraph* in a 2010 report, this law has never been repealed (Samuel 2010).
13. Edith Rabatjoie (who has escaped from Adèle's custody) also appears dressed as a man in this final sequence, having followed Adèle and Ripol accompanied by Adèle's treacherous ex-employee Albert. Although originally intended to be the eponymous figure of this series as noted above, Edith does not reappear after the first album and hence is not sufficiently developed as a character to make a detailed examination possible.

NOTES

14. 'Ma pauvre enfant'.
15. It is interesting to note that in an intriguing twist later in the same album, Adèle is taken hostage by Esperandieu, and it is, in turn, from him that she is rescued by the *pithécanthrope*.
16. This quotation is provided solely in English by Laity.
17. 'D'un point de vue féminine, la bande dessinée était pratiquement un désert. Il y avait eu Bécassine, et puis Barbarella, et entre les deux, rien ou presque. Je me suis dit que j'allais créer une sorte de Brindavoine au féminin'.
18. 'ce que l'imaginaire collectif reconnaît spontanément comme tel: une créature qui fait exception à ce qui est perçu (à tort ou à raison) comme ordre naturel'.
19. Jones discusses unmarried female detective characters from the Anglo-American literary tradition in her article: 'Agatha Christie's Miss Marple; Stuart Palmer's Hildegarde Withers; Patricia Wentworth's Miss Silver; and Heron Carvic's Miss Seeton' (Jones 1975: 107). Single female investigator characters are not as prominent in the French detective genre in literature, although Charles Exbrayat's Imogène McCathery is one example.
20. 'On imagine mal Sherlock Holmes aller chercher ses enfants à l'école'.
21. It is interesting to note that in Luc Besson's cinematic adaptation of the Adèle Blanc-Sec narrative (the film, also entitled *Les Aventures extraordinaires d'Adèle Blanc-Sec*, is largely a composite of the first and third albums, with original elements incorporated), Adèle has a twin sister she battles to save throughout the story. This vision of Adèle as a figure with noble motivations and positive, compassionate relationships with other people is quite different from her self-interested, misanthropic BD incarnation.
22. As indicated by Screech, the figure of Clara Bernhardt is a reference by Tardi to the popular *Belle Époque* actress Sarah Bernhardt (2005: 149). It is interesting that Tardi features in *Les Aventures extraordinaires d'Adèle Blanc-Sec* a reference to Bernhardt, an openly bisexual, trouser-wearing woman whose most controversial acting choice famously saw her interpret the traditionally male-reserved role of Hamlet in 1899. It is possible that Bernhardt's real-life transgression of traditional gender performance inspired the personality of Adèle Blanc-Sec.
23. 'Rendue à moitié folle par la perte de sa beauté'.
24. This is similar to Mulvey's theory that one of the 'avenues of escape' for the male unconscious from the castration anxiety provoked by the sight of the female body is 'investigating the woman, demystifying her mystery' (1989: 21). This is counterbalanced by the saving or punishing of the 'guilty' woman, as described above.
25. The naked female form is seen in two further albums. In *Momies en folie*, an unidentified nude female is sacrificed by a satanic cult, and in *Tous des monstres!* a woman (later discovered to be Mireille Pain-Sec) is shown naked as she models for a life art class.
26. The 'iconic' status of this image is defended by the fact that it is one of the few direct strip-to-screen transpositions between the BD series and Besson's filmic adaptation.

27. For a comprehensive consideration of the trope of the bather in painted art, see Nochlin 2006.
28. Interestingly, in *Le Labyrinthe infernal*, Brindavoine is also shown in the bath, this constituting the first and only view of a naked male figure in the series. Brindavoine additionally falls under Schlesser and Sécheret's description of the 'monstrous' in Tardi's work, for very different reasons than Adèle: he is an amputee, having voluntarily infected his arm with gangrene to escape the horror of the First World War trenches. The view of Brindavoine in the bath appears to take on a different symbolic meaning to that attached to Adèle's 'purifying' bathing ritual. In these frames Brindavoine's injured body is clearly shown for the first time, and the reader's eye is drawn to his mutilated 'monstrosity'. The figure of Brindavoine in *Les Aventures extraordinaires d'Adèle Blanc-Sec* is intriguing and warrants further examination. Due to the female focus of the current study, however, this must be undertaken elsewhere.

Chapter 5 – Beyond Bonemine: An Introductory History of Female Secondary Characters in the Francophone Bande Dessinée

1. 'la traitrise, la fourberie'.
2. 'la sensibilité, la fragilité, la coquetterie, l'intuition et…l'art d'attirer des problèmes'.
3. This strip was an influence for Jean-Claude Forest's later science-fiction *bandes dessinées*, particularly *Barbarella*.
4. Although the 1949 law was ostensibly created to protect children from 'immoral' influence, as Simone Castaldi notes in an international aside in *Drawn and Dangerous: Italian Comics of the 1970s to 1980s*, the law also allowed the communist French government of the time to 'prevent the diffusion of American comics and what was perceived to be their treacherous capitalist-imperialist ideology' (Castaldi 2010: 33).
5. 'Jacobs est un cochon!'
6. 'intournables classiques du 9e art'.
7. 'Woman Smurf'.
8. Known in the English-language translations as Papa Smurf, Lazy Smurf and Handy Smurf.
9. For a more detailed discussion of *Pilote*'s pivotal role in the *bande dessinée* of the 1960s and beyond, see Michallat 2018.
10. 'L'un des premiers auteurs de bande dessinée dont l'œuvre a su ménager aux femmes une place de choix'.
11. Crepax and Pratt shared influences when it came to female figures, both basing characters on American actress Louise Brooks (inspiration for Crepax's Valentina and Pratt's Louise Brookszowyc).
12. For more information on the Comics Code, see Beaty 2005.
13. 'Réservé aux adultes'.

14. One of the founding artists of *L'Écho des Savanes* was Claire Bretécher, illustrating that women too may be responsible for variously 'unfeminist' images. More examples of this are considered in Chapter 10.
15. From the evidence amassed thus far in this original historical account of women secondary characters, it appears that Annie Pilloy's observations about female figures and hair colour in *bandes dessinées* for children are also applicable to strips for more mature audiences.
16. As Groensteen (2013) has noted, one element of both of the above-noted trends (and, indeed, other genres since the 1960s 'adult revolution' of the *bande dessinée*) that did allow women characters a prominent place, interestingly, was album covers, which disproportionately featured minor female figures in varying states of undress, often accompanied by guns or other weaponry, as an eye-grabbing marketing tactic.

Chapter 6 – A Study of Stereotypes: The Secondary Female Characters of Astérix

1. See also Bruno (2002) for a very brief but useful summary of female depiction in the series.
2. For an analysis of Cleopatra's depiction in *Astérix et Cléopâtre*, however, see Lipani-Vaissade 2011: 137.
3. 'Falbala', significantly, means 'furbelows' or 'frills', thus attributing to this first named female figure frivolous or ornamental connotations.
4. 'rien moins qu'un dictionnaire exhaustif des personnages d'Astérix'. It should be noted that this 'exhaustive' dictionary seems to omit many minor characters (male and female) from Astérix and Obélix's overseas adventures; however, the 10:1 male/female ratio it suggests would seem to be a fairly indicative average of all albums.
5. 'On nous a souvent reproché la faible présence féminine dans les aventures d'Astérix. Mais il faut bien voir que nos personnages sont pour la plupart burlesques. Ce sont des caricatures. Pour notre part, nous tenons trop la femme en estime pour la mettre dans des situations grotesques et lui donner une image qui la dénaturerait […]'.
6. 'si des imbéciles écrivent un jour l'histoire de notre village, ils n'appelleront pas ça les aventures d'Abraracourcix le Gaulois !!!'.
7. It has been suggested that the couple of Mr and Mrs Agecanonix represents a subtle parody of Goscinny's relationship with his wife who was fourteen years his junior (Rouvière 2006: 202).
8. 'Au lieu de dire des sornettes, aide-moi plutôt à plumer ce poulet!'
9. The rolling pin is also a symbol of female force in the British strip *Andy Capp*, which shows the eponymous Andy facing his rolling-pin-wielding wife Flo when he stumbles home late from the pub.
10. The name of this character is a clear reference to Verdi's opera *La Traviata*, which, adapted from Dumas' *La Dame aux camellias*, tells the story of a Parisian courtesan.

11. The publication of *La Rose et le glaive* – a narrative that satirizes the emergence of feminism in society – in 1990 is somewhat curious, coming two decades after the publicizing of the feminist cause in France following May '68 and the formation of the *Mouvement de libération des femmes* (MLF). The narrative may have been inspired by the visible inclusion of feminist interests in politics during the 1980s – Mitterrand created a Ministry of Women's Rights soon after his election, for example – and by the emergence of some high-profile female politicians, such as Edith Cresson (the first female Minister of Agriculture in France and later the first and, to date, only female Prime Minister), who was not well-received in her domain. Several online *Astérix* fan sites suggest that Maestria, a prominent female figure in *La Rose et le glaive*, is a caricature of Cresson; however, Uderzo has never confirmed this.
12. One well-known example of the mocking of educated women in French-drawn art is Daumier's 1844 series of caricatures on the *bas-bleu* (from the English 'blue stocking'. The term was used to refer to a woman of letters and took on a pejorative connotation). Daumier's collection shows, for example, an image of a man whose trousers have been thrown at his head by an angry wife and one of a young child stuck headfirst in a pail of water while her mother sits at a desk, writing. Some narrative elements of *La Rose et le glaive* are reminiscent of such caricatures.
13. As an unmarried woman (as noted in Chapter 4), Adèle Blanc-Sec would seem to correspond also to the basic criteria of the 'woman alone' type. However, in keeping with her generally ambiguous representation in other respects, Adèle's characterization and, particularly, her interactions with other figures do not place her as a traditional example of this type as Maestria is. Most notably, she is neither mocked nor pitied; rather, as indicated, this element of her 'monstrosity' is neutralized by her nude beautification.
14. 'Un village peuplé d'irréductibles Gaulois résiste encore et toujours à l'envahisseur'.

Chapter 7 – Secondary Women in *Urban Realism:* La Vie de ma mère

1. This work is named after a repeated exclamation of the principal character that translates in English to 'on my mother's life'.
2. 'mon petit'.
3. As noted, the title of the work, *La Vie de ma mère*, constitutes the phrase that Kevin repeats consistently in his narration to attest to the truth of his testimony. It is possible, however, that it also refers in a subtler way to Kevin's struggle to find a maternal figure in his life.
4. 'Allez, on s'arrache! La thune, je l'ai!'.
5. 'Chez moi, on est pas cistra, la preuve, Nathalie, une fois, elle est sortie avec un black'.
6. Ferguson (1981: 7) draws a clear distinction between the 'seductress', who wields her power over men, and the 'sex object', who is powerless and is used by men. 'Kept women' and prostitutes are often examples of the 'sex object' type.
7. 'un art fondé sur l'image davantage que sur le langage (par opposition au roman)'.
8. 'Elle l'a largué vite fait, son black, Nathalie. Maintenant, elle vit avec un portos, Antonio!'
9. 'qu'elle aille pas croire que je voulais lui faire des trucs dégueulasses …'.

10. 'afin justement d'éviter l'écueil de la simple répétition en images du récit d'origine'.
11. 'Dans la plupart des albums, les visages et les corps féminins demeurent privés d'existence individuelle, tant ils obéissent aux mêmes schémas, aux mêmes clichés de la séduction inexpressive'.
12. 'la meuf elle avait la terreur, elle bougeait plus ni rien'.
13. It is noted in the preceding chronology of female secondary characters in the *bande dessinée* that in the heroic fantasy genre, sexual violence against women is shown in several strips. The depiction of this sexual violence is often eroticized and thus greatly differs from Chauzy and Jonquet's shocking, realist depiction of rape in *La Vie de ma mère*.
14. 'Dans la cour, j'ai vu Clarisse. Elle m'a fait un sourire, et dans ma tête, ça s'est tout brouillé avec le sourire que la meuf de Livry-Gargan elle m'avait fait quand j'avais sonné à son portail, la vérité ! Y a son visage qui s'est mélangé à çui de Clarisse, c'était style un cauchemar'.

Chapter 8 – Black Secondary Women in the Works of Warnauts and Raives: The Eroticization of Difference

1. Nevertheless, lesbian characters depicted by male creators still remain quite rare. See p. 29, p.33, pp.148-149 and p.210 (endnote 29) for further discussion on this matter.
2. The symbolic potency of fruits (and other foods) in artistically conveying exotic 'difference' to European audiences goes beyond the simple visual suggestion seen in 'Congo blanc'. In *Consuming the Caribbean: From Arawaks to Zombies*, Mimi Sheller indicates the widespread exploitation of the exoticism of creole foods in literature seeking to display an Othered, romanticized image of the Caribbean (2003: 186 [see also Britton 1996]).
3. Baligi's pose here may also echo a trend in colonial art, as Willis and Williams note that 'in Orientalist art, the odalisque pose of a recumbent woman was used to draw immediate parallels to the sexually available woman' (2002: 42). The pose was earlier established in artworks eroticizing the female form regardless of race, however – one thinks particularly of Goya's *La Maja nuda* (*c*.1797–1800) – and would later find its way into photography. See particularly Man Ray's pictures of Kiki de Montparnasse in the early 1920s.
4. The extensive exhibition of (and reproduction of images depicting) Sarah Baartman – a nineteenth-century Khosian woman whose display to fascinated spectators in western Europe earned her the nickname 'The Hottentot Venus' – is a clear example of this. For a fuller account of Sarah Baartman's life, see Hobson (2005). For a comprehensive historical study of the photography and exhibition of the black female body, see Williams and Willis 2002.
5. It is also interesting to note when considering the Black Venus narrative in cinema the attention drawn to this figure in 2010 by *La Graine et le mulet* director Abdellatif Kechiche's film *Vénus noire*, which told the story of Sarah Baartman, the 'Hottentot Venus' (see Note 4, above).

6. 'Demain' and 'Tu es mon homme'.
7. The difference between Baligi and Isabelle's levels of verbal expression recall Spivak's observation in influential essay 'Can the Subaltern Speak' that the female (post-)colonial figure is doubly silenced – that both her race and her sex render her unable to express herself in obtaining representational systems (Spivak 1993: 82–83). Juxtaposed against Isabelle's dialogue, Baligi's almost total silence stems from her position as both black and female.
8. 'cette saleté de négresse'.
9. 'C'est grotesque, tu aimes la baiser, c'est tout…c'est uniquement sexuel!'
10. 'Je ne peux pas…pardonne-moi…Louis'.
11. 'Parce que le fait qu'elle soit black ne compte pas dans ton désir de la revoir?'
12. That Souana notes her participation in an *Antillaise* dance troupe is significant and recalls to an extent a narrative device employed in colonial cinema to remind the audience of the underlying 'primitive and sexualized' nature of women of African origin who have adapted to life in France. In pre-war French films featuring female characters of colonial origin such as Grémillon's *Daïnah la métisse* (1931) and Gréville's famous *Princesse Tam-Tam* (1935) starring Josephine Baker, it is through the women's frenetic performances of their native dances that their 'intrinsically wild and eroticized' dispositions are made evident.
13. 'Ce pays? Mais c'est la France'.
14. 'Ce pays est la Guadeloupe. Il n'y a que "vous" pour croire que nous sommes vraiment ici en France. Vous et quelques hommes politiques intéressés'.
15. 'C'est le climat. Ça les rend nerveux, les pauvres chéris'.

Chapter 9 – Secondary Women in the BD New Wave: The Female Figures of Le Combat ordinaire

1. Nonetheless, as Grove notes, Larcenet is slightly unusual as a part of this new *bande dessinée* direction, in that his work has almost always been published by mainstream houses such as Delcourt and Dargaud (2010: 189).
2. Grove also links the aforementioned focus on artists – 'the promotion of an independent BD d'*auteur*' (2010: 52) – and the limited budget of some strips of this new movement of *bande dessinée* production to similar features in the emergence of the French cinematic 'New Wave'.
3. This is comparable to Baru's *L'Autoroute de Soleil* (1995) in which, as Miller notes, the end of traditional male employment in the north-east of France is symbolized by the demolition of the blast furnace at the local steelworks of the principal characters Karim and Alexandre (2007: 75). The demise of traditionally 'male' heavy industry jobs used as a narrative premise is also seen in turn-of-the millennium cinema, for example Abdellatif Kechiche's 2007 film *La Graine et le mulet*.

4. 'Ooooh mais tu m'as l'air bien pâle! Tu ne dois pas bien manger, toi. Depuis tout petit, tu as des problèmes avec la nourriture. Et ta constipation, ça va mieux ? Ooh! Et puis tu ne t'es pas rasé et tes vêtements ne sont pas repassés…'.
5. 'Oh ! Mon dieu…comme je suis inquiète pour toi !'.
6. 'Les racines, c'est bon pour les ficus!'.
7. 'une femme se présente à la présidentielle, dis donc! …et elle a une vraie chance, c'est pas une figurante, tu te rends compte?! Évidemment, toi, tu l'aurais détestée…'.
8. 'Parfois, je pense à toi…où est-ce qu'il a disparu, toutes ces années, le garçon timide qui avait demandé ma main à mon père dans son costume de messe? Faut-il que la vie t'ait laminé…qu'elle te soit passée dessus comme un train…pour être devenu cet égoïste abruti, haineux et sans compassion aux côtés duquel j'ai tout raté…'.
9. 'Les Français ont tellement peur pour leurs maisons qu'ils en oublient que ce sont nos parents qui les ont construites'.
10. In Miller's aforementioned post-colonially-focused analysis of *Le Combat ordinaire*, she proposes a different interpretation of this episode, suggesting that Marco's collapse could be 'read as a symptom of his terror at the possibility of becoming a father himself' but that it is also possible to interpret it as 'an unconscious fear of acknowledging the dual identity embodied by the little girl' (2007: 170).

Chapter 10 – The Women that Women Draw: An Introductory History of Female Characters Drawn by Women Artists in the Francophone Bande Dessinée

1. As noted in the Introduction and in the Chapter 2 study of Bécassine, although this character was originally conceived in 1905 by a male-female creative team, Jacqueline Rivière and Joseph-Porphyre Pinchon, the principal creative pair behind the long-running series and the most well-known depictions of the character was to be artist Pinchon alongside Maurice 'Caumery' Languereau. Thus, Bécassine is discussed in Section 1 of this book, focusing on male-drawn strips.
2. 'Youpi! Vite mon masque au concombre!'
3. 'la belle fée avait pour nom Claire Bretécher, et, en quelques coups de son crayon magique, elle transforma ce qui aurait pu être doux et fade en quelque chose de relevé, d'appétissant, et d'incroyablement farfelu.'
4. The feud between rival gang leaders Manda and Leca over 'Casque d'Or' – the nickname of prostitute Amélie Élie – was also made into a film in 1952 (simply entitled *Casque d'Or*), directed by Jacques Becker.
5. 'Depressing'.
6. 'cette soi-disant nouvelle presse percluse des plus vieux et des plus crasseux fantasmes machos'.
7. 'fétichisme, sexisme et infantilisme'.

8. Cestac's series *Harry Mickson*, created at the end of the 1970s and regularly published throughout the 1980s, focused on the comedic exploits of the male principal figure (although a certain androgynous ambiguity is present in the series due to Cestac's bulbous style and choice of anthropomorphized characters), whilst Puchol's darkly-humoured, realist strips of the 1980s (*Ringard!*, *Les Traquenards*, *Dessous troublants*) featured both male and female characters without a particular focus on either).
9. In 1982, Claire Bretécher was awarded a special Angoulême festival '10th anniversary' prize similar to the 'Grand Prix' as it granted her the honour of co-presiding over the following year's festival alongside the 'traditional' Grand Prix winner, Paul Gillon.
10. See Chute (2010: 20–24) for more discussion of the history of US women's autobiographical strips.
11. 'semblait peu imaginable'.
12. 'La bande dessinée féminine' n'est pas un genre narratif [...] Publier des collections 'féminines' est misogyne'.
13. Her friends Valou and Suzanne tell her briefly in *Lucie: La Funambule*, for example, that they are entering into a civil union (2004: 45).
14. 'semble avoir "autorisé" d'autres jeunes femmes à travers le monde à s'exprimer à travers la bande dessinée'.
15. 'L'appellation "girly" ne fait que renforcer les clichés sexistes'.

Chapter 11 – The Rise and Fall of Ah! Nana: France's First and Only All-Female illustré

1. An interesting point to note is that the writer of the *BD Guide* article chose to cite the editor-in-chief using her married name, which never appeared in any issue of *Ah! Nana*: the latter always used her maiden name of Janic Guillerez in the pages of, and in reference to, the journal.
2. Both articles are condensed versions of Masters dissertations produced by their respective authors, which partially or wholly take *Ah! Nana* as their subject. See Delaborde 2005; Talet 2004.
3. As noted above, some male artists were invited to contribute to *Ah! Nana*, this occasionally resulting in male/female collaborations within the *illustré*. The journal also regularly featured strips by American women artists, which appeared in French translation. In order to remain within the defined limits of this project, however, only strips created entirely by women and originally written in French will be analysed in the following case studies.
4. 'Elles étaient quelques dessinatrices, coloristes et journalistes à se plaindre réciproquement de devoir assumer les phantasmes masculins déguisés en règle d'or de la presse. Nous passâmes aux actes, esquissant une idée de journal [...] Les Humanoïdes bourrés de soupçons offrirent leur imprimeur. Merci quand même'.

NOTES

5. 'Nazism today'.
6. 'Unfashionable Fashion'.
7. 'Men'.
8. 'Sex and Little Girls', 'Cruel France', 'Homosexuality, Transsexuality' and, finally, 'Incest'.
9. 'Sado-masochist bande dessinée artists: a bunch of impotent men?' (note the play on words in the original French provided by the word 'bande').
10. Janic Guillerez was, at the time of *Ah! Nana*'s conception, both the typographic designer for *Métal Hurlant* and the partner of its editor-in-chief Jean-Pierre Dionnet. Anne Delobel, editorial secretary for *Ah! Nana*, also performed this role for *Métal Hurlant* and was the colourist for her partner Jacques Tardi, an artist who contributed to both publications (Delaborde 2005: 25). For more information on the connection between *Ah! Nana*, *Métal Hurlant* and Les Humanoïdes Associés, see the dissertations by Delaborde and Talet noted above.
11. 'le parti affiché de déshumanisation qui apparait, dès le premier examen de la revue, et n'existe qu'au détriment de la femme, traitée en femme objet'.
12. 'Rosie the Riveter' was an important pre-feminist icon in the United States, symbolizing the American woman who took on traditionally 'male' jobs in factories during the Second World War. It was also the title of a strip by Trina Robbins, which had appeared in *Ah! Nana* under the translated title of 'Rosie la riveteuse'.
13. '*Ah! Nana* – le seul journal de bandes fait par des femmes!'; 'Interdit par des hommes!!!'
14. '*Ah ! Nana* va mourir ... La censure s'exerce, une fois encore. Entre deux revues de cul, nous tombons'.
15. '[o]n n'as pas l'habitude de voir des femmes ruer dans les brancards. Les dessins, les textes, souvent d'un humour vengeur et iconoclaste, nous valent d'être punies'.
16. 'Bonne Fête Papa'.
17. 'Ne vous étonnez point de découvrir en une seule fois autant de dessinatrices. On en recense officiellement cinquante en France, mais nous sommes certaines que vous êtes bien plus nombreuses. Mesdames, nous vous attendons'.
18. Although Chantal Montellier is now one of the most prolific female artists in francophone *bande dessinée* history, at the time of *Ah! Nana*'s creation, she had published very little. Her *Andy Gang* strip, which would later be made into two albums published by Les Humanoïdes Associés, was originally created for *Ah! Nana*.
19. In 1970, the law regarding 'paternal authority' over children was replaced with one respecting 'parental authority', thus allowing mothers equal decision-making rights over their families. Abortion was legalized in France in 1975, eight years after the legalization of the contraceptive pill, in 1967.
20. '[p]atiemment', 'avec persévérance', 'encore' and 'toujours'.
21. 'Mais enfin, il est bien quelque part, ce prince charmant!'.
22. 'Je ne vois rien venir!'.
23. 'Toujours rien! Je sens que je vais me décourager'.
24. 'Toujours dérangée! ... En tout cas, je ne partage pas mon gâteau!'.

25. 'Opération No. 5: Mettre légèrement les joues en relief à la lame de rasoir. Estomper…'.
26. Mona's first strip for *Ah! Nana* was announced in the third issue, as 'Edith Orial' noted the arrival of a new artist from Lebanon. Other than her country of origin, however, no information from either the pages of *Ah! Nana*, *bande dessinée* encyclopaedias or online research has been found.
27. 'salope'.
28. 'La salope, regardez ce qu'elle lui fait faire'.
29. 'elle jouit, elle jouit'.
30. 'Et voilà les amis, l'histoire triste et exemplaire d'Angélique […] Perchées sur des talons hauts, fagotées dans nos jupes, paralysées par nos ceintures, soutiens-gorges et corsets, la mode nous livre pieds et poings liés à nos agresseurs'.
31. 'Oh! Mais c'est le MLF! Ne regardez pas Soeur Immaculé, le pape l'a interdit!'.
32. 'Aimez-vous les filles! Dehors vous autres'.
33. 'Et rappelez-vous, pouvoir courir, sauter, c'est prendre son pied!'.
34. The link between the Catholic church and the denial of sexual pleasure is one seen elsewhere in Mona's work for *Ah! Nana* as her first strip for the journal, published in the third issue, features an interview with a doctor discussing the 'dangers' of sexual pleasure, before a priest appears to add that carnal pleasure is a 'mortal sin' ('un péché mortel') (Mona 1977a).
35. 'de mon temps', '… comme le temps passe …'.
36. 'Finalement, je vous ai trouvés, vous vous cachiez si bien derrière vos habitudes. Mais moi, je ne me laisse pas faire facilement par des exorcismes!'.
37. 'Ordre!', 'Dieu', and 'Famille'.
38. In this way, the message of the strip is similar to that found in *Le Combat ordinaire* concerning the evolution of women in the face of the decline of the traditional male. Capuana's strip focuses on an embodied and sexually aware conception of female 'emancipation', however, which is missing from Larcenet's work.

Chapter 12 – Murdering the Male Gaze: Chantal Montellier's Odile et les crocodiles

1. Her 2008 BD adaptation of Kafka's *The Trial*, co-created with David Zane Mairowitz, was originally published in English, however.
2. That the introduction to this album is written by Montellier may be considered symbolic in itself, as, like other contemporary female artists, several of Montellier's albums contain introductions by prominent male figures in the *bande dessinée* industry. Her inaugural published album *1996* (1978), for example, contains a preface by Jean-Claude Forest. *Social Fiction*, published in 2003, but regrouping into one tome three older albums – *1996*, *Wonder City* and *Shelter* (these are the original titles of the [French-language] strips) – features an introduction by Jean-Pierre Dionnet. Montellier's authorial preface for *Sorcières mes soeurs* in 2006 asserts the validity of her own voice within the *bande dessinée* industry.

3. 'La revue de BD féminine 'Ah! Nana' tombait [...] sous les coups d'une censure exclusivement masculine [...] La société patriarcale a d'excellents réflexes, dommage qu'ils lui servent surtout à briser les talents de ses femmes'.
4. 'Les bûchers de l'inquisition brûlent toujours, même si ceux qui les attisent ont remisé leurs déguisements au vestiaire et semblent être des nôtres'.
5. 'dynamique entre répétition et narration'.
6. Artemisia Gentileschi also became the subject of a 1997 film by Agnès Merlet, simply entitled *Artemisia*. As the title of this film suggests, Merlet approached the figure of Gentileschi in a more direct way than Montellier, whose references to the artist are interwoven within narratives focusing on other women figures. For a discussion of such references in *Faux Sanglant*, and symbolism in the wider album, see Miller (2001).
7. 'Odile B., ce n'est pas moi'.
8. For a lengthier discussion of the effect of Montellier's chosen colour scheme on the atmosphere of the album, see Smolderen (1984).
9. Nguyen and Sohet describe New Realist *bandes dessinées* as works that 'display critical ways of looking at and dealing with the reality of an urban and industrial society' (2003: 115). Chantal Montellier's work, in particular, 'brings New Realism to its extreme by emphasising the themes of social violence and exclusion aimed at visible minority groups and the mentally ill' (2003: 115).
10. 'comme le sort de toutes les femmes'.
11. 'Outre ses mille deux cents boutiques, le centre met à votre disposition [...] ses nombreuses salles de cinéma, son théâtre [...] et ses call-girls maison'.
12. 'Tous les dimanches matin, un prêtre en habit assure un service religieux, avec chant choral préenregistré. Un distributeur automatique d'hosties est à votre disposition au rayon: articles religieux'.
13. The dystopian society evoked here recalls that represented in Godard's 1965 film *Alphaville*.
14. Perhaps a reference to *Animal Farm*, this is not the only nod to George Orwell's work found within the album; graffiti references to his earlier work *Keep the Aspidistra Flying* are visible on the walls in certain scenes (see 2008: 35, for example).
15. 'Mes violeurs, eux, étaient des "fils de bonne famille", des violeurs de luxe – pour une pauvre fille comme moi, presque une aubaine! [...] je n'étais plus une femme salie mais une sale provocatrice! ...'.
16. In this way, Montellier's use of the *nouveau réaliste* style contrasts with the work of Yves Klein, the pioneer of *nouveau réalisme*. In 1960, Klein famously used nude female models as 'live brushes' (their bodies were covered in paint and then pressed against material to leave a brightly coloured impression), an artistic process that attracted criticism for its literal 'objectification' of women and their nude forms.
17. 'un accident sexuel'.
18. 'Votre plaisir seul guide votre vie ! Vous souhaitez que tout le monde vous aime! [...] Sans doute les traces d'une pathologie hystérique ...'.

19. Montellier's mediation of the viewer's gaze upon the naked figure of Odile in this panel via the look of these symbolic male figures in the foreground presents the character very consciously as the subject of a gaze defined by a gendered hierarchy. The formation of the panel in this way alters the view of Odile's nakedness from other examples of female nudity previously analysed in this study, in which the view of the exposed female is presented directly for the 'delectation' of the reader, and recalls Mulvey's observation in relation to cinema that a first challenge to the established conventions of looking in film would be to 'free the look of the camera into its materiality in time and space and the look of the audience into dialectics and passionate detachment' (1989: 26).
20. The pornographic presentation of some of these women – in provocative poses, wearing skimpy undergarments or bondage gear – contrasts their depiction from other exposed images of women already examined in this book, such as the images of Adèle Blanc-Sec considered in Tardi's series. In *The Female Nude: Art, Obscenity and Sexuality*, Lynda Nead differentiates between the 'female nude as a symbol of the pure, disinterested, functionless gaze and of the female body transubstantiated; and, on the other hand ... images of pornography, the realm of the profane ... where sensual desires are stimulated and gratified' (1992: 85). As discussed in relation to Tardi's work, the female nude provides an idealized and thus 'contained' view of the female form by removing 'all abhorrent reminders of her fecund corporeality ... secretions, pubic hair, genitals ...' (Ussher 2006: 3). The sexualized images shown (and critiqued) by Montellier, in contrast, precisely highlight the corporeality of the exposed women to invite a sexual response and thus are not intended to act as 'containing' or 'regulating' depictions of women.
21. 'ça manque de femme ici! [...] les femmes, plutôt que de leur faire faire le ménage, j'ai toujours mieux à leur proposer'.
22. 'conquérir, bien sûr d'une façon symbolique, le droit de regarder au lieu d'être regardée, au lieu d'être celle qu'on juge'.
23. 'Remarque que moi, j'aime mieux les grosses, mais enfin ... on fait avec ce qu'on a, pas vrai?'.
24. 'Une femme, ca se fabrique de A à Z! [...] Elle devient la toile et moi le peintre'.
25. This 1936 novel by George Orwell (translated into French as *Et vive l'aspidistra!* [only the last two words, without the 'Et' appear on the wall behind Odile's head]) tells the story of a writer who attempts to shun the economic impetus of twentieth-century life.
26. 'chaque mot, chaque phrase que j'écrivais me libérait un peu de ma peur. Je reprenais espoir [...] Je me disais que peut-être, grâce à ça, je n'aurais plus jamais envie de tuer ...'.
27. 'ton corps est mots'.
28. 'A mon avis il faut être soit très bestiale, soit très masochiste pour accepter de faire l'amour avec un homme ... avec une femme, par contre ...'.
29. However, it should be noted that Montellier's physical depiction of Odile is not incongruous with that of other characters throughout her work.
30. See, for example, those by Bagieu, Motin or Diglee. See pp. 150-151 for a discussion of so-called 'chick-BD'.

NOTES

Chapter 13 – Everyday Extremes: Aurélia Aurita's Fraise et chocolat

1. '[C]e livre a fait un BUZZ'.
2. See, for example, *L'Epinard de Yukiko* (2001).
3. 'L'histoire que vous venez de lire est une fiction, car je n'ai jamais, bien évidemment, de toute ma vie, repassé une seule des chemises de Frédéric'.
4. '[certaines planches] montrent que l'auteure sait dessiner plus académiquement'; 'entre esquisse et caricature'.
5. See, again, the analysis of Forest's *Barbarella* in Chapter 3, in which this erotic 'freezing' effect is, in contrast, very much encouraged.
6. Reyns-Chikuma and Gheno briefly refer to this feature of *Fraise et chocolat* in their work on Aurita and state it to be one of the reasons for the commercial success and attention – the 'buzz' – surrounding the book following its 2006 publication (2013: 109).
7. 'J'aimerais être avec quelqu'un … Mais avoir plein d'amants !!! A eux, je donnerais mon corps … mais mon fantasme c'est de réserver mon âme à une et une seule personne'.

Conclusion – Problem Solved?

1. 'Ah, et pour une fois c'est une fille qui parle'.
2. 'Ho j'aimerais bien savoir faire parler mes personnages féminins aussi bien que ça. Oui, mais elle, elle est une fille alors tu parles, ça vient tout seul'.
3. 'Jusqu'au jour où vous découvrez que quelqu'un l'a déjà fait et à ce moment-là vous vous sentez "autorisé" à le faire à votre tour'.

References

Algoud, A. (2010), *Petit dictionnaire énervé de Tintin*, Paris: Editions de l'Opportun.

Andrieu, O. (1999), *Le Livre d'Astérix le Gaulois*, Paris: Albert René.

Anon. (1919), *Lili*, Paris: Société parisienne d'édition.

Anon. (2017a), *Astérix. Le site officiel*, http://www.asterix.com/asterix-de-a-a-z/les-personnages/. Accessed 23 November 2017.

Anon. (2017b), *L'essentiel à propos de Tintin et Hergé*, https://fr.tintin.com/essentiel. Accessed 11 December 2017.

Aurita, A. (2006), *Fraise et chocolat*, Liège: Les Impressions Nouvelles.

Aurita, A. (2007), *Fraise et chocolat 2*, Clamecy: Les Impressions Nouvelles.

Aurita, A. (2009), *Buzz-moi*, Liège: Les Impressions Nouvelles.

Barecca, R. (2013), Preface, in P. Dickinson, A. Higgins, P.M St. Pierre, D.Solomon and S.Zwagerman (eds), *Women and Comedy: History, Theory, Practice*, Maryland: Fairleigh Dickinson University Press; Rowman & Littlefield, pp. xi–xviii.

Beaty, B. (2005), *Frederic Wertham and the Critique of Mass Culture*, Jackson: University Press of Mississippi.

Beaty, B. (2007), *Unpopular Culture: Transforming the European Comic Book in the 1990s*, Toronto: University of Toronto Press.

Bechtel, G. (2003), *Les Quatre Femmes de Dieu: La putain, la sorcière, la sainte et Bécassine*, Paris: Pocket.

Bhabha, H. (2004), *The Location of Culture*, London: Routledge.

Boy, F. (2009), *Les femmes dans la bande dessinée d'auteur depuis les années 1970: Itinéraires croisés: Claire Bretécher, Chantal Montellier, Marjane Satrapi*. s.l.:s.n., dumas-00712333.

Brauer, F. and Callen, A. (eds), (2008). *Art, Sex and Eugenics: Corpus Delecti*, London: Ashgate.

Bretécher, C. (1972), *Les États d'âme de Cellulite*, Paris: Dargaud.

Breton, A. (1962), *Manifestes du surréalisme: édition complète*, Paris: J.-J Pauvert.

Britton, C. (1996), 'Eating their words', in *ASCALF Yearbook 1*, s.l.:s.n., pp. 15–23.

Brogniez, L. (2010), 'Féminin singulier: les desseins du moi. Julie Doucet, Dominique Goblet', *Textyles*, 36-37, pp. 117–38.

Bruno, P. (2002), 'Astérix, devant nous, le sauveur de la France?', *Le Français aujourd'hui*, 136(1), pp. 104–09.

REFERENCES

Capuana, C. (1977a), 'Visite inattendue', *Ah! Nana* (no.3), pp. 18–27.

Capuana, C. (1977b), 'Untitled', *Ah! Nana* (no.6), Back Page.

Carrier, M. (2004), '*Persepolis* et les révolutions de Marjane Satrapi', *Belphégor: Littérature Populaire et Culture Médiatique*, 4:1, Web.

Carroll, N. (1990), 'The Image of Women in Film: A Defense of a Paradigm', *The Journal of Aesthetics and Art Criticism*, 48:4, pp. 349–60.

Castaldi, S. (2010), *Drawn and Dangerous: Italian Comics of the 1970s and 1980s*, Jackson: University Press of Mississippi.

Catel, V. and Grisseaux, V. (2004), *Lucie: La Funambule*, Paris: Casterman.

Caumery, M. and Pinchon, J. (1921), *Bécassine voyage*, Paris: Librairie Henri Gautier.

Caumery, M. and Pinchon, J. (1993), *Bécassine pendant la Grande Guerre*, Paris: Hachette/Gautier-Languereau.

Caumery, M. and Pinchon, J. (2015), *Bécassine. L'Intégrale - Livre I*, Paris: Hachette Livre/Gautier-Languereau.

Chauzy, J.-C. and Jonquet, T. (2003a), *La Vie de ma mère: Face A*, Paris: Casterman.

(2003b), *La Vie de ma mère: Face B*, Paris: Casterman.

Chute, H. (2010), *Graphic Women: Life Narrative and Contemporary Comics*, New York: Columbia University Press.

Ciuraru, C. (2011), 'The Story of the Story of O', http://www.guernicamag.com/features/2772/ciuraru61511/. Accessed 21 November 2011.

Cixous, H., Cohen, K. and Cohen, P. (1976), 'The Laugh of the Medusa', *Signs*, 1:4, pp. 875–93.

Claveloux, N. (1977), 'La Conasse et le Prince Charmant', *Ah! Nana* (no.2), pp. 27–31.

Collectif des créatrices de bande dessinée contre le sexisme (2016), 'Collectif des créatrices de bande dessinée contre le sexisme: Historique', https://bdegalite.org/historique/. Accessed 3 Novembre 2017.

Cone, A. (2011), 'Strange Encounters during Wartime: Bécassine chez les Turcs', *European Comic Art*, July, 4:2, pp. 181–97.

Cooper, S. (1995), 'Myths of Female Sexuality', in J.Magonet (ed.), *Jewish Explorations of Sexuality*, Oxford: Berghahn, pp. 157–64.

Cvetkovich, A. (2008), 'Drawing the Archive in Alison Bechdel's *Fun Home*', *Women's Studies Quarterly*, 36:1, pp. 111–28.

Darrow, M. H. (2000), *French Women and the First World War: War Stories of the Home Front*, Oxford: Berg.

Davreux, H. (2006), *Bécassine ou l'image d'une femme*, Paris: Editions Labor.

Delaborde, B. (2005), *Le magazine Ah! Nana (1976-1978)*, s.l.:Université Marc Bloch – Strasbourg II.

Delaborde, B. (2006), 'Ah! Nana - Les femmes humanoïdes', *Neuvième Art*, January, 12, pp. 68–73.

Delabre, A. (2009), 'BD: Blan et Galou présentent leur nouvel album', http://www.tetu.com/actualites/france/bd-blan-et-galou-presentent-leur-nouvel-album-15999. Accessed 29 July 2012.

Denni, M. (2001), 'Fillette 1909-1942', *Le Collectionneur de Bandes Dessinées*, 93, pp. 20–28.

Doan, L. L. (1991), *Old Maids to Radical Spinsters*, Chicago: University of Illinois Press.

Eagleton, M. (2003), 'Literature', in *A Concise Companion to Feminist Theory*, Oxford: Blackwell, pp. 153–72.

Eyers, T. (2012), *Lacan and the Concept of the 'Real'*, New York: Palgrave MacMillan.

Ferguson, M. A. (1981), *Images of Women in Literature*, 3rd ed., Boston: Houghton Mifflin Company.

Filippini, H. (2006), *Encyclopédie de la bande dessinée érotique*, Paris: La Musardine.

Finet, N. and Tardi, J. (2010), *Le Livre d'Adèle*, Paris: Casterman.

Forest, J. -C. (1982), *Le Miroir aux tempêtes*, Poitiers: Editions du Fromage et Albin Michel.

Forest, J. -C. (1994), *Barbarella* (Edition Intégrale: Premier Tome), Geneva: Les Humanoïdes associés.

Forsdick, C. (2005), 'Exoticising the Domestique: Bécassine, Brittany and the Beauty of the Dead', in C.Forsdick, L.Grove and L.McQuillan (eds), *The Francophone Bande Dessinée*, Amsterdam: Rodopi, pp. 23–37.

Frémion, Y. (2005), 'Yves Gohanne, dessinatrice mystère', *Le Collectionneur de Bandes Dessinées*, 106, p. 47.

Gaumer, P. (2010), *Dictionnaire mondial de la BD*, Paris: Larousse.

Gaumer, P. and Moliterni, C. (1994), *Dictionnaire mondial de la bande dessinée*, Paris: Larousse.

Gaumer, P. and Moliterni, C. (1997), *Dictionnaire mondial de la bande dessinée*, Paris: Larousse.

Genette, G. (1987), *Seuils*, Paris: Editions du Seuil.

Goscinny, R. and Uderzo, A. (1970), *La Zizanie*, Paris: Lombard.

Goscinny, R. and Uderzo, A. (1975), *Les aventures d'Astérix: Astérix chez les Helvètes, Le Domaine des Dieux, Les Lauriers de César, Le Devin, Astérix en Corse*, Paris: Dargaud.

Goscinny, R. and Uderzo, A. (1990), *La Rose et le glaive*, Paris: Les Editions Albert René.

Groensteen, T. (1980), *Tardi*, Paris: Magic Strip.

Groensteen, T. (1999), *Système de la bande dessinée*, Paris: Presses Universitaires de France.

Groensteen, T. (2000), *Astérix, Barbarella et Cie*, Angoulême: CNBDI.

Groensteen, T. (2013), 'Femme (1): représentation de la femme', http://neuviemeart.citebd.org/spip.php?article677. Accessed 16 February 2018.

Groensteen, T. (2014), 'Femme (2): la création au féminin', http://neuviemeart.citebd.org/spip.php?article727. Accessed 16 April 2018.

Groensteen, T. (2015), 'Femmes et bande dessinée: rencontre avec Thierry Groensteen', https://www.youtube.com/watch?v=w1oZrb3klk. Accessed 30 July 2019.

Grove, L. (2005), *Text/Image Mosaics in French Culture: Emblems and Comic Strips*, Aldershot: Ashgate.

Grove, L. (2010), *Comics in French: The European Bande Dessinée in Context*, Oxford: Berghan.

Guesdon, Y. (2014), *Coiffes de Bretagne*, Spézet: Coop Breizh.

Haederli, A. (2008), 'De Bonemine à Maestria: Les Femmes dans Astérix', *Uniscope*, April, 533, p. 7.

REFERENCES

Hannah, M.-K., Hunt, K. and West, P. (2004), 'Contextualising Smoking: Masculinity, Femininity and Class Différences in Smoking in Men and Women from Three Générations in the West of Scotland', *Health Education Research*, pp. 239–49.

Heller-Nicholas, A. (2011), *Rape-Revenge Films: A Critical Study*, Jefferson: McFarland.

Hobson, J. (2005), *Venus in the Dark: Blackness and Beauty in Popular Culture*, London: Routledge.

Hutcheon, L. (2013), *A Theory of Adaptation*, London: Routledge.

Jacobs, B. (2007), *Childfree Women: An Archetypal Perspective*, Ann Arbor: Pro Quest.

Jones, M. J. (1975), 'The Spinster Detective', *Journal of Communication*, June, 25:2, pp. 106–12.

Jonquet, T. (2001), *La Vie de ma mère*, Paris: Gallimard.

Joubert, B. (2006), *Histoires de censure: Anthologie érotique*, Paris: La Musardine.

Kunzle, D. (1986), 'Marie Duval and Ally Sloper', *History Workshop Journal*, 21:1, pp. 133–40.

Ladurie, I. L. R. (2016), 'L'autoreprésentation féminine dans la bande dessinée pornographique', *Revue de recherche en civilisation américaine*, 6, Online.

Laity, K. (2002), 'Construction of a "Female Hero": Iconography in *Les aventures extraordinaires d'Adèle Blanc-Sec*', *International Journal of Comic Art*, Spring, pp. 163–69.

Lambiek (2009), *Lambiek Comiclopedia*, http://lambiek.net/artists/l/layjanine.htm. Accessed 3 July 2012.

Larcenet, M. (2004a), *Le Combat ordinaire*, Paris: Dargaud.

Larcenet, M. (2004b), *Le Combat ordinaire 2: Les Quantités Négligeables*, Paris: Dargaud.

Larcenet, M. (2009), *Le Combat ordinaire 4: Planter des clous*, Paris: Dargaud.

Larcenet, M. (2011), *Le Combat ordinaire 3: Ce qui est précieux*, Paris: Dargaud.

Lathers, M. (2010), *Space Oddities: Women and Outer Space in Popular Film and Culture, 1960-2000*, New York: Continuum International.

Lefèvre-Vakana, P. (2003), 'Les Dessous de Barbarella', *Le Collectionneur de Bandes Dessinées*, 99, pp. 38–41.

Lefèvre-Vakana, P. (2004), *L'art de Jean-Claude Forest*, Paris: Editions de l'An 2.

Lehembre, B. (2005), *Bécassine: Une légende du siècle*, Paris: Gautier-Languereau.

Lemaire, T. (2009), *Thierry Groensteen: 'Les auteurs femmes sont très fréquemment réorientées vers l'illustration jeunesse'*, http://www.actuabd.com/Thierry-Groensteen-Les-auteurs. Accessed 3 September 2012.

Lemke-Santangelo, G. (2009), *Daughters of Aquarius: Women of the Sixties Counterculture*, Lawrence: University Press of Kansas.

Lenfant, C. (1978), 'Editorial', *Ah! Nana* (no.9), p. 2.

Lightman, S. (2014), *Graphic Details: Jewish Women's Confessional Comics in Essays and Interviews*, Jefferson: McFarland.

Lipani-Vaissade, M.-C. (2009), 'La Révolte des personnages féminins de la bande dessinée francophone', *Le Temps des médias*, 12, pp. 152–62.

Lipani-Vaissade, M.-C. (2011), 'Les femmes dans Astérix: uniquement des emmerdeuses?', in *Le Tour du monde d'Astérix*, Paris: Presses Sorbonne Nouvelle, pp. 131–48.

McCloud, S. (1994), *Understanding Comics*, New York: Harper Perennial.

McKinney, M. (1997), 'Métissage in post-colonial comics', in *Post-Colonial Cultures in France*, London: Routledge, pp. 169–89.

McKinney, M. (2000), 'The Representation of Ethnic Minority Women in Comic Books', in J.Freedman and C.Tarr (eds), *Women, Immigration and Identities in France*, Oxford: Berg, pp. 85–102.

McKinney, M. (2011), *The Colonial Heritage of French Comics*, Liverpool: Liverpool University Press.

Menu, J. -C. (2005), *Plates bandes*, Paris: l'Association.

Michallat, W., (2018) *French Cartoon Art in the 1960s and 1970s:* Pilote hebdomadaire *and the Teenager* Bande Dessinée, Leuven: Leuven University Press.

Miller, A. (2001), 'Chantal Montellier's Faux Sanglant: Sex, Death, Lies and Video Tape', *French Studies*, LV:2, pp. 207–20.

Miller, A. (2007), *Reading Bande Dessinée: Critical Approaches to French-language Comic Strip*, Bristol: Intellect.

Minne, S. (2010), 'Stratégies éditoriales et représentations de l'homosexualité dans la bande dessinée lesbienne et gay francophone', *Image & Narrative*, 11:4, pp. 171–84.

Moi, T. (1995), *Sexual/Textual Politics: Feminist Literary Theory*, London: Routledge.

Moliterni, C.et al. (2004), *BD Guide 2005*, Paris: Omnibus.

Mona (1977a), 'Un médecin nous révèle', *Ah! Nana* (no.3), p. 47.

Mona (1977b), 'Une Histoire exemplaire', *Ah! Nana* (no. 4), pp. 89–92.

Montellier, C. (1984), *Odile et les crocodiles*, Paris: Les Humanoïdes associés.

Montellier, C. (1994). *L'Ile aux démons: une aventure de Julie Bristol*, Paris: Dargaud.

Montellier, C. (2006), *Sorcières, mes sœurs*, Antony: La Boîte à Bulles.

Montellier, C. (2008), *Odile et les crocodiles*, Paris: Actes-Sud.

Montellier, C., Claveloux, N., Cestac, F. and Puchol, J. (2012), *27 ans plus tard toujours aussi 'Navrant'*, https://associationartemisia.wordpress.com/2012/01/27/27-ans-plus-tard-toujours-aussi-navrant/. Accessed 5 October 2017.

Morgan, H. (2009), 'Graphic Shorthand: From Caricature to Narratology in Twentieth-Century Bande dessinée and Comics', *European Comic Art*, 2:1, pp. 21–39.

Mulvey, L. (1989), *Visual and Other Pleasures*, London: Macmillan Press.

Mulvey, L. (2009), *Visual and Other Pleasures*, 2nd ed., Basingstoke: Palgrave Macmillan.

Nead, L. (1992), *The Female Nude: Art, Obscenity and Sexuality*, London: Routledge.

Nguyen, N.-H. and Sohet, P. (2003), 'Social Criticism in a Singular Mode of Expression: The Art of New Realist Cartoonist Chantal Montellier', *International Journal of Comic Art*, 5:1, pp. 115–33.

Nochlin, L. (1996), 'Women, Art and Power', in N.Bryson, M. A.Holly and K.Moxey (eds), *Visual Theory*, Gateshead: Polity Press, pp. 13–46.

REFERENCES

Nochlin, L. (2006), *Bathers, Bodies, Beauty: The Visceral Eye*, Cambridge: Cambridge University Press.

Oksman, T. (2016), *'How Come Boys Get to Keep Their Noses?': Women and Jewish American Identity in Contemporary Graphic Memoirs*, New York: Columbia University Press.

Orial, E. (1976), Editorial, *Ah! Nana* (No.1), p. 3.

Parris, M. (2009), 'Of Course Tintin's Gay: Ask Snowy', http://entertainment.timesonline.co.uk/tol/artsandentertainment/books/article5461005.ece. Accessed 11 December 2009.

Peeters, B. (1991), *Case, planche, récit. Comment lire une bande dessinée*, Tournai: Casterman.

Peeters, B. (1994), 'Le Visage et la ligne: zigzags töpfferiens', in T.Groensteen and B.Peeters (eds), *Töpffer: l'invention de la bande dessinée*, Paris: Hermann, pp. 1–64.

Pieterse, J. N. (1995), *White on Black: Images of Africa and Blacks in Western Popular Culture*, New Haven: Yale University Press.

Pilloy, A. (1994), *Les Compagnes des heros de B.D. Des Femmes et des bulles*, Paris: Editions L'Harmattan.

Pollock, G. (2003), 'The Visual', in M.Eagleton (ed.), *A Concise Companion to Feminist Theory*, Melbourne: Blackwell Publishing, pp. 173–94.

Pomerleau, L. (1989), 'Pierre Christin and Enki Bilal: Called to Comics', *The Comics Journal*, May:129, pp. 62–67.

Rancour-Laferriere, D. (2011), *The Sign of the Cross: From Golgotha to Genocide*, London: Transaction.

Rand, N. and Torok, M. (1994), '*The Sandman* looks at 'The Uncanny'. The Return of the Repressed or of the Secret; Hoffmann's question to Freud', in S.Shamdasani and M.Münchow (eds), *Speculations after Freud: Psychoanalysis, Philosophy and Culture*, London: Routledge, pp. 185–203.

Renaud, J. and Dufaux, J. (1990), *Jessica Blandy 6: Au loin, la fille d'Ipanema*, Paris: Dupuis.

Renaud, J. and Dufaux, J. (1992), *Jessica Blandy 7: Repondez, mourant…*, Paris: Dupuis.

Renaud, J. and Dufaux, J. (2006), *Jessica Blandy Tome 24: Les Gardiens*, Marcinelle: Dupuis.

Reyns-Chikuma, C. (2016), 'De Bécassine à Yoko Tsuno: Réflexions sur les stéréotypes, les oublis et la renaissance de quelques héroïnes créées par des auteurs masculins', *Alternative Francophone*, 1:9, pp. 155–70.

Reyns-Chikuma, C. and Gheno, M. (2013), 'De 'Fraise et chocolat' à 'Buzz-moi' d'aurélia aurita [sic]. D'un journal érographique à la mise en scène d'une mise à nu dans le contexte du « tout dire »', *Image [&] Narrative*, 14:1, pp. 105–29.

Ribémont (1929), 'Nigaude et Malicette XXXIX', *Fillette*, 20 October, pp. 2–3.

Robbins, T. (1993), *A Century of Women Cartoonists*, Northampton: Kitchen Sink Press.

Robbins, T. (1999), *From Girls to Grrrlz: A History of Women's Comics from Teens to Zines*, San Francisco: Chronicle Books.

Robbins, T. and Yronwode, C. (1985), *Women and the Comics*, New York: Eclipse Books.

Robertson, S. L. (1994), 'Matriarchy and the Rhetoric of Domesticity', in *The Stowe Debate: Rhetorical Strategies in Uncle Tom's Cabin*, Amherst: University of Massachusetts Press, pp. 116–40.

Rollet, B. (1999), 'Unruly Woman? Josiane Balasko, French Comedy, and *Gazon maudit* (Balasko, 1995)', in P.Powrie (ed.), *French Cinema in the 1990s: Continuity and Difference*, Oxford: Oxford University Press, pp. 127–36.

Roof, J. (2002), *All about Thelma and Eve: Sidekicks and Third Wheels*, Urbana: University of Illinois Press.

Rouvière, N. (2006), *Astérix ou les lumières de la civilisation*, Paris: Presses universitaires de France.

Sabin, R. (1993), *Adult Comics*, London: Routledge.

Sabin, R. (1996), *Comics, Comix & Graphic Novels*, London: Phaidon.

Samuel, H. (2010), 'Paris trouser ban for women could be lifted', http://www.telegraph.co.uk/news/worldnews/europe/france/7677686/Paris-trouser-ban-for-women-could-be-lifted.html. Accessed 27 July 2012.

Schofield, H. (2004), 'Titeuf storms French comic world', http://news.bbc.co.uk/2/hi/3658750.stm. Accessed 27 July 2012.

Screech, M. (2005), *Masters of the Ninth Art: Bandes dessinées and Franco-Belgian Identity*, Liverpool: Liverpool University Press.

Sécheret, L. and Schlesser, T. (2010), 'Tardi, un carnaval des monstres', *Sociétés et Répresentations*, May:29, pp. 79–98.

Séraphine (1999), *Ascension*, Pantin: Dargaud.

Sharpley-Whiting, T. D. (1999), *Black Venus: Sexualized Savages, Primal Fears and Primitive Narratives in French*, Durham: Duke University Press.

Sheller, M. (2003), *Consuming the Caribbean: From Arawaks to Zombies*, London: Routledge.

Simon, J. (2008), 'Le Combat Ordinaire de Marco… euh…. Manu Larcenet: Une BD réalité à dimension autofictionnelle', *Image & Narrative*, 22, Online.

Smolderen, T., (1984), 'Odile et les crocodiles', *Les Cahiers de la bande dessinée*, June/July, Volume 58, p. 57.

Sohet, P. (2007), *Images du récit*, Montréal: PUQ.

Spivak, G. C. (1993), 'Can the Subaltern Speak', in L.Chisman and P.Williams (eds), *Colonial Discourse and Post-Colonial Theory*, London: Harvester Whitesheaf, pp. 66–111.

Stam, R. (2013), 'Adaptation and the French New Wave: A Study in Ambivalence', *Interfaces*, 34, pp. 177–97.

Steel, J., (2005), 'Let's Party! Astérix and the World Cup (France 1998)', in *The Francophone Bande Dessinée*, Amsterdam: Rodopi, pp. 201–18.

Talet, V. (2004), *Les magazines* Métal Hurlant *et* Ah! Nana: *deux experiences dans l'univers underground en France 1975-1987*, s.l.:Université d'Avignon.

Talet, V. (2006), 'Le magazine *Ah! Nana*: une épopée féministe dans un monde d'hommes', *CLIO: Histoire, femmes et sociétés*, 24, pp. 251–72.

Tannahill, L. (2016), 'Bécassine, a *bande dessinée* pioneer', *Studies in Comics*, 7:2, pp. 221–35.

Tardi, J. (1976), *Tous des monstres!*, Paris: Casterman.

REFERENCES

Tardi, J. (2007a), *Adèle et la bête*, Paris: Casterman.
Tardi, J. (2007b), *Le Noyé à deux têtes*. Paris: Casterman.
Tardi, J. (2007c), *Le Savant fou*, Paris: Casterman.
Tardi, J. (2007d), *Momies en folie*, Paris: Casterman.
Taylor, K. L. (2007), *The Facts on File Companion to the French Novel*, New York: Facts on File.
Tensuan, T. M. (2006), 'Comic Visions and Revisions in the Work of Lynda Barry and Marjane Satrapi', *Modern Fiction Studies*, 52:4, pp. 947–64.
Tishkoff, D. (2005), *Madonna/Whore: The Myth of the Two Marys*, Bloomington: AuthorHouse.
Ussher, J. M. (2006), *Managing the Monstrous Feminine: Regulating the Reproductive Body*, New York: Routledge.
Various (eds), (1998), *Astérix. Un mythe et ses figures* [special issue], *Ethnologie française*, 3:2.
Vitruve, R. (2001), *Bécassine, oeuvre littéraire*, Paris: La Pensée universelle.
Warnauts, E. and Raives, G. (1994), *Equatoriales*, Tournai: Casterman.
—— (1996), *Lettres d'Outremer*, Tournai: Casterman.
Ways of Seeing (Episode 2) (1972), John Berger (writer and narrator), Michael Dibb (producer), s.l.: BBC.
Wilk, S. R. (2000), *Medusa: Solving the Mystery of the Gorgon*, Oxford: Oxford University Press.
Williams, C. and Willis, D. (2002), *The Black Female Body: A Photographic History*, Philadelphia: Temple University Press.
Zancarini-Fournel, M. (2005), *Histoire des femmes en France: XIX-XXe siècle*, Rennes: Presses universitaires de Rennes.

Index

A

abortion (depictions of in *bandes dessinées*), 147

absence of women characters from *bande dessinée* scholarship, 8, 14, 16–17, 17–18, 49, 50–51, 81, 140, 152

'action' women in the *bande dessinée*, 5, 30

adaptation, 114–115, 116–117, 118, 190

Adèle Blanc-Sec, 6, 27, 61–75, 146, 167, 190, 220n13

    Adèle et la bête, 64–75

    characterization of, 62–71

    cinematic adaptation of, 217n21, 217n26

    gender blurring of, 67–71

    monstering of, 71–75

adult shift in *bande dessinée* readership, 5–6, 10, 23, 24–25, 49, 87, 89, 96, 141–142, 209n19, 213n5, 219n16

Ah! Nana, 63, 144–145, 152–165, 191, 192

    creation of, 153–154

    censorship of, 155, 167

    study of *bandes dessinées* in, 156–164

Alix, 86

androgynous women in *bandes dessinées*, 67–68, 143–144, 169, 190, 191, 217n22

Angoulême festival, 31, 147, 210n27, 224n9

Arabelle, 23, 209n18

Association (L'), 93

Association Artemisia, 167, 208n14

Astérix le Gaulois, 87, 93, 96–107, 142, 212n29

    Bonemine, 97, 98, 99, 100, 104, 106

    Falbala, 97, 99, 219n3

    Latraviata, 101

    La Rose et le glaive, 103–107

    Madame Agecanonix, 99, 219n7

    Maestria, 103–105

    mothers of Astérix and Obélix, 100–101

Aurita, Aurélia, 149–150, 189, see also '*Fraise et chocolat*'

autobiography, 147, 149, 180, 181–183, 193

Aventures de la petite Shirley (Les), 19–20

Aya de Yopougon, 31, 150, 210n27

B

bande dessinée grid (evolution of), 16, 17, 18, 19, 20, 23, 35, 39, 190, 209n18

Barbarella, 24–25, 49–60, 70, 88, 184–185, 190

    Barbarella (bande dessinée), 54–60

    Barbarella (film), 37, 50, 213n10, 215n24

    characterization/sexualization of, 52–54, 55–60, 190

    'grounding' of, 52–54

'bathers' in visual art, 74–75, 218n27

Beaty, Bart, 210n26, 218n12

Bécassine, 10, 15, 16, 21, 32, 34–48, 54, 62, 70, 190

Bécassine (*Cont.*)
   Bécassine pendant la (Grande) Guerre, 43–47
   Breton stereotypes, 35–36, 38, 40–41, 45
   defeminization of, 39–42
   dehumanization of, 45–48
   Loulotte, 41–42, 43
   Madame de Grand-Air, 43
   Marie Quillouch, 40, 45, 211n21
Berger, John, 2, 3
Bhabha, Homi, 122
Bilal, Enki, 28, 185
Blake et Mortimer, 85–86
blogs (of or about *bandes dessinées*), 150
Boilet, Frédéric, 180, 182, 185
Boudjellal, Farid, 92
Bourgeon, François, 27, 185
Bretécher, Claire, 141–143, 144, 152, 166, 191, 219n14, 224n9
Butler, Judith, 67, 68

C
Capuana, Cecilia, 156, 159–160, 163–164
caricature, 4, 105, 114–115, 190, 220n12
Catholic influence on *bande dessinée* production, 15, 21–22, 34, 211n11, 211n13
Catholicism and attitudes towards sex, 162, 226n34
Caumery, see 'Bécassine'
censorship, 22–23, 49, 50–51, 85–86, 87, 89, 90, 94, 98, 152, 155, 167, 213n5
Cestac, Florence, 145, 146–147, 224n8
Chauzy, Jean-Christophe, see '*La Vie de ma mère*'
Chute, Hillary, 8, 185, 224n10
Cixous, Hélène, 183, 191
Claveloux, Nicole, 143–144, 145, 157, 158–159, 191

Collectif des créatrices de bande dessinée contre le sexisme, 148, 150, 207n9
comedic origins of the *bande dessinée*, 5
Combat ordinaire, Le, 130–137
   older female characters in, 132–134, 137 see also 'stereotypes of women/mother'
   representations of evolution of female roles in, 133–134, 135–136, 137, 226n38
   reflections on social class in, 131, 135
   reflections on changing male societal roles in, 131, 133–134, 135–136, 222n3
'Congo blanc', see '*Equatoriales*'
Corto Maltese, see 'Pratt, Hugo'
Crepax, Guido, 25, 89, 174, 185, 214n15, 218n11

D
Davreux, Hélène, 26, 35, 36, 41
degeneration theory, 212n25
Despentes, Virginie, 180
Dionnet, Janic, see 'Guillerez, Janic'
Doucet, Julie, 147, 149, 180
Durga-Rani, 20–21

E
economic viability of the *bande dessinée*, 10, 96
Epoxy, 25, 49
elderly women in *bandes dessinées*, 24, 28, 81, 132–134, 163
Equatoriales, 92, 119–125, see also 'stereotypes of women/Black Venus'
Espiègle Lili (L'), 15–17, 32, 41, 207n9
everyday life in the *bande dessinée*, 82, 93, 107, 130, 143, 148, 183, 184

F
Famille Fenouillard (La), 210n1

INDEX

female detective characters in *bandes dessinées*, 24, 32, 61, 146, 166, 217n19
feminist politics in France, 26, 158, 220n11, 225n19
Ferguson, Mary, 43, 99, 100–101, 102, 105, 114–115, 132, 157, 220n6
Forest, Jean-Claude, 24, 27, 142, 185, 214n18, 218n3, 226n2, see also 'Barbarella'
Fraise et chocolat, 149–150, 180–188, 189
    autobiographical form of, 180–183
    challenging of idealized female in, 183–186
    challenging of sexual myths in, 186–188
    'quotidian' rendering of sex in, 183–184
Freud, Sigmund, 60, 186, 215n31
Flash Gordon, 26, 84
Frustrés, Les, 143, see also 'Bretécher, Claire'

G

Gaston Lagaffe, 86, 93, 94
gaze (female), 175, 192
gaze (male, theories of), 2–4, 51, 55–60, 121, 186, 187, 190, 192, 214n21, see also 'Barbarella/characterisation/sexualisation of', 'gaze (female)' and '*Odile et les crocodiles*'
Gentileschi, Artemisia, 167–168, 176, 227n6
Giffey, René, 16, 19, 213n8
'girly' *bande dessinée*, 150–151, 179, 192, 228n30
girls (young) in *bandes dessinées*, 16–20, 21–22, 24, 30, 32, 43, 81, 93, 94, 135–136, 141
Goetzinger, Annie, 31, 144, 151, 152
Goscinny, René, 1, 4, 5, 22, 24, 87, 142, see also '*Astérix le Gaulois*'
Groensteen, Thierry, 7, 21, 23, 24, 28, 49, 61, 65, 72, 88, 149, 191, 208n10, 213n5, 219n16
Grove, Laurence, 24, 130, 207n8, 209n15, 209n21, 222n1, 222n2
Guillerez, Janic, 153, 154, 224n1, 225n10

H

hair colour in *bandes dessinées*, 81, 83, 219n15
Hergé, 1, 4, 5, 26, 215n1, see also '*Tintin (bande dessinée)*'
historical realism (genre of *bande dessinée*), 91, 92, 94, 130
heroic fantasy (genre of *bande dessinée*), 28, 29, 91, 92, 93, 94, 130, 221n13
Histoire d'O, 172, 174

I

illustrés, 14–15
    Bernadette, 141
    Echo des Savanes (L'), 90, 219n14
    Epatant (L'), 83, 207n9
    Fillette, 15–16, 17, 18, 19, 20, 21, 23, 140, 141, 207n9, 208n4
    Journal de Mickey, 18, 19, 84
    Lili, 17
    Line, 23–24
    Métal Hurlant, 90, 154–155, 156, 225n10
    Pilote, 24, 28, 87, 88, 90, 96, 141
    Semaine de Suzette (La), 15–16, 19, 21, 23, 140, 208n4, see also 'Bécassine'
    Tintin, 24, 28, 85, 91
'images of women' criticism, 8–9, 193
'importance of influence' in *bande dessinée* creation, 6, 7, 27, 49, 70–71, 190–191, 192, 193

J

Jeanette Pointu, 28–29
Jessica Blandy, 29
Jodelle, 25, 49, 63
journals (of *bandes dessinées*) see 'illustrés'
Julie Bristol, 146, 166–167

K
Kominsky-Crumb, Aline, 147, 180, 185

L
'lack' (woman as), 3, 6, 72, 73, 186–187, 192
La Femme piège, 28, 29
Larcenet, Manu, 93, 130, 191, 222n1, 226n38, see also '*Combat ordinaire (Le)*'
Laureline, see '*Valérian*'
Lehembre, Bernard, 36, 38, 42
Lejeune, Philippe, 181
Lettres d'Outremer, 125–129
LGBTQ women in *bandes dessinées*, 29, 33, 94, 144, 148–149, 151, 157, 210n29, 221n1
Line, 23–24
Little Annie Rooney, 18–19
Losfeld, Eric, 24, 25, 50, 63, 142, 209n20
Loi du 16 juillet 1949 sur les publications destinées à la jeunesse, 5, 22–23, 25, 33, 50, 85, 86, 87, 94, 209n15, 218n4

M
Manara, Milo, 25, 185
manga, 149
McKinney, Mark, 91–92, 94, 126, 209n10
McCloud, Scott, 214n19
menstruation (depictions of in *bandes dessinées*), 146–147, 180, 183
menopause (depictions of in *bandes dessinées*), 147
Miller, Ann, 28, 91, 93, 135, 181, 223n10, 227n6
Moebius, 1, 90, 215n1
Mona, 160–162, 226n26
Montellier, Chantal, 8, 142–143, 145, 146, 155, 156, 191, 208n14, 215n2, 225n18, see also '*Odile et les crocodiles*'
Mulvey, Laura, 2, 215n30

on castration anxiety, 3–4, 59–60, 72, 217n24
on women as spectacle, 2–4, 55, 56–57, 186–187, see also 'gaze (male, theories of)'
on the 'freezing' effect of female erotic spectacle, 55–56, 185
on creating new forms of looking, 6, 228n19
on the positioning of women in phallocentric society, 2, 56, 186–187

N
Natacha, 25–26
'Navrant', 145, 174
Nead, Lynda, 75, 228n20
Neaud, Fabrice, 149, 180
'New Wave' *bande dessinée*, 130, 222n2, see also 'everyday life in the *bande dessinée*'
Nochlin, Linda, 105, 218n27
Nigaude et Malicette, 17–18
Ninette et Clo-Clo, 17, 19

O
Odile et les crocodiles, 145, 166–179
critique of 'male gaze' in, 174–176, 22n19
feminist intertextual references in, 172–174, 175, 176
nouveau réaliste style of, 166, 170, 227n9, 227n16
rape/revenge theme in, 171–172, see also 'rape (representations of in *bandes dessinées*)'
references to George Orwell in, 227n14, 228n25

P
Passagers du vent (Les), 27
phallocentrism, 2–3, 5, 56, 69, 71, 72, 78, 177, 189–190, 191, 208n11

INDEX

Peeters, Benoît, 6, 207n7
Pilloy, Annie, 7, 9, 79, 81–82, 83, 85, 219n15
Pinchon, Émile-Joseph-Porphyre, see 'Bécassine'
Pollock, Griselda, 2, 6
Polly and her Pals, 19
Pratt, Hugo, 88–89, 218n11
Pravda, 25, 49, 63, 142
prefaces (of *bandes dessinées*), 142–143, 148, 167, 169–170, 181, 189, 226n2
pregnancy (depictions of in *bandes dessinées*), 135, 214n17
Prudence Petitpas, 24
Puchol, Jeanne, 145, 147, 167, 191, 224n8

Q
Quatre Punaises au club, 146

R
rape and sexual violence (representations of in *bandes dessinées*), 29, 91, 94, 116–117, 161–162, 170–172, 221n13, see also '*Odile et les crocodiles*'
Raives, Guy see '*Equatoriales*' & '*Lettres d'Outremer*'
readership of *bande dessinée* (by gender), 4–5, 15–16, 18–19, 82, 149, 207n9
Rivière, Jacqueline, 15, 34–35, 36
Robbins, Trina, 89, 145, 156, 157, 225n12
Rose et le glaive (La), 103–107

S
Sadoul, Numa, 61, 215n1
Satrapi, Marjane, 7, 149, 150, 191
science fiction (genre of *bande dessinée*), 28, 30, 49, 156, 213n9
scopophilic pleasure and reading *bandes dessinées*, 56–57, see also 'gaze (male, theories of)'

sexual act (in *bandes dessinées*), 50–51, 58–59, 89, 90, 91, 111, 120–121, 126–127, 149, 156, 160, 180–181, 183–187
Sfar, Joann, 181, 189, 191
stereotypes of women, 99, 102, 115, 118, 122–123, 129, 187, 190, 191–192
    Black Venus, 122–125, 127–128, 129, 221n4
    childless woman, 71, 72, 105
    damsel in distress, 69–70
    dominating wife, 99–101, 219n9, 220n12
    educated woman, 104–105, 220n12
    Madonna/whore, 111–114, 116, 117, 187
    militant feminist, 104, 177
    monstrous woman, 71–75, 220n13
    mother, 41–42, 99, 100–101, 132, 135, 157
    nude woman, 2, 73–75, 88, 102, 122, 128, 184–185, 220n13, 227n16, 228n20
    powerful woman, 105, 107
    social class, 15, 17–18, 23, 43, 62, 108, 109, 111–112, 113, 124–125, 135, 143, 172
    woman alone, 71–72, 104–105, 220n13
    woman as erotic spectacle, 55–60, 174–175, 178, 184–185, 221n3, 222n12, 228n20
    woman as victim, 158–162, 168, 173
    'woman on a pedestal', 99, 101, 144
Schtroumpfs (Les), 85, 86–87, 93
Séraphine, 148
Sorcières, mes soeurs, 167
Sylvie, 23

T
Tanx/Tanxx, 150
Tardi, Jacques, 27, 61, 63, 70–71, 115, 167, 190, see also '*Adèle Blanc-Sec*'

Titeuf, 92–93
Thorgal, 91
Tintin (bande dessinée), 18, 38, 83, 120, see also 'illustrés/*Tintin*'
Trondheim, Lewis, 1, 93, 94

U
Uderzo, Albert see '*Astérix le Gaulois*'
underground comics (American), 89–90, 147, 156
Ussher, Jane, 42, 67, 73, 74, 228n20

V
Valérian, 88
Vie de ma mère (La), 94, 108–118, 190
    adaptation of, 113–117
    secondary women in see 'stereotypes of women/Madonna/whore' and 'stereotypes of women/social class'

W
Warnauts, Eric, see '*Equatoriales*' & '*Lettres d'Outremer*'
Ways of Seeing, see 'Berger, John'
Winnie Winkle, 17, 18, 33, 208n8
women of colour in *bandes dessinées*, 31, 91–92, 94, 119–129, 135, 145, 150, 151, 157, 180, 182, see also 'stereotypes of women/Black Venus'
women's experiences of WWI, 44, 216, 211n18

Y
Yoko Tsuno, 26, 90

Z
Zoubinette, 20, 23, 24